106

MW01069249

Lawsuits

by Victoria E. Green, J.D.

ALPHA

A member of Penguin Group (USA) Inc.

To my parents, Phyllis and Leslie Green, with much love and many thanks.

ALPHA BOOKS

Published by the Penguin Group

Penguin Group (USA) Inc., 375 Hudson Street, New York, New York 10014, USA

Penguin Group (Canada), 90 Eglinton Avenue East, Suite 700, Toronto, Ontario M4P 2Y3, Canada (a division of Pearson Penguin Canada Inc.)

Penguin Books Ltd., 80 Strand, London WC2R 0RL, England

Penguin Ireland, 25 St. Stephen's Green, Dublin 2, Ireland (a division of Penguin Books Ltd.)

Penguin Group (Australia), 250 Camberwell Road, Camberwell, Victoria 3124, Australia (a division of Pearson Australia Group Pty. Ltd.)

Penguin Books India Pvt. Ltd., 11 Community Centre, Panchsheel Park, New Delhi—110 017, India

Penguin Group (NZ), 67 Apollo Drive, Rosedale, North Shore, Auckland 1311, New Zealand (a division of Pearson New Zealand Ltd.)

Penguin Books (South Africa) (Pty.) Ltd., 24 Sturdee Avenue, Rosebank, Johannesburg 2196, South Africa

Penguin Books Ltd., Registered Offices: 80 Strand, London WC2R 0RL, England

International Standard Book Number: 978-1-61564-038-6
Library of Congress Catalog Card Number: 2010902233

12 11 10   8 7 6 5 4 3 2 1

Interpretation of the printing code: The rightmost number of the first series of numbers is the year of the book's printing; the rightmost number of the second series of numbers is the number of the book's printing. For example, a printing code of 10-1 shows that the first printing occurred in 2010.

Printed in the United States of America

Note: This publication contains the opinions and ideas of its author. It is intended to provide helpful and informative material on the subject matter covered. It is sold with the understanding that the author and publisher are not engaged in rendering professional services in the book. If the reader requires personal assistance or advice, a competent professional should be consulted.

The author and publisher specifically disclaim any responsibility for any liability, loss, or risk, personal or otherwise, which is incurred as a consequence, directly or indirectly, of the use and application of any of the contents of this book.

Most Alpha books are available at special quantity discounts for bulk purchases for sales promotions, premiums, fund-raising, or educational use. Special books, or book excerpts, can also be created to fit specific needs.

For details, write: Special Markets, Alpha Books, 375 Hudson Street, New York, NY 10014.

Publisher: *Marie Butler-Knight*

Associate Publisher: *Mike Sanders*

Senior Managing Editor: *Billy Fields*

Senior Acquisitions Editor: *Paul Dinas*

Development Editor: *Jennifer Moore*

Production Editor: *Kayla Dugger*

Copy Editor: *Jan Zoya*

Cover Designer: *Kurt Owens*

Book Designers: *William Thomas, Rebecca Batchelor*

Indexer: *Celia McCoy*

Layout: *Brian Massey*

Proofreader: *John Etchison*

Contents

Introduction

A storm knocks your neighbor's tree into your house. Your business partner doesn't cough up his share of this year's taxes. You want to spend more time with your children, but your ex isn't cooperating. Civil lawsuits happen when you least expect them, and always at the most stressful time possible. It's a chicken and the egg issue: does the lawsuit cause the stress, or is the stress causing a lawsuit? As with so much in law, the answer is probably somewhere in between. The lawsuit definitely causes stress on its own, but it's also a way to relieve stress by resolving the underlying problem. This book is for you, whether you've found yourself in the middle of a lawsuit or are just curious about what really happens.

This book will help you understand the ins and outs of the American litigation system. It's set up to be as useful as possible, making your journey as straightforward as it can be. You don't need to read it front to back; you can pick the part that has the information you need most and start there. Although this book isn't a replacement for personalized legal advice, it's designed to help you answer the basic questions about lawsuits and provide background information to help you make intelligent decisions about your own situation.

How This Book Is Organized

Turn to **Part 1, Should You Sue?,** to answer the big question of whether or not to file a suit in the first place. To make that decision, you need to know the basics about lawsuits. The chapters in this part cover the mechanics of how a lawsuit starts, as well as the minimum criteria for filing suit in the first place.

The key to a winning lawsuit is provable damages, and here you'll find out everything you need to know about them. This part also walks you through what happens when you're sued, from the first steps you should take to how to tell if you've been slammed with a "frivolous" lawsuit. It also addresses nuts-and-bolts questions like "How long will my lawsuit take?"

Finally, you'll learn about the various kinds of civil lawsuits—class action, contract cases, personal injury, and family law—and how you can use them to resolve different kinds of problems.

Not every lawsuit requires a lawyer, but how do you decide when it makes sense to go it alone? **Part 2, Legal Representation,** helps you make an informed decision. It also gives you pointers on finding a lawyer if you decide to hire one and introduces you to the people you're likely to encounter during a lawsuit, from court personnel to the professionals who work with lawyers.

Finances are a big factor when deciding whether or not to hire an attorney. Predicting how much a lawsuit will cost isn't easy, but this part walks you through not only the costs of working with a lawyer but the additional fees you'll run into along the way. You can use this information to get a general sense of just how much money your lawsuit will end up costing you.

Part 3, The Legal Environment, gives you a more thorough understanding of how the U.S. justice system works, including the difference between small claims court and the regular court system. This part offers a step-by-step guide to how the court system is set up and how cases move through the system. You also learn about the most important rules that govern lawsuits, so that you can avoid losing on common technicalities.

Part 4, The Trial Process, deals with all facets of the trial itself. You start at the beginning of the beginning, with pretrial settlements, and move on to getting the case ready to go to court and the court proceedings that lead up to trial. You also get an introduction to what counts as evidence and how to establish that evidence for presentation at the trial.

This part also covers how the final decision is actually made by the court and how you might go about appealing that decision if you disagree with it. In addition to the purely legal consequences of the lawsuit, the aftermath of the lawsuit includes effects on your business and personal relationships, your finances, and your credit. This part helps to prepare for those after-effects, so you won't be caught off guard.

And what if worse comes to worst, and you suspect that your attorney is the reason you didn't get what you were hoping for? You might have a case against your attorney for legal malpractice. You can use this part as a guide to help you through the complexities of malpractice actions.

Part 5, Alternatives to Filing Suit, explains negotiation, mediation, and arbitration techniques. You may wish to turn to negotiation at several points throughout the lawsuit. And because many courts require some form of mediation before they'll let you go forward with a lawsuit, you need to learn how it works and how it can help—or hurt—your case. Finally, you get the scoop on the newest way to solve legal problems outside of court: arbitration. You may have agreed to arbitration rather than standard court procedures in a contract you've signed, and you'll need to know what to expect.

Your journey began with a problem. Hopefully, this book will help you find a solution.

Extras

Throughout this book, you'll find the following "sidebars" highlighting helpful or interesting information:

DEFINITION

Turn to these boxes for a quick explanation of terms that are important to grasping the overall concepts in the legal process. (You'll find even more definitions in Appendix A, at the back of the book.)

IN THE KNOW

Here you'll find insider tips and advice to help you move forward.

PITFALLS

These boxes serve as warnings about things that will waste your time or pose an ethical dilemma.

JUST THE FACTS

Just for fun, these sidebars are packed with interesting legal trivia.

Acknowledgments

This book could not have been written without the help and support of many people. In particular, I would like to thank Nina L. Kaufman, Esq., for making this opportunity available to me. Thanks are also due to my agent, Claire Gerus, and especially to my editor, Paul Dinas, for shepherding me through the process. Without Paul's generous help and guidance, this book would never have been written. I must also thank Jennifer Moore, my development editor, for her contributions to this book. For his thoughtful improvements to the text, I am deeply grateful to Jonathan A. Green, an outstandingly fine attorney and writer.

Thanks are also due to the many teachers who have pushed and pulled me through my education. I would especially like to acknowledge Mrs. Taft and Mr. Wilson, my high school English teachers, forever without first names but forever gratefully remembered for forcing high standards of literacy on me and generations of Phase Five students. My professors at the Boston University School of Law are also due many thanks for introducing me to the seamless web of the law. Professor Neil Hecht's kindnesses were only outmatched by the clarity of his explanations. I have done my best to model my own teaching and writing style after his. The lawyers who took over my training after law school, Lawrence Imerman, John Forczak, and Norman J. Rice, initiated me in the mysteries and realities of the practice of law. I can never thank them enough.

Last but certainly not least are the people who have enriched my life and made it possible for me to write this book. The late Lawrence Hatzenbeler quite literally changed my life with his perceptive and generous help. Steven Hanley and Steven Nickoloff provided tremendous support throughout the writing process. Most of all, my family has given me unstinting support and love, along with the occasional kick in the pants—exactly what I needed for this book and for my life. My love and thanks go to them all.

Trademarks

All terms mentioned in this book that are known to be or are suspected of being trademarks or service marks have been appropriately capitalized. Alpha Books and Penguin Group (USA) Inc. cannot attest to the accuracy of this information. Use of a term in this book should not be regarded as affecting the validity of any trademark or service mark.

Should You Sue?

This portion of the book deals with the basics underlying all lawsuits. You'll learn how lawsuits start and what you need to successfully begin one. You'll also find out what types of lawsuits are used to solve specific problems. Most important, you'll learn about the one thing every lawsuit must have to succeed: damages.

How Lawsuits Start

In This Chapter

- Why "Can I sue?" is the wrong question
- Understanding the legal time frame
- Defining your goals
- Avoiding frivolous lawsuits

Civil lawsuits start with a problem. It can be a problem between two people or shared by two million people. The problem can involve the government or business, or both.

Before people sue, they usually try to resolve the problem on their own. When that doesn't work, a lawsuit is a way to solve the problem and enforce its solution.

You Can Sue for Anything— But Can You Win?

The number-one question people ask lawyers is "Can I sue for that?" The number-two question is "Can he sue me for that?" The short answer to both questions is "yes." You (and he) can sue for anything.

The more important question is whether or not you (or he) will win. The answer to that is "It depends." A lawyer can tell you what the law is on a particular topic, and, based on the facts you describe, can make a prediction about what is going to happen. The problem is that it's only a prediction, and it's about as accurate as a good weather forecast. Like an unexpected cold front, surprises come up that range from undiscovered facts to a witness falling apart on the stand.

The potential for winning your lawsuit is also called "having a good case." In order to have a good case, you need all the parts that make up a case.

What Makes Up a Case

To have a case, you need three things:

- A problem
- A loss
- A law

If you're missing any one of these three things, you don't have a case, even if the other parts are very strong. Let's take a closer look at each of these elements.

A Problem

You need a problem that is either an ongoing problem or has already happened. The law doesn't provide solutions to potential problems that may or may not happen in the future, except when there's evidence that the potential future problem is part of a current dispute, like setting future visitation rights and schedules in a divorce case. If there's only an imagined future problem, you don't have a case.

A Loss

You need to have suffered a loss or been hurt somehow. This is called "having damages," which will be covered in detail in Chapter 3. If you haven't been hurt or lost something like money, you have no case.

A Law

There needs to be a law of some sort that says that the kind of damage you suffered is something where the law allows for a remedy. In other words, if there is a problem and you have been damaged due to the problem, there has to be a law that addresses that problem. For example, your feelings may have been hurt (there's the hurt or loss) by someone wearing an ugly outfit (there's the problem), but there's no law that says this is a loss that someone else has to take responsibility for. You'll recover nothing in this situation.

Once you've got these three things, you need to take one more step to ensure you have a good case: you need to make sure the facts of the situation meet the requirements of the law that provides recovery for your sort of problem. To see whether that's true, a lawyer analyzes your problem by breaking down the relevant law into its smallest parts, called elements, and applies your facts to each element. If all the facts don't match up with all the elements of the law, there is no case under that law. It's important to know that when the facts change, so does whether or not there's a case under that law. That's why it's so important to tell your lawyer the whole truth when you meet, and to include even minor details.

IN THE KNOW

Feel free to tell your lawyer everything, no matter how embarrassing or confidential. He cannot tell these things to anyone else—even the police—without your permission because of attorney-client privilege. That means the lawyer must keep what you tell him private, unless you give the okay to let other people know. There are exceptions, as with everything in law, but they're very limited: only if you threaten immediate serious harm to others can the attorney breach that confidentiality.

When a lawyer says "You have a good case," she means that your facts match up very well with the elements of the law in question, and that your damages are the kind for which the law allows recovery. More than that, though, the lawyer also usually means that your facts are strong and persuasive, and that your loss is big enough to make it worthwhile to pursue your case in court. You certainly don't want to spend more money on an attorney than what you could hope to receive as damages.

How Long Will This Take?

There's no telling how long any one case will take. So many factors go into determining when a case ends that the best anyone can do is make a guess. Among the factors that determine how long a case will take are …

- How busy the court is.

- If the court set its own deadlines that you have to follow.

- How many problems you want to solve.

- How willing both sides are to compromise.

- How much time you have available. (Are you willing and able to take more time?)

- How complex the problems are you want to solve.

- What kind of problem you have.

For example, if the court is really busy, your case is going to have to wait—the court won't be able to put it at the top of the pile unless there is a very compelling reason. Similarly, if you have a case involving 20 people as parties, it's going to take more time to sort through than if there were only 2 people. If you are involved in a child custody dispute, it can continue until the child turns 18. If the other side isn't willing to compromise, you can spend a great deal more time on a case than you had originally planned.

JUST THE FACTS

If the case is a criminal law case, then by law you have the right to a "speedy trial." You don't have this right in a civil case.

The longer the case takes, the more money it will cost you, both in attorney fees and in lost opportunities like work. You are, to some degree, in control of how long the case will take in that you can always agree to end the case at any time. You might not get what you originally wanted, but you can get out. If you have plenty of time on your hands, you might be more willing to let a case play out over a long period of time.

What Do You Really Want to Achieve?

It should be easy to say what you want to achieve with a lawsuit: you want to solve the problem that brought you to court in the first place. In reality, that's often not the only goal you have in going to court. You may see yourself as a champion of justice. You may want to get back at the jerk who put you in this lousy position. You may see this as a way to make some money.

Lawsuits take up a great deal of time, money, and energy; the more honest you are about your goals in bringing a lawsuit, the better able you'll be to make a decision about how and when to end it.

You've Been Sued—Now What?

The most important thing to do once you've been sued is respond to the court. If you do not respond, you'll lose by default, like a little league team that doesn't show for a game. The loss will count against you, regardless of how unjust or untrue the claims in the lawsuit are, and you'll have to pay whatever damages were claimed against you. (Defaults and damages are covered in Chapter 3).

You can make a response with or without a lawyer (see Chapter 4 for advice on picking a lawyer). If it's a criminal lawsuit and you're the defendant, it's in your best interest to have an attorney and to read *The Complete Idiot's Guide to Criminal Lawsuits*. The book you're holding in your hand only covers civil lawsuits, and while having a lawyer will make your experience significantly easier, it's highly unlikely you'll end up in jail as a result of a civil lawsuit.

 PITFALLS

You can end up in jail due to a civil lawsuit if you're found in contempt of court! Always behave respectfully while in the courthouse, no matter how you feel or what happens. Disrespectful or disruptive behavior is considered a criminal offense in court.

If you have insurance, call your insurance carrier. Typically, if you are in a car accident, your auto insurance company will handle the lawsuit by assigning you an attorney and taking care of the case. Likewise, if someone is hurt on your property, call your homeowner's insurance carrier. Even if the insurance company won't defend the case, you have to tell them about the lawsuit as soon as possible.

 IN THE KNOW

You can still be defaulted while you are trying to get your insurance company to answer the complaint and defend you. Be sure that they are going to answer; otherwise, you need to make arrangements to answer the complaint, either on your own or by getting an attorney.

Frivolous Lawsuits

Why do the courts let someone start a lawsuit for something that's clearly stupid? It has to do with the American belief in the importance of access to justice. Everyone is entitled to approach the court for anything. There is no prescreening process to keep some people or claims out. Because of this, the court can't immediately determine whether the claims made are pointless or not. The court has to examine every case that's filed on an individual basis. The court doesn't really begin that examination until the other side, the *defendant*, responds to the *plaintiff's* claims.

> **DEFINITION**
>
> The **plaintiff** is the person or entity that starts the lawsuit; the **defendant** is the person or entity that's being sued and has to respond to the plaintiff's claims.

Likewise, the court can't tell from the fact that a suit was filed whether the facts claimed are true or not. Although the courts are open to everyone, including the stupid, the misguided, and the obnoxious, the courts are not particularly fond of stupid, obnoxious lawsuits. To address this issue, all courts have a version of a federal court rule called Rule 11. Rule 11 strikes down any lawsuit or part of a lawsuit that's brought without supporting evidence or without real law behind it. It also eliminates lawsuits or parts of lawsuits that are brought only to harass or are otherwise frivolous. The problem is, the court has to examine the suit before it can decide to use Rule 11 or its equivalent. This means the stupid, obnoxious suit goes forward until the other side asks for a decision under Rule 11.

If the court finds part or all of a case to be frivolous or unfounded, it will rule to *strike* the relevant portion of the case. The bonus to Rule 11 is that in addition to striking the case, the court can fine the offending party. The fine can include attorney fees for the party that had to come to court to defend itself against a frivolous case. The question is, what makes a case frivolous?

> **DEFINITION**
>
> To **strike** means to take out or remove something from a lawsuit or part of a lawsuit. When an attorney says, "Strike that," after a statement, it means "ignore that statement."

What Makes a Frivolous Suit

Nonlawyers tend to think a frivolous lawsuit is one where the parties should just grow up and stop whining instead of suing. Lawyers see whining as part of human nature. For a lawyer to classify a lawsuit as frivolous, the following conditions must be met.

- There is no law that supports making this a lawsuit.

- The facts don't fit the law you're claiming to sue under.

- The only motivation for the suit is to embarrass or harass the defendant.

When any of these things are true, the case is considered to have no merit. When a lawyer knows the case has no merit, he is prohibited by law and ethics from starting the case. The lawyer has a responsibility to check that the facts are at least based on something that might be true. This doesn't mean the attorney has to decide whether or not the claim is true—that's the court's job. It means that before filing a divorce case seeking custody of children, the attorney must check to see that the parties were legally married and have children, not that one party is genuinely an unfit parent.

When a judge decides that an argument in a case is frivolous, she is not saying that the argument is wrong or that the other side is right. Instead, she is saying that the frivolous argument is not even an argument at all. It's as meaningful as giving the judge a recipe for chocolate chip cookies. They may be good cookies, but the recipe is not a legal claim. For attorneys, being told by a judge that an argument or case is frivolous is a complete humiliation. The attorney is basically being told that he has no idea what he's doing.

JUST THE FACTS

The legal community in any area, no matter how big it seems, is still a relatively small group. Lawyers know each other, or know someone who knows someone. When a lawyer messes up, the rest of the legal community finds out quickly, even if they weren't there. This is a real motivation to avoid making basic mistakes, like bringing a frivolous suit.

Why Stella Won When She Spilled the Coffee

The lawsuit that's often held up as an example of lawyers gone wild with frivolous lawsuits is Stella Liebeck's suit against McDonald's. Stella, who was in her late 70s at the time, bought a cup of coffee at a McDonald's drive-through window. Her grandson was driving and pulled over so she could add cream and sugar to her coffee. When Stella took the lid off the cup, the coffee spilled onto her lap and legs. At this point, the case definitely sounds like the very best definition of an "Oh, grow up and stop whining" kind of frivolous case. If that's all that happened, there would have been no legal claim, and it would be a frivolous case in legal terms, too.

Unfortunately for Stella, the spilled coffee was so hot that it instantly burned through her skin to the muscle layer. The damage wasn't just on the inside of her legs—her genitals suffered severe burns, too. She ended up in the hospital needing skin grafts to replace the skin that was burned off. She also needed painful debridement treatments, which involve scraping off the burned areas to keep them clean and healing properly.

Stella contacted the McDonald's restaurant where she bought the coffee and asked them for two things. First, she wanted them to turn the temperature down on their coffee so other people wouldn't get scalded. Second, she wanted McDonald's to pay for the things her insurance wasn't covering. McDonald's refused. Stella had to be talked into suing McDonald's, which she finally agreed to do.

It turns out that the McDonald's in question knew about other people claiming they were getting burned from the coffee, and that this restaurant kept the coffee at near boiling temperatures, a practice the coffee industry does not recommend for safety reasons.

You may still think Stella's case is stupid, but it's not frivolous under the legal definition. The three main reasons to find a lawsuit frivolous don't apply.

First, there was a law that supported making this a lawsuit. Product liability and negligence law state that if you're going to sell something, it has to be safe for ordinary use. Ordinary use of coffee includes drinking it—and spilling it, too.

Second, the facts fit the law Stella sued under. She bought coffee intending to drink it, and it wasn't safe to drink because it was sold too hot. By the way, McDonald's had two arguments for selling the coffee so hot that it could cause severe burns. First, they said the coffee tasted better if it was made super-hot, and second, it had to be served that hot to remain drinkably warm once the purchaser had reached their destination.

Finally, Stella's only motivation for the suit was not to embarrass or harass McDonald's. She had suffered an injury and wanted to be reimbursed for the expense it caused her. She also wanted to make sure that no one else was similarly injured. You might still think it was something she should have expected, and she should have just shut up and paid for it herself, but legally, she had every right to sue, and the suit was not legally frivolous.

The case would've been different if she'd dripped ketchup from her burger onto her clothes. Yes, there would have been an injury of sorts—her clothes would've gotten dirty—but it's not an injury that the law provides a remedy for. Getting dirty while eating is an ordinary risk of eating. Ending up in the hospital with severe burns isn't.

In the end, the jury was horrified by the injuries Stella suffered, and by McDonald's refusal to make the coffee a safe temperature. They awarded Stella $200,000 to compensate her for her injury. Because the jury decided she was 20 percent at fault for spilling the coffee herself, the damages were reduced by 20 percent to $160,000. That wasn't what got critics really exercised, though. Stella was also awarded $2.7 million dollars in damages to punish McDonald's for being so irresponsible.

The $2.7 million was later reduced to $480,000, three times Stella's compensatory damages. After the judgment, to avoid dealing with a further appeal, McDonald's and Stella negotiated a settlement, which remains confidential, so no one is really sure how the case ended.

Because it sounds stupid and frivolous in the nonlegal sense to sue for spilling coffee on yourself, this case became the poster child for American greed and eagerness to sue over anything.

Why You Need to Show Up Anyway

You can't do anything to avoid a frivolous lawsuit. The best you can do is point out to the court why, legally, the lawsuit is frivolous. Regardless of how stupid the suit seems to you, and regardless of whether it fits the legal definition of frivolous, you still need to show up in court and defend yourself against any lawsuit filed against you. The only thing worse than a frivolous lawsuit is losing a frivolous lawsuit because you didn't fight it properly.

The Least You Need to Know

- The most important question to ask in a lawsuit is "How likely am I to win?"
- In order to have a valid case, you must have a law to sue under and facts that fit every part of the law.
- There is no way to predict how long a lawsuit will take.
- Legally frivolous lawsuits are more than just stupid; they have no basis in law.

Kinds of Lawsuits

In This Chapter

- The difference between civil and criminal lawsuits
- The most common types of civil lawsuits
- Class action lawsuits

There are almost as many kinds of lawsuits as there are problems, but in general, lawsuits fall into established categories to make it easier to solve the problems presented.

Civil Suits vs. Criminal Suits

The law can be divided into two major categories: civil and criminal. The same event can lead to both criminal and civil lawsuits. This is because the same event or behavior can hurt both the individual and society at large.

To protect society at large, there are statutes that forbid and punish certain behaviors and turn them into crimes. Without a specific statute criminalizing a specific behavior, there is no crime. For example, there are statutes that say if two people get into a fight, and one breaks the other's arm, the act was a crime. On the other hand, there is no statute that says that in a verbal fight, the act of calling someone stupid is a crime. Without a statute criminalizing the act, the government will not step in and sue the person accused of that act.

When the act hurts an individual, whether or not there is a statute making the act a crime, it falls under civil law. The government will not act on the injured person's behalf if there is no criminal statute. Instead, the person who was hurt has to act against the person who hurt him by bringing a case to court. This can be done even if there is a criminal action brought by the government for the same act.

The most famous example of an act with both civil and criminal consequences was O. J. Simpson's murder trial. There was not enough evidence to find him *guilty* beyond a reasonable doubt of killing his wife, Nicole Brown Simpson, and her friend, Ronald Goldman. The criminal consequence—jail time and possible fines—was not imposed. However, a lower level of proof is needed to find someone responsible in a civil case. There was enough evidence to find him *liable* for the deaths of Brown Simpson and Goldman. The civil consequence—payment of damages—was imposed on O. J. The problem, as in many civil cases, is collecting payment.

DEFINITION

Someone who is **guilty** is criminally responsible for an act that is against the law. Someone who is **liable** is civilly responsible for a particular act (or failure to act) that the law requires.

Tort Law: Personal Injury and Property Damage

When people are hurt or their property is damaged, it falls under the area of law known as tort law. There are two kinds of torts: intentional, where the person intended the act that caused the harm; and accidental, which is usually called *negligence* in the legal field.

DEFINITION

Negligence is when a person has a responsibility to pay attention and be careful in his actions but fails to do so and causes an injury to another.

Accidents Will Happen

Not all injuries are caused by accidents. However, accidents are the major source of personal injury and property damage. Regardless of whether the injury was caused by someone behaving negligently or caused by someone's intentional behavior, if someone else caused the injury, that person is responsible for making up for the damage the injury caused. That's known as "making you whole again."

What Do You Have to Prove to Win?

To win an accidental or negligence personal injury case, the following three things must be proven:

- The person who caused the injury had to have some sort of relationship with the injured person or place that gave him a duty to be careful or avoid harm.

- The person (who usually becomes the defendant) has to violate or breach that duty to be careful or avoid harm.

- That violation or breach of duty has to cause injury.

If you're missing any one of these things, or if you can't prove them adequately, you'll lose your case.

Is Your Case Worth Pursuing?

Knowing what you have to prove is the first step in deciding whether your case is worth pursuing. Was there a duty? Was it violated, or, as attorneys say, *breached?* Did that breach of duty cause your injury? If you can show all that, you've passed the first step in determining whether the case is worth pursuing.

DEFINITION

Breached means broken, violated, or contrary to what was supposed to happen.

The next step is the one that often seems unfair or unjust, because it's all about the money. Does the defendant have any money to pay for your injury? Is there an insurance policy, or a house, or a bank account? You can have the best case in the world in terms of the three elements we talked about, but if your defendant has no assets, why spend your time, money, and energy pursuing a case? Defendants who have no assets are called "judgment-proof" in legal slang; it's recognition that you can't get money from a stone. If the defendant has no assets, you can have the biggest *judgment* in the world and it won't do you any good.

DEFINITION

A **judgment** is a court order that declares one party the winner of a lawsuit, and usually awards the winner money that the loser must pay. A judgment can be enforced by the courts through actions like garnishments (taking money that's owed to the loser) and auctions.

Who Will Pay?

Your defendant may be judgment-proof, but look to other parties who might be involved, too. Consider insurance companies, friends or family members who lent the car involved in the accident, and anyone else present when the accident happened. They may have some responsibility for the accident, too, and if they do, they can help pay for it.

PITFALLS

Just because your defendant has no assets now doesn't mean she won't hit the lottery jackpot next week. If you fail to sue within the time granted by statute and your defendant comes into money, you won't get any of it. It may be worth suing just in case.

Once you have the judgment, you can start the *collections* process.

Your defendant may not have money in the bank, but if he's employed, there's a ready source of partial payment of your judgment: his paycheck. You can do what's called *garnishing* any sum of money that is owed to the defendant; it doesn't have to be his paycheck. It can be a tax refund, proceeds from the sale of a car or house, or any money owed to the defendant by anybody. There are some exceptions, like Social Security checks, but for the most part, anyone who owes your defendant can be made to pay you instead of him.

DEFINITION

Collections is the process of getting money owed to you from the person or entity that owes it. **Garnishing** is taking something from a third party who owes it to your defendant before the third party gives it to the defendant.

If your defendant has insurance, but the insurance doesn't cover the entire amount of the judgment, the defendant still owes the entire amount of the judgment. Many people believe that all anyone can get is the insurance money, but that's absolutely wrong. If you have a $500,000 judgment, and the defendant has a $300,000 insurance policy, the policy will have to pay out 100 percent to you, and the defendant still owes you $200,000. You can collect on that the same way you would collect on any judgment, via garnishment or seizure of assets.

Seizure of assets means that you get a court order authorizing you to take some object that belongs to the defendant and either keep it as payment (called "satisfaction" of the debt) or sell it to get cash (liquidation of the asset). If you don't get enough money from the sale of that object or asset, you can continue to get court orders to seize assets until the debt is paid off.

Medical Malpractice

Medical malpractice is a form of personal injury, but it has special rules because there are two reasons you might not get the results you want from medical treatment: bad luck or bad treatment. If you just have bad luck, that means you got the treatment you would've received from any competent doctor, and it simply didn't work. You may have ended up injured or not cured, but it's not legally actionable. If it's bad treatment, meaning you didn't get the kind of treatment any competent doctor would've given, then you have a case.

It's Different from Other Personal Injuries

Remember that in ordinary personal injury cases, all you need to show is that there was a duty to be careful that the defendant violated or breached. With medical malpractice, to show that the medical professional breached his duty to be careful, you also have to prove that the medical care you received was not up to the standards of the medical community.

Was It Bad Luck or Bad Medicine?

Medicine is based in science, but science hasn't come up with the cure for everything. People still die or react badly to a drug or treatment that others do well with, and there's not much we can do about it. What we can and do act on is making sure that the treatment people get is as safe and effective as possible.

However, deciding whether you or your loved ones were treated responsibly is difficult; it requires an evaluation by another doctor. That doctor reviews the medical records and, based on community standards, advises the lawyer whether the treatment was up to par. If one doctor doesn't believe that the treatment was bad, a lawyer may seek a second opinion, but that's relatively rare. Lawyers develop a trust with the doctors they work with in evaluating cases; if the doctor doesn't think there's a case, the lawyer is likely to believe her.

JUST THE FACTS

One of the problems with medical malpractice suits is that doctors dislike second-guessing other doctors, because they know it could be their mistake on trial next time. As a consequence, not many doctors are willing to testify about what kind of care another doctor gave a patient. Because doctors who are willing to serve as "expert witnesses" in trials are not all that common, they often get a lot of work from lawyers who need a case evaluated. This fact is often used in court, albeit not always successfully, to try to show that the doctor's evaluation isn't reliable.

Who Can You Sue?

You can sue the doctor, the nurse, the hospital …. You can sue anyone or any entity that provided medical care to you. Your best bet is to sue them all, because it's often hard to prove who exactly was at fault for the ultimate injury. For example, had the doctor provided better supervision of the nurse, the nurse's mistake might have been caught and reversed. Sue them both!

Who Will Pay?

Doctors frequently have malpractice insurance policies that will pay up to a certain amount, called the per-incident value of the policy. The amount depends on how much the doctor decided to spend on his insurance. Remember that if the insurance doesn't cover the entire judgment, the defendant still has to pay the remaining amount. Often, for practicality's sake, when the case is settled, it's settled for an amount that the insurance will cover. Because many lawyers take on medical malpractice cases on a contingent fee basis (see Chapter 5 for a discussion of how lawyers are paid) the money will be paid directly to the lawyer, who will then pay it to you.

Product Liability

When a product hurts someone, the manufacturer may be held responsible if the product was defective in some way. The defect might be a bad or dangerous design, or it might have been put together badly or with substandard materials. The defect might even be in the instructions or warnings if they make the product dangerous to use.

It's not enough for the product to be defective. In order to have a case, the product has to hurt someone. Only people who have actually been hurt by the product can successfully sue under product liability. If you notice the problem with the item, and (intelligently) don't use it and therefore don't suffer an injury or loss, you may get your money back for your purchase, but you won't win big in a lawsuit.

IN THE KNOW

If you have a product liability issue, you might also want to contact the Consumer Product Safety Commission at www.cpsc.gov. It's the branch of the government that works with manufacturers to issue recalls of dangerous and defective products. Not only will you help other people, but you might help your lawsuit.

Problems with Proof

The biggest problem with product liability is proving that the product was defective when it left the manufacturer. If the product was altered in some way after it was purchased, whether by the retailer or the purchaser, the manufacturer can argue that the product was safe when it left his hands. If that's the case, then you may have to look to the retailer as a possible defendant. You may also have to do extra work to show that any changes to the product after it left the retailer or manufacturer didn't affect the product and its basic flaws, and that the problem is still the manufacturer or retailer's responsibility.

Can Your Claim Be Treated as a Class Action Suit?

If enough other people have suffered the same kind of injuries from the same defect, it might be exactly the sort of situation class action suits were designed to address. Defining "enough" is difficult because it varies from one case to another. Class actions usually work with hundreds or thousands of plaintiffs. To convince an attorney to take your case, you may need to do some research to discover these other potential plaintiffs. You can use anything from advertising to word of mouth. Using the Internet is the most modern way to inform people about the situation. You can set up a website so that people can find you and information about the suit you're planning to file. You can create a discussion group to let people know you've got an option they might want to consider. See the discussion later in this chapter about class actions for more information about how they work.

Contracts

A contract is an agreement between two or more people to do (or not do) a specific thing. There must be a negotiated or bargained-for exchange, whether it's an exchange of promises or acts.

In the early days of the movies, Sam Goldwyn, of the famous Metro Goldwyn Mayer studios, famously said, "An oral contract isn't worth the paper it's written on." Most people believe that oral or spoken contracts aren't real contracts and cannot be enforced. This is absolutely not true. While there are problems proving what the contract was really about, an oral contract is a real contract. The court is perfectly capable of making a decision about who's telling the truth and who's not.

Do You Really Have a Contract?

How do you know that you really have a contract? Sometimes you will have a piece of paper titled "contract" or "agreement," but other times you'll just have a handshake or an informal agreement. If there was no negotiation or if the parties didn't really come to an agreement that both understood, then there's no contract.

Proving the Elements of a Contract

The basic things you must prove to show that there was a contract are that there was an agreement of some sort, that you had a meaningful negotiation, and that you exchanged something of value. One major element in proving this is showing that both parties agreed and understood what they were getting into when they made the contract. Lawyers call this "a meeting of the minds." If both sides didn't really agree, then there's no contract. Look at what the initial offer was; did both sides think it was for the same thing? If one side thought "my car" meant the Buick, and the other side thought it meant the Ferrari, there's no meeting of the minds, and no contract.

The next thing to look at is whether the offer was accepted exactly as it was made. If instead of just saying "Yes," or "I agree," the other side says, "Yes, but can I also have a full tank of gas," that's actually considered a rejection of the old offer and making a new offer. Unless the new offer is accepted, the old offer was rejected and no contract exists. Negotiation seems like it is …

1. An offer

2. A counteroffer

3. Another offer

4. Another counteroffer

… until an agreement is reached. In legal terms, a negotiation is actually …

1. An offer

2. An implied rejection

3. A new offer

4. Another implied rejection

5. Another new offer

… until both sides agree to the offer.

The next major element in the definition of a contract is the exchange of something of value, called "consideration" It's not enough to have the word "consideration" in the contract—you'll see a lot of preprinted contracts that say "For one dollar and other good and valuable consideration"—but that doesn't mean consideration existed. You have to exchange something that's legally allowed (so no crack cocaine), but the court won't really look at whether the exchange is equal unless you're arguing that the exchange is so unequal that it amounts to fraud.

The court also won't look at what the exchange itself is and whether or not it's a foolish thing for one side to do—again, unless you're claiming fraud. If you want to buy an elephant, no one's stopping you. Sure, it might be tough to find a place to keep it, and keeping it clean, healthy, and fed might bankrupt you, but it's a free country.

You also need to show that you were ready, willing, and able to perform your side of the contract, or that there was a really good reason why you weren't going to. Once you've done that, you've shown all the elements needed to prove a contract exists.

No Punitive Damages Allowed

In contract cases, you get either money or performance. You might get the money you were owed under the contract, or the money you had to spend because the other side didn't live up to the contract. You might also get an order from the court saying that the other side has to do what they promised to do under the contract, like build a retaining wall to keep their land from sliding into yours.

What you won't get is extra money to punish the other party for breaking the contract. This is business, and all you get is what you bargained for. Punishment is for bad behavior that injures people, which, admittedly, failing to live up to a contract does. The difference is that in contracts you're expecting something, and there's always the possibility that the other side won't come through for you. It's business, not a surprise.

Will Contests

When a person dies with a will, she's said to die testate. Her will has to be proven to be her actual last will and testament, and that proving gets done in probate court. Probate actually means proving.

Just because a person has left a clear will stating where and how she wants her possessions divided after death doesn't mean that the people left behind agree with the terms of the will. When they disagree, they challenge or contest (pronounced *kon-TEST*) the will. This kind of lawsuit is called a will contest (pronounced *KON-test*).

How Probate Court Differs from Other Courts

Probate courts only deal with people who can't make decisions for themselves and their possessions, whether it's because of age (too young), disability, or death. Probate courts tend to be separate from ordinary, general trial courts. They have separate rules about how things are done and may even have a clerk and an office separate from the general court's clerk and office.

Time Frame

Probate courts seem to take longer than most other trial courts to get things done, particularly when it involves a will. This is often because wills get lower priority over living people who have immediate crises. Because will contests can continue as long as there are people willing to argue and have money to pay the lawyers, they can take anywhere from a few months to several years to resolve.

Family Law

Family law is the generic term for any problem dealing with marriage, children, and divorce. This is actually a very complex area of law. For example, divorce lawyers not only need to be familiar with the laws of divorce, but they also need to know about tax law, retirement benefits law, and insurance law so that they don't accidentally ruin someone's financial future.

Divorce

There are two ways to end a marriage: annulment and divorce.

Annulment is very rare. It's a legal declaration that the marriage never happened because of some major flaw in the ceremony. For example, if the parties were too drunk to know what they were doing, they didn't knowingly consent to be married, and the marriage can be annulled. Most of the time, though, marriages are done properly, and the only way to legally end the marriage is through the courts via divorce. Even if you were only married for one day, you are likely to have to get a divorce to legally end the marriage.

Divorce usually requires that you be a resident of the county and state for a specific period of time before you can start proceedings. This is so the court has the power to hear and decide your case (also known as jurisdiction, discussed in more detail in Chapter 7).

Child Custody

There can be issues of child custody even without divorce. Parents who never married, parents who are separated, parents who have been accused of negligence or abuse, and parents who are absent for whatever reason can pitch a family head-first into a dispute over who takes the children.

There are two types of custody: physical custody, where the child is physically with the custodian; and legal custody, where the child may not be physically with the custodian, but that custodian has the right to make major decisions about the child's life. What school the child goes to, medical treatment, extracurricular activities, and religious matters are all under the control of the person with legal custody.

JUST THE FACTS

Other types of custody you may be familiar with, like joint custody or sole custody, describe how many people are involved in custody of the child, not what kind of control the person has over the child.

Emancipation of Minors

Until a child turns 18, most states consider him a minor. Minors are under the control of their parents or guardians; they cannot decide whether or where to go to school, make decisions about their own medical treatment, or sign a binding contract for anything other than necessary food, clothing, and shelter. To get free of that control before age 18, the minor must apply to the court for emancipation.

Class Action

If enough other people have suffered the same kind of injuries from the same defect or event, it can be more efficient to create a class action suit than to have each person sue individually. Class action suits take all the people who have a similar claim and officially turn them into a single plaintiff, in a process called certifying them as a class. Usually one person's name appears as the lead or name plaintiff in the case name.

Class action suits are more efficient for the courts and for the defendant, because they only have to deal with one case instead of thousands. The advantage to the plaintiffs is that the cost of a lawyer and pursuing the case is spread around a group, although frequently these cases are taken on a contingent fee basis. (See Chapter 5 for a discussion of how contingent fees work.) Also, the potential payoff, judgment, or settlement is often much higher than it would be for one person's injury, another advantage to the plaintiffs.

Requirements to Create a Class Action

The requirements for creating a class action have one thing in common: fairness. Turning one person's lawsuit into a group's lawsuit has to be fair to everyone, including the plaintiffs, the defendant, and the court. Class action suits are fair to the court when there are so many plaintiffs that individual lawsuits would overwhelm the court. They're fair to the plaintiffs when there are common claims that are typical of the plaintiffs (or defendants) and when the named plaintiff is able to protect the interests of everyone in the class. Class action suits are fair to the defendant when the suit will focus on the common claims rather than on each individual plaintiff's facts. If you can show all of these things, then you can create a class action suit.

When pursuing a class action lawsuit, you must provide notice to the potential class of plaintiffs. Notice has to be given at least two different times. First, class members should get notice that the case is being pursued, and at the same time give them the option to pursue their claim on their own, called "opting out." In addition, any time there is a proposed settlement, the court usually orders that a notice be sent to all the members of the class.

Certifying the Class

For a class action suit to work, the class has to be approved or certified by the court. This is done after the complaint has been filed. The attorney then makes a formal request of the court for certification. The defendant may object to the certification on the grounds that the requirements for creating a class action aren't met. The defendant may also question whether the named plaintiff is representative of the group, or question the ability and resources of the attorney handling the case for the group.

Shareholder Suits and Derivative Actions

When you buy stock or shares in a corporation, you become an owner of that corporation. The more stock you buy, the bigger a share of the corporation you own. Once you've paid for the stock, your financial obligation is over. You are protected from losing anything other than the amount of money you invested in the stock. If the corporation owes someone money, that creditor cannot come directly to you for payment. This is because you are protected from having to pay for anything other than the shares of stock that you own through limited liability. In exchange for that protection, you do not have the power to directly manage the corporation. You have the power to vote for people to manage the corporation, and you have the power to request that the corporation consider doing something, but you can't force the corporation to do anything without getting the agreement of the other shareholders.

The people you elect to run the corporation have duties to you and to the corporation, including the duty to deal fairly and loyally with the corporation and the shareholders. You have rights, too: the right to get your share of profit when the corporation declares a dividend, and the right to look at the corporation's accounting books, among others. When your rights aren't respected, or if the people running the corporation aren't dealing fairly and loyally with the corporation or stockholders, you have a right to sue.

Suing for Your Own Losses

As a stockholder, you have specific individual rights. If the corporation's actions harm you or trample on your rights, you have an action against the corporation. It's called an individual or direct action, because the right to act comes directly from you, the plaintiff, an individual. For example, if you asked to see the books of the corporation and were refused, that's an individual wrong. If you didn't get paid your share of the profits when everyone else did, that's an individual wrong. You can sue the corporation directly to recover your profits or to force them to let you look at the books. This is more common with smaller corporations, because larger corporations tend to have mechanisms in place to make sure these sorts of mistakes don't happen.

Suing for the Corporation's Losses

Stockholders also have rights that they get through, or derive from, the corporation. These are called derivative rights. If the corporation won't act in its own best interest (maybe because it would hurt one of the people in power in the corporation), a shareholder can sue to force the corporation to act. For example, if the corporation loaned money to its president, who hasn't paid it back, the board of directors may not want to sue to get the money back to avoid hurting the president. However, it's in the corporation's best interest to get paid back. As a stockholder, or as a member of a group of stockholders, you can use the rights you derive from the corporation and sue on its behalf.

The Least You Need to Know

- The same action can result in both civil and criminal lawsuits.
- Even if someone cannot pay off a lawsuit now, she might be able to pay it off later.
- Probate or will contests are usually held in a separate civil court.
- Class actions are only created if they're fair to all parties.

Damages and How You Get Them

In This Chapter

- Understanding damages
- Different kinds of damages
- Why you need to show damages
- Why you need to mitigate damages

The court can't turn back the hands of time. The court can't unhurt your back, can't regrow the tree your neighbor cut down, and can't uncrash your car. What the court can do is say "we're going to put a dollar amount on that claim" to resolve the issue. The court can also resolve issues by making people do (or preventing them from doing) specific acts. For example, if no dollar amount would resolve the problem of the cut tree, the court might order your neighbor to plant a new one. But before the court can order action, someone has to suffer a loss, called damages. This chapter is about what kind of loss or damages you need in order to have a "good" case, and what the court can order done to "make good" your loss.

No Harm = No Damages = No Case

If you haven't already suffered some kind of loss, or there isn't some ongoing issue that directly affects you, the law doesn't have the ability to help you. The law isn't concerned with an imaginary future; it works based on what's happened in the past and makes very few predictions. For example, the law will not tell someone not to follow you tomorrow if he's never followed you in the first place. As far as the law is concerned, if you haven't been hurt, you don't have a loss. If you don't have a loss, then you don't have a problem. No harm and no problem mean no damages, and if you don't have damages, you don't have a lawsuit.

Is the Loss Worth Anything?

Be wary, though: even if there is harm, the damages can still be zero, or a very small amount. How can that be? In a lawsuit that uses a jury, it's up to the jury to decide how much the damage is worth. The jury is entitled to say, "You're right, plaintiff, you were harmed and had a loss, so you win on principle, but the loss isn't worth very much." The loss can be so difficult to put a price tag on that the jury awards $1—or 1¢—to the plaintiff. Cases where the defendant lied about the plaintiff, committing defamation, are often in this category.

A less common way for a winning plaintiff to fail to get monetary damages is if the plaintiff is so obnoxious throughout the trial that the jury ends up hating him. Juries have to follow the law, so they're forced to find in favor of the party who's right according to the law and the facts. In one case, the jury had to find that the plaintiff was a victim of a wrongful citizen's arrest, because the law and the facts said so. Ordinarily, this would be a big financial win. Unfortunately for the plaintiff, he was such a jerk throughout the proceedings that the jury refused to give any monetary damages. In fact, the jury asked if they could make the plaintiff pay the defendant's attorney fees!

The lesson here is that if your attorney tells you to "tone it down" or in any way to change your behavior, take a good look at yourself to see why she might be suggesting this. She's the expert on what works in court, and the way you see yourself and your behavior might not be the way others see you. It might be worth making a change to improve your chances of winning your case.

Types of Damages

Two types of losses result in damages: those that can be fixed with money, and those that can only be fixed by action. Some courts have the ability to award money damages. Some courts have the ability to make someone do something. Some courts can give you both kinds of solutions.

Whatever solution the court comes up with, when the court makes its decision, it is called "awarding relief." Whatever kind of relief you want, lawyers lump it all together and call it "damages," because it's the easiest way to understand what the court requires in order to consider your case. Ultimately, without some form of damages for which the court can give you a remedy, your case will be dismissed.

Monetary Damages

Losses that can be fixed with money are called "monetary damages." The big issue with monetary damages is usually over just how much money it will take to fix the problem. If you paid $1,000 for a television this morning, and the television doesn't work this afternoon, it's pretty easy to say you have suffered monetary damages in the amount of $1,000. On the other hand, if you paid $1,000 for a painting 10 years ago that was damaged today, it's much harder to say what your damages are. Is it the $1,000 that you paid 10 years ago? Or is it more, because the art gained in value over the years? It might even be worth less than the $1,000 you paid, based on the current market value for paintings.

Arguments over monetary damages are common. Even with what seems like a straightforward case, people start bringing up issues like original value versus replacement cost, and whether the replacement should be priced out for a brand-new one or one that's the same age as the one that was lost. On top of that, some things are not easily put into dollars and cents. For example, how do you put a value on a broken leg? These are legitimate issues, and the courts are used to dealing with them. It's unusual for a case to proceed without significant discussion of what the correct amount of damages should be.

Nonmonetary Damages

The other kind of loss is fixed with action, and is called nonmonetary damage. The solution for nonmonetary damages is referred to as injunctive relief or equitable relief. Here, you're not asking for a sum of money; you're asking that someone do (or not do) something she should or shouldn't have in the first place. For example, your neighbor may start building a pizza oven on your side of the property line. What you want is the removal of the pizza oven, and the restoration of your part of the property. Your solution is a court order called an "injunction," which forces the other side to do the specific thing that will fix the problem.

Injunctions are used for everything from family law issues to high finance. They're a very flexible—and very powerful—tool. Injunctive relief can be used together with monetary damages so that the court can create a complete solution to a party's problem.

PITFALLS

In order to get equitable relief, you have to come to the court with clean hands. This means that as far as this case is concerned, you've acted in good faith and behaved ethically throughout. If you've got dirty hands, the court won't award you equitable relief.

Preventing Damages Before They Begin

In law, there's always an exception to prove the rule. The rule here is that there has to be some harm before there is a lawsuit. The exception is in situations where there isn't necessarily harm in the classic sense of loss, but there certainly is a problem that needs a solution. In these cases, there's another kind of solution the courts can provide, one that is intended to prevent any damage to either side before it can start. The solution is called "declaratory relief." It works by asking the court to make a decision as to what your rights and the other side's rights are in a particular situation. The court then "declares" what your rights are and issues an order that makes that declaration clear. It's not really granting relief from damage or loss, because there wasn't any; it's one of the few times the court acts without real damage or loss.

Getting You to Where You Were

One way to ask for damages is to ask to be taken back to where you were before the conflict started. These damages are called "compensatory damages." Compensatory damages literally compensate you, or make up for, what you lost. In order to get these kinds of damages, you have to show where you actually were before everything began. You also have to show how the other side took you away from that place. For example, if you claim that someone's bad actions resulted in you losing income for a year, you're likely to have to show things like tax returns to prove where you were financially.

JUST THE FACTS

Many people object to showing their tax returns and other private data, but the court isn't going to just take your word for how much you made last year when there's a very easy way to determine exactly how much you did make. You can ask the court to seal that portion of the record that includes your tax return, and for permission to block out your Social Security number if those are concerns for you. In fact, most courts nowadays have rules that prohibit revealing birth dates and Social Security numbers in any public court file.

Another example of getting you to where you were would be repairing the damage to your car as a result of an accident. If the car was completely totaled, giving you the Kelley Blue Book value of the car gives you the monetary value of what you lost. You're technically in the same place you were before the accident happened. Of course, that doesn't compensate you for the time it took to sue, or your attorney fees, or anything else; you can ask for that as part of the consequential damages you suffered as a result of the injury.

You can also ask to be reimbursed for the additional, secondary losses the original injury led to. These are called "consequential damages." Lawyers say that consequential damages "flow" from the injury, or say that "but for" the injury, these secondary losses wouldn't have happened. If you're a plumber, and you purchase a brand-new truck that's a lemon, you'd say, "I want the purchase price of this truck back." That would be dealt with through compensatory damages. However, what if you were unable to work for a week because you had no work truck? But for the lack of a good truck, you could've made a week's income. Your loss of income for that week is a consequential damage.

IN THE KNOW

When you negotiate a contract, for yourself or for your business, it's a good idea to specify that you'll get consequential damages if the other side doesn't live up to the contract. Often, unless the contract states that consequential damages are available, the court won't allow them in contract cases.

Keep track of your consequential damages carefully. Although the court may not allow you to recover all of them, you may be able to deduct some of them from your taxes. Check with your attorney and tax preparer before trying to make these deductions, because there are always exceptions.

Getting You to Where You Should Be

The other major kind of monetary damages doesn't look at where you were before the incident happened; it looks at where you would be if the incident hadn't happened or if things had happened the way they were supposed to. This is most common in contract cases, where it's easy to see where you planned to be at the end of the contract.

Suppose you contract with someone to build a house, and the contractor runs off without finishing the job. If you were supposed to have a completed house at the end of the contract, the court can give you damages against that contractor in the amount that it will take to get you a completed house.

The major issue with these kinds of damages is that you'll have to find some way to show how much it will cost to get you to the end result. You'll often need to hire an expert to testify as to how much this will cost or take. These experts can charge anywhere from $100 an hour on up, but you might be able to recover the cost of hiring the expert as part of your damages. You might still need to show tax returns or other proof of income to give a valid starting point. You're also likely to have to show what your costs were to make up for what you lost in the incident. These are all matters of proof, and your attorney can best tell you what you'll need to show in your particular case.

The Ford Pinto Case and Punitive Damages

As noted in Chapter 2, contract cases don't allow damages as punishment for what happened. In a contract, you're considered a business person, and your harm is considered limited to the contract and anything the lack in the contract caused. In other cases, particularly tort cases, the defendant can be punished for his behavior by having to pay more money on top of the damages that he directly caused. These are called punitive damages.

The most famous case of punitive damages, and a good example of the kinds of cases that get awarded punitive damages, is the Ford Pinto case. Ford Motor Company designed and manufactured a subcompact car called the Pinto in the 1970s. The design called for the gas tank to be placed right in front of the rear bumper. In some rear-end collisions, the gas tank exploded, killing or severely injuring the people in the car.

Ford knew about this problem, and employees discussed changing the position of the gas tank to prevent this kind of injury. They looked at the cost of redesigning the car, including retooling the manufacturing plant. While the per-car price was low, the overall cost of making the change was high. In fact, Ford estimated that it would be cheaper to pay off people whose loved ones were injured or killed than it would be to change the design and manufacture of the car. Ford decided not to make the change.

During a 1981 lawsuit against Ford for a death and a serious injury caused by rear-end-collision gas-tank explosion, this cost-saving measure was discovered. The jury was horrified that Ford decided to save about $11 per car rather than save a human life. The jury wanted to send a strong message to Ford—and to other manufacturers—that following an economic analysis that valued money over life was not acceptable. To do that, they awarded the largest amount of punitive damages ever at that time, $125 million. Although the judge reduced the punitive damage award, manufacturers got the message.

The Ford Pinto case is exactly the sort of situation that punitive damages are intended to address. Punitive damages are given when the defendant's actions were the cause of injury and were really outrageous. The defendant's act has to cause reasonable people to think that the plaintiff deserves more than just compensatory damages to repay whatever the injury cost. Those reasonable people (usually the jury) have to believe that an example must be set so that other potential defendants don't copy this defendant's behavior, thinking they'll get away with it.

Liquidated Damages

When you can say exactly how much the damage is worth in dollars and cents, you've got "liquidated" damages. Technically, liquidated damages aren't really a category of damages the way that punitive or consequential damages are. Instead, they're a way of talking about whether the damage can be paid for in money or whether you require some form of injunctive relief. Cash is considered a liquid asset, because it can flow freely from one person to another without any argument about how much a dollar is actually worth. One dollar is 100 cents, and that's that. You can still argue about how much a dollar can buy, but it's always going to be worth 100 cents.

Sometimes, contracts will say how damages are to be calculated if there's a breach of contract. That, too, is a form of "liquidated damages." When you negotiate a contract, it might be a good idea to state that if one party fails, they have to pay a specific amount as liquidated damages. Figure out how much the contract is worth as a whole, and then add in whatever you think you might need if the contract falls through. That might include money to compensate you for the time you spend trying to get someone else to finish the contract, and money you might spend on a lawsuit.

For example, if you're paying $100,000 to someone to build your house, the contract is worth $100,000. How much time and energy do you think you'll spend trying to get a new contractor? Put that into a dollar amount, and add it to the $100,000. Add in what you think it might cost to hire an attorney to help you with the case.

PITFALLS

Try to remain reasonable when calculating the amount of liquidated damages to specify in a contract. Remember that contract cases don't allow punitive damages. If you get greedy about the liquidated damages, the judge is likely to strike the entire amount down as disguised punitive damages. It might be reasonable to double or triple the amount of the contract, but then again, it might not. The law always looks to the individual facts of the case for what's reasonable.

Your Duty to Minimize Your Damages

The defendant is responsible for repairing or making good the injury that he caused, but only the injury that he caused. You, as the injured person, have a duty to make sure you don't make the injury worse. This is called a duty to "mitigate damages." There is an old saying in law, "One who seeks equity must do equity." That means if you want the court to act fairly to you, you have to act fairly to the other side. Mitigation of damages is part of that process.

A perfect example is seen in landlord-tenant lease cases. Suppose there is a one-year lease for an apartment. If the tenant moves out with six months to go on the lease, the landlord has to try to re-rent the premises for a reasonable rate. This doesn't mean that he has to do a full-on media attack to try to rent the property, but he has to make a good-faith effort to rent it for as much as reasonably possible. The amount the former tenant owes is reduced by the amount the landlord is able to get for the apartment, but the landlord's cost for re-renting the apartment is the former tenant's responsibility.

The duty to mitigate damages applies in every case, in one form or another. If your key supplier fails on you, the law will not reward you for sitting around whining about it. You have to try to find a new supplier to make sure you don't fail on your other contracts. The law will allow you to recover everything you spent to get that new supplier, but again, you have a duty to make sure you tried to get a good deal to minimize the damage.

A practical reason to minimize or mitigate your damages is that it's going to take quite a while to get the money back from the person who injured you. The money is coming out of your pocket first. Don't spend more than you can afford to fix the problem if at all possible.

IN THE KNOW

It's okay to take the most expensive quote as long as there's a good reason for it beyond making the other guy pay.

Can I Get My Attorney Fees Paid?

Attorney fees are often seen by the parties as a sort of consequential damage in their case. Unfortunately, attorney fees are usually *not* something you can get as an item of damage. Again, there are exceptions that we'll get to in a minute. The United States has what is called "the American rule," which states that because you don't need an attorney to use the courts, you don't get your attorney fees paid as part of your damages. It's your choice to use an attorney, and while it's usually a wise choice, it's not a requirement. If it's not a requirement, it's not considered a form of damage.

The exceptions usually fall under two categories:

- There is a contract that says the loser has to pay attorney fees.
- There is a law in the case that says the loser has to pay attorney fees.

A perfect example of a law that requires payment of attorney fees as damages is the Federal Magnusson Moss Warranty Act. Suppose you buy a car, and that car is a lemon. Suppose the manufacturer can't or won't fix the car, even though there is a warranty on it. This is exactly the kind of situation that the Magnusson Moss Warranty Act addresses. This act says that if the manufacturer loses, they have to pay attorney fees as part of damages.

Why? There are two big reasons behind this part of the Magnusson Moss Act. First, manufacturers who make a warranty should live up to their warranties. Second, it's typically a "little guy" who's going to have to go up against a "Goliath," with unlimited resources. If the "little guy" had to pay an attorney by the hour to sue over a product that only cost $1,500 to begin with, "David" could never afford to sue "Goliath."

Can I Get My Interest Paid?

When it comes to lawsuits, interest falls into three general categories:

- Interest as an item of damage
- Prejudgment interest
- Judgment interest

Suppose you purchase a car, and have to take out a loan. If the car is defective, you want to return the car. If you purchased the car for $25,000, you want your damages to include the purchase price. However, you also are paying interest on the loan. In order to make sure you are made whole, you need to make sure you get your interest payments back. This is an example of interest as an item of damage.

Now suppose you loaned $1,000 to a friend, who was to pay it back by December 31. Suppose she doesn't repay that loan. You want interest on that money. That is prejudgment or presuit interest. Many states have specific laws that cover what situations allow for this kind of interest, and in what amount.

Finally, suppose you file a lawsuit and you win. You will get an order from the court saying you win—a judgment. Until that judgment is paid, you get interest on the amount of money awarded in the judgment. This is called judgment interest. Again, different states have different laws that cover interest in this situation.

JUST THE FACTS

The judgment interest rate is set by law and is usually the prime interest rate (the rate the government lends money to banks) plus a few percentage points. As the prime interest rate changes, so will the judgment interest rate. That makes calculating the interest owed very tricky!

Pro Rata Damages

Part of being fair to both sides is making sure the damages paid by the defaulting side are accurate. Sometimes the court will only allow that damages be charged for the actual time you suffered them on a daily basis. This is called "pro rata" (literally, "by the rate") or proportional damages. In order to pro rate the damages, your costs must be liquidated. This is often used in cases where it's easy to liquidate the damages, like in a contract case. It isn't often used in personal injury cases, because the cost of the damages suffered doesn't stop when the lawsuit is over.

Documenting Damages

When you've been injured in any way, you need to track what the injury is and what it has cost you. This is called documenting your damages. Documenting your damages is an important part of proving that you have a case. Not only does your documentation show that you have suffered a loss that can be remedied by the court, but it will help provide the evidence that's needed to prove the loss and the amount of damages.

Make sure you take the following actions:

- Keep all the receipts relating to the injury, and make copies of them.
- Take pictures of your injuries or of the damaged items.
- Keep a phone log of any calls you make to get the damage repaired.
- Keep copies of all e-mails sent and received in repairing the damage.
- Get more than one estimate or see more than one doctor.
- Keep any letters or estimates given to you.
- Document why you chose the repair shop or supplier you did, especially if it was the most expensive one.

Take Notes

Be as polite as possible in working with everyone you encounter as a result of the injury. The more polite and reasonable you are, the more cooperation you're likely to get out of them. It's a good idea to get a simple notebook or legal pad, and write down the names of people you deal with, along with the date and time and what was said, every time. Be sure to ask for names, spellings, and job titles. That way, the next time you deal with that company or person, you can pick up quickly where you left off. You're also more likely to get good service if the person on the other end realizes you're keeping track of everything.

Because of the use of cell phones, it's also a good idea to keep a small notebook with you at all times in case you need to write something down and you're not with your main notes and files. It's possible but not likely that these notebooks might be admitted as evidence themselves (see Chapter 11 for more on evidence). Even if they're not evidence themselves, these notebooks are going to be an outstanding resource for you and your attorney as you try to get evidence together for the trial.

Keep Files

As you deal with the events that lead up to your lawsuit and with the lawsuit itself, it's extremely important that you keep track of all the paperwork generated. The least you should do is toss them all in the same place, whether that's a box or a bag. That's not the best solution, but if you're under too much stress to do more than that, at least you're not throwing things away. A better idea is to get an expandable file folder, preferably the kind with a flap that keeps the papers inside. You don't need to buy the legal size unless you're trying to keep larger items inside; lawyers use regular 8.5×11 paper now, like everyone else.

If you have items that are too large or bulky to go in the files, write down in your notebook where they are. In the stress of the lawsuit, you may not immediately remember. It's helpful to know that at one point you did have the item, and to know where it was last.

Using Electronics Wisely

If you use the computer or a smart phone or the like to keep track of things for your case, back up frequently. And don't just back up to one kind of media or to one place. Back up online, to another hard drive, to CDs, to hard copy, and to a USB drive. Be aware that you may have to produce your hard drive and backups to the other side during discovery (see Chapter 10 on the pretrial process for more on discovery).

The Least You Need to Know

- If you can't show legally sufficient damages, you have no case.
- Damages can take you back to where you were before the incident happened, or take you to where you should've been at the end of a contract.
- Punitive damages aren't allowed in contract cases.
- You have a duty to minimize or mitigate your damages.

Legal Representation

Many people are more comfortable in a lawsuit with a lawyer at their side, but do you really need one? This part tells you how to decide whether or not to get a lawyer, and the kinds of things to look for if you do decide to hire one. You'll find out how much everything in a lawsuit costs, and who's involved in the process.

Do You Really Need a Lawyer?

In This Chapter

- The pros and cons of going without a lawyer
- The many types of lawyers
- Questions to ask when choosing a lawyer
- What to watch out for in a lawyer you hire

You don't need to hire a lawyer to go to court any more than you need to hire an electrician to install a light switch. However, the more complex the job, the better an idea it is to hire a professional. They're more likely to have the tools at hand and do a faster, neater job than you would.

Advantages and Disadvantages of Going Without

The obvious advantage of going without a lawyer is financial. You won't be spending any money on legal fees. You also won't be at the mercy of the lawyer's schedule for return calls, meetings, or setting court dates. You may even get some slack from the court on the format of your paperwork because you don't have a lawyer. However, you won't get any leeway on due dates or showing proper respect for the court.

There are two major disadvantages to going without a lawyer, and they're summed up in this joke: Joe spent four hours trying to get the power back on in his house. He called the power company, and they swore there was nothing wrong with the grid, so he called an electrician to come right away. The electrician came, spent three minutes looking at Joe's setup, flipped a switch, and the power came on. Joe was thrilled—until the electrician gave him a bill for $250. "All you did was flip a switch! It only took you three minutes! How can you charge $250?" The electrician replied, "It's not $250 for three minutes; it's $250 for knowing to flip the switch."

IN THE KNOW

If there is a law library nearby, particularly one that's geared toward practicing lawyers rather than a law school, it will have a lot of resources available to help you go it alone.

In many cases, the nonlawyer doesn't know what switches to flip and can spend several hours on a case without ever getting the job done. Many people recognize this, and feel intimidated about even trying to go it without a lawyer. The problem is that lawyers aren't cheap, and free lawyers aren't available to the majority of the population. Remember, though, there are many lawyers at many price points, and they are often willing to negotiate their fees.

PITFALLS

Beware of using public paralegal services for litigation. Paralegals are prohibited by law from giving legal advice to solve your current problem and prevent future problems. Plus, because paralegals aren't licensed, there's no guarantee of basic competence. Last, most paralegals are not covered by professional insurance. You can sue, but you're not likely to recover much money.

Finding a Lawyer

There are as many ways to find a lawyer as there are lawyers and cases. Lawyers advertise in places like the Yellow Pages, newspapers, magazines, and even on Craigslist. It never hurts to check out an advertised attorney, but there are other ways of finding a lawyer as well.

Word of Mouth

The most common way to find a lawyer is by word of mouth. Start with the professionals you already use, like accountants, bankers (and bank tellers), and stock brokers. They may have used a particular attorney and had a good experience, or they might have a client whose expertise they respect. Move on to asking friends and family whether they've used a lawyer they would recommend to you. It's not enough to ask whether they know any lawyers. It's important to find out what their experience was like, and whether they would recommend that lawyer to someone else.

Essentially, ask everyone you know, everywhere you go. The same names may start to pop up over and over again. That's a good sign that this attorney has a good reputation and might be a good fit for you.

Remember that just because the attorney lost a case for someone doesn't mean that she is incompetent. Fifty percent of all people who go to court lose their cases—it's just the way things work. It's more important to find out answers to the following questions:

- Does the attorney or her staff return calls?

- Does the attorney meet deadlines?

- Does the attorney treat clients respectfully?

- Were the fees charged fairly?

- Did the attorney give a clear accounting of time and money?

- Did the attorney seem knowledgeable?

- Did the attorney seem confident in court or in negotiations?

Bar Associations

Look online or in the Yellow Pages for *bar* associations such as state and county bars for where you live. Many of them have referral programs, which attorneys sign up for. Unless the attorney signs up for the program, the bar association won't refer cases to her. Because of this, most of the attorneys who are in the referral program tend to be newer, or looking to build up their practice. Some very fine lawyers are involved in these referral programs. As with any attorney you consider hiring, be thorough in asking the questions listed later in this chapter.

DEFINITION

A **bar** is a way of referring to attorneys as a profession or group, or a group made up of attorneys.

Legal Services Plans

In a legal services plan, sometimes called a legal insurance plan, you pay either an annual lump sum (usually between $100 and $300) or a monthly fee that divides the annual fee into payments. This entitles you to specific legal services. You may, for example, be entitled to have a simple will drawn up, have legal documents reviewed, and have letters and phone calls made on your behalf. For other legal problems, you'll be given a highly discounted hourly rate, sometimes less than $100 per hour.

Some people find these services very helpful, and there are some very good attorneys who work with these services. However, you will have less choice in the attorney who provides your service, and if you have a major case, you may prefer to interview attorneys and find one with expertise in your specific problem.

A legal insurance program will only refer you to an attorney who has signed up to take cases from them for a prepaid price. With most legal insurance plans, there is no opportunity to choose the lawyer who will be assigned to the case, although there may be a provision for switching attorneys if the relationship is not working out.

If you need more than the service agreed to in the insurance contract, you will have to come to an agreement with the attorney about how that service will be given and paid for. Check with the specific insurance carrier to see what its guidelines are for those instances.

The advantage to legal insurance plans is that the attorney is preselected and available at need. The disadvantage is that there is a limited selection and the attorney might not be the best for the situation.

Legal Aid

Legal aid began as assistance for low-income people, typically those living at or below the poverty level. However, there are legal aid programs for people in specific situations other than just low income. For example, legal aid groups provide service for the elderly, for artists, for family law issues, and so on. Some law schools also operate legal aid programs in which attorney-supervised law students provide legal services.

Finally, there are legal services dedicated to providing service to particular groups of people, like union members, students, and others. Check to see if any group you're involved in has such a legal clinic; they're often excellent.

Most of these groups are staffed by very dedicated attorneys and paralegals who are often highly skilled in their area of law. Unfortunately, they are often burdened with very high caseloads so attorneys aren't able to spend as much time as they would like on individual cases. It can be difficult to get hold of the attorney or paralegal handling a particular case because of the high caseload.

Solo Attorneys

Solos, or sole practitioners, have no other attorneys working with them. They may have secretaries or paralegals, or no one at all. This can result in lower fees and more personal attention. It can also mean the attorney is overwhelmed and has no help. Check to see which category your attorney falls into.

Large Firm vs. Small Firm

Sometimes a referral will not be to a particular lawyer, but instead to a law firm. Firms have reputations, and the individual attorneys in the firm can usually be relied upon to fit that reputation. For example, some firms have a reputation for aggressiveness, and most of their lawyers are aggressive. Be aware that "aggressive" doesn't necessarily translate to "effective." An attorney who's devoted to maintaining a reputation for aggression may not be willing to compromise when you are.

JUST THE FACTS

Companies made up of lawyers are called law firms, not law companies. Who knows why? It's just one of those things.

When a referral is to a particular attorney, you still need to consider what kind of firm they're affiliated with and how that firm will fit your needs.

The definitions of "small," "medium," and "large" firms vary depending on the part of the country. In big cities, large may mean over 150 lawyers; in smaller cities, large may mean over 30. Regardless, the larger the firm, the more expensive it will be. A sole practitioner might charge anywhere from $75 to $450 per hour, or more if she's a very well-known attorney. Attorneys in large law firms generally charge from $250 to $750 per hour or more.

The advantage to a law firm over a sole practitioner is depth; if your attorney becomes ill or has a conflict, another attorney is available to take her place. Firms also tend to have more administrative support, which can make your case run more smoothly. Realistically, the number of lawyers in the firm is less important than the kind of staff support the attorney has. Lawsuits are complex, requiring careful organization and attention to detail. If the attorney doesn't have a lot of staff support, ask how he manages detail. Many lawyers' offices are highly computerized, which can make up for not having much in the way of a human staff.

Because legal help is a service, in the end, the most important factor is the attorney himself, not the size of the firm. The number of attorneys in a firm bears little relationship to the skill of the attorney. Some highly skilled lawyers practice on their own, and others practice in a large firm. Focus on the attorney first, and the firm itself second.

The Famous Lawyer

There's an ad on local TV in which two insurance executives find out that a particular lawyer is on the case. "Oh, no! We'd better settle now!" they exclaim. That's everyone's fantasy of the big-name lawyer; people will tremble at her name, and give in immediately. The irony is that the lawyer on the other side has her ego on the line. She may fight harder than usual to prove that she's up to the famous lawyer's weight.

The reality is that the lawyer's reputation will have some effect on the case, but not necessarily enough to make the case an instant win. Famous lawyers cost more, and are often worth the money. But don't let the fame prevent you from insisting on the same kind of service you would expect from any lawyer. Your attorney should return phone calls, answer your questions, and give enough time and attention to your case to make it a success.

When Is a Lawyer Supplied?

In criminal cases, you have a right to an attorney, and the judicial system must provide you with one. This is not true in civil cases. Because the only thing at stake is money, not physical freedom, there is no constitutional right to representation. However, you might have an arrangement in a contract that supplies you with an attorney when you need one.

Insurance Company Attorneys

Your homeowner's or auto insurance policy probably provides for an attorney to defend you if you're sued for an event that's covered by your policy. These attorneys are usually very experienced in defending the type of claim made under the policy. Their primary client, however, is the insurance company.

In-House Corporate Attorneys

If you work for a corporation and are sued for something the corporation is responsible for, the corporation might provide attorneys to defend you and the corporation. Some corporate attorneys focus more on transactions and negotiations than on lawsuits, and so they hire outside counsel to represent them in lawsuits. When the attorney represents the corporation, the primary client is the corporation. This means there may be some conflict between the corporation's interests and your interests; you might want to hire a separate attorney if you believe you have interests that differ from those of the corporation.

Third-Party Attorneys

Your main attorney might hire a specialist to represent you. This legal subcontractor is usually hired because of her expertise or because she is licensed in another state where your primary attorney isn't licensed. Unlike attorneys provided for you under insurance plans or by corporations, this attorney hasn't been paid for ahead of time. You will have to pay this attorney separately, unless you have an agreement with your primary attorney that you will only be paying his fees, and that he will pay any other attorneys who work for him out of what you pay him.

Interviewing Prospective Lawyers

One of the advantages—and disadvantages—of today's legal market is that there are so many attorneys available. It's an advantage because you are likely to find an attorney whose experience and style work well for you. It's a disadvantage because in order to find that attorney, you might have to interview more than you'd like to.

IN THE KNOW

Keep track of the attorneys you interview and the answers they give to your questions. Write everything down! That way you'll have a basis for comparison and making your choice will be that much easier.

Past Experience

As with investments, in law, past performance is no guarantee of future success. However, law is one of those areas where experience helps develop judgment and ability. An attorney is legally allowed to take a case in an area in which he has no experience, as long as he works to develop expertise in that area. If your attorney has no experience with your type of case, ask him the following questions:

- How do you plan to make up for your lack of experience?

- Do you have other, more experienced attorneys you can call on for help?

- Do you have enough time to learn what you need to in order to be an effective advocate for me?

- Will I be billed for the extra time it takes for you to learn this new area?

Regardless of whether the attorney has experience in your topic, ask him these questions:

- What sorts of other cases have you handled?

- What courts have you appeared in?

- How many trials have you done?

- What sort of support services do you have to keep you on track?

- How have you handled problems with too much work and not enough time in the past?

- What kind of help will you provide in completing interrogatories (see Chapter 7)?

- Do you have malpractice insurance?

PITFALLS

Not all states require that attorneys maintain malpractice insurance in order to practice law. Ask your attorney whether she carries insurance, and how much it's for. If there should be a malpractice claim, at least there'll be money available to collect if you win.

Success Rate

It's legitimate to ask about the attorney's success rate, keeping in mind that batting .500 isn't all bad. No one can have a 100 percent success rate just by the very nature of the law. We have a system where one side wins and the other side loses, and someone's going to be on the losing side every time. Losses can have more to do with specific fact patterns than the attorney's skills, so be more concerned with past experience, client recommendations, and how confident you feel with the attorney herself.

Client Recommendations

Another way to evaluate a potential attorney is by talking to previous clients. Because of attorney-client confidentiality, the attorney must get permission from clients before referring prospective clients to them for questions. Many clients prefer not to discuss their case once it's over, so don't expect a long list of people to call. If you can't get any client recommendations, this may be a sign that it never occurred to the attorney to get permission from previous clients, or it may be a sign that the attorney doesn't have any clients whom he believes would be willing to say positive things about him. You should be able to get some sort of client comment, even if it's from a client survey, before hiring the attorney.

Cost and Billing Practices

Don't be shy about talking about how much this is going to cost you, and how you'll be billed. See Chapter 5 for a thorough discussion of costs and how you can pay an attorney. The big thing to remember is that this is a negotiation. There are enough attorneys out there that you should be able to find a good one who's willing to work with you on how much your case will cost and how the payment is going to be worked out. If you're determined to have a particular lawyer, though, you have less room for negotiation. Negotiation means just that—not screaming and telling the other person he's taking advantage of you. Ask if there's room for discussion on price and payment method. It can't hurt, and it might help.

Who Will Be Handling Your Case?

Some law firms have people who specialize in finding clients, while other lawyers actually handle the case. Ask about whether other lawyers will be working on your case and whether their cost is the same as, or different from, that of the attorney you're currently talking to. Who will be "point man" or your point of contact for the case? Is there a paralegal or legal assistant who will be doing much of the non-court-appearance work? Find out. These are legitimate questions to ask, and if the attorney becomes uncomfortable, that's a warning sign. You might prefer to have a firm that's up front about these sorts of issues.

It's also important to make sure the person you're planning to hire is licensed as an attorney. The Internet makes that an easy task. See the helpful websites in Appendix B for a list of contacts to check in your state to find out whether or not an attorney has a current license.

The next issue to investigate is whether the attorney has had any disciplinary action taken against her. The fact that a complaint has been filed against an attorney isn't that big a deal. As with lawsuits, anyone can file a complaint (sometimes called a grievance) against an attorney, even if there's no basis for it. If the attorney has been practicing long enough, chances are excellent that at least one client has complained, usually because of fees. The big question is whether there was a basis for the complaint and how the complaint was resolved.

In particular, you want to know whether the attorney was disciplined in any way. You're better off finding one who's never been disciplined. If you still want to use this attorney, ask her why she was disciplined and whether the underlying problem has been resolved. Some very fine attorneys were ill and unable to handle their practice properly for a while, or are recovering alcoholics who are now able to provide outstanding legal services. The bigger problems come with attorneys who improperly took client money. That indicates at the very least a problem with accounting, if not worse. While it's true that mishandling client money might have been because of a problem that's now resolved, more often it indicates a lack of basic honesty and responsibility. Again, there are many attorneys available who haven't had this kind of problem; you're better off using one of them rather than an attorney who can't handle client money properly.

The Least You Need to Know

- There are many attorneys available; you're not stuck with the first one you meet.
- Interview several attorneys before you settle on one.
- Ask questions and write down the answers when you interview attorneys.
- Make sure your attorney is licensed and insured.

How Much Does Justice Cost?

In This Chapter

- Making sense of attorneys' fees
- Deciding which way you'll pay
- Uncovering other costs
- Considering nonmonetary costs
- Getting the best value for your dollar

Among themselves, lawyers semi-jokingly ask, "How much justice can the client afford?" Sadly, it's not much of a joke. Even if the attorney provides free services, the courts charge money to hear your case and for every request (motion) you make along the way. Getting justice also requires work that we tend to take for granted; we forget that making copies and phone calls, sending mail and messages, and getting places costs money.

Lawyers, like plumbers and doctors, expect to be paid for their work. Unlike plumbers and doctors, the service the lawyer provides isn't always clear-cut or well defined, which makes it difficult to get a clear idea of what a fair price for the service will be. In this chapter, you'll learn what options you have in paying for your attorney's time and advice, what kinds of additional costs to expect, and how to reduce your costs.

How Much Does a Lawyer Cost?

There is no one legitimate price for legal services. Costs vary based on the following variables:

- Where you are (East and West Coast lawyers charge more)
- The lawyer's level of experience
- The lawyer's reputation
- The size of the law firm and the lawyer's position in it
- The complexity of the case
- How much competition there is for legal services
- How much the case is worth in terms of a cash judgment

Fees are negotiable, as are methods of payment. Generally, you'll be paying in cash. However, some attorneys take credit cards, some will create a payment plan, some will take a lien (like a mortgage) on property to secure payment, and a few will even take service or items in trade.

Most attorneys will want you to pay something before they begin work on your case. At the very least, the payment agreement must be set and signed before they begin work.

Hourly Fees

The classic way to pay an attorney is by the hour. With an ordinary hourly wage, people are paid for the amount of time they are at work, whether they're surfing the web or actually working. An attorney's time is accounted in *billable hours*, which means you'll only pay for the time the attorney is actually working on your case. Attorneys' hourly rates range from a low of about $100 per hour to $1,500 per hour or more. Average rates tend to be about $250 to $300 per hour for a reasonably experienced lawyer in the Midwest.

DEFINITION

Billable hours are hours or parts of hours spent working strictly on a specific case.

The attorney will track her time, often with special computer software, to be sure you're being accurately charged for the time spent on your case. At the end of the month, or your agreed-upon billing period, you'll get a bill specifying how the attorney's time was spent on your case and totaling the amount you owe.

Most attorneys have a minimum billable hourly period, so a four-minute phone call won't be billed at exactly four minutes. A typical minimum period is either 15 minutes (0.25 hour) or 6 minutes (0.10 hour), because those are the easiest to calculate against the hourly rate. Your charge will be rounded up to the nearest minimum period, so your 4-minute call will be billed at 6 minutes—or 15 minutes—depending on your agreement.

Per-Service Hourly Fee

A variation on the standard hourly fee is an hourly fee that changes based on the task performed. For example, an attorney might charge $400 per hour for court appearances, but $250 per hour for research on your case and $300 per hour for meeting with you. If you're working with a lawyer on this basis, expect to get very detailed bills showing exactly what was done and what rate you were billed for it.

Flat Fees

Another way to pay a lawyer is the same way you pay for any large purchase: a set price, called a flat fee. When the lawyer can easily predict the amount of time and complexity of a particular case or service, he's more willing to quote a flat fee. You're unlikely to get a flat fee for most litigation, since there's no way of knowing at the beginning how long the lawsuit will take or how complex it will get. Flat fees are common for lawsuits like basic divorces without children and collection cases where the lawyer is suing so you get paid on a debt. There are also nonlawsuit legal proceedings that don't have a plaintiff or defendant, but require a court appearance. These include matters like bankruptcy filings, immigration applications, and applications for probate for wills, and they also often use a flat-fee payment structure.

It's almost impossible to say what a reasonable flat fee would be for any particular case without looking at the case itself. That being said, it's not unusual for flat fees to range from $750 to $15,000, with the higher end being for more complex divorce and bankruptcy cases.

JUST THE FACTS

Some attorneys do nothing but simple flat-fee cases, referring more complex cases out to other lawyers. Those lawyers will have advertisements that read something like "Divorce—No Kids—$2,500."

Flat-fee agreements often specify how many visits or phone calls the fee includes. Keep careful track of your phone calls and visits in that case, because the agreement you sign is likely to include additional fees if you make more calls than the agreed-upon number. The agreement is also going to include added fees for further services if the case becomes more complex, or if you require something beyond what was initially agreed upon.

Retainer Fees

Regardless of whether you pay an attorney an hourly or flat fee, the attorney is likely to ask for a retainer as an up-front payment or deposit for her services. Retainers are usually an amount that covers at least 5 hours of the attorney's time, but more often 10 hours or more. For example, if you're paying $250 per hour for attorney fees, you're likely to be asked for $2,500 as a retainer. In a flat-fee case, the retainer is likely to be 50 percent of the entire fee.

The money you pay as a retainer will be used to pay the hourly fees until it's used up. Retainers are essentially advance payments against billable hours. Once the retainer is used up, the attorney will ask for more money to be used as a further advance payment against billable hours. If you were paying a flat fee, your next payment would be the next portion of the fee that was due.

PITFALLS

Protect yourself! Some attorneys will ask for the entire fee before starting any work. This is a negotiable point, and one you should consider before agreeing to hire the attorney in case you're not happy with the service you're getting.

Check the agreement you sign carefully; the retainer can be either nonrefundable or refundable. If it's nonrefundable, even if the attorney does no work on your case, the attorney is permitted to keep the money. If it's refundable and the case is not a flat-fee case, then any money that was unearned or left over at the end of the case (or when you and the lawyer part ways) is returned to you. This is a point to negotiate with the attorney before you sign the agreement.

Contingent Fees

When you see an ad on TV saying "You don't pay unless we win," what you're seeing is an offer to do legal work for a contingent fee. This means the attorney fee depends on, or is contingent on, your winning money in the lawsuit. The lawyer's share of the win is usually one third to one half of the total. It's important to know that the attorney fee is the only thing you won't pay unless you win. You'll still have to pay for the attorney's other costs and your own court costs, which we'll talk about later in this chapter.

The ads on TV are usually for torts or personal injury cases, like dog bites, slip and falls, professional malpractice, or *product liability*. There are some kinds of cases where contingent fees are absolutely forbidden, both as an ethical and legal matter. In particular, divorce cannot be done as a contingent-fee case because then the lawyer will want to make sure the divorce goes through.

DEFINITION

Product liability is the legal term for a type of tort in which someone suffers an injury as a result of a faulty product. When a manufacturer creates a product that will hurt people even if it's used properly, the manufacturer is responsible.

Let's take an example of how a contingent-fee case would work. In a personal injury case, handled on a contingency-fee basis, the lawyer's fee is usually 33⅓ percent of the amount recovered, after payment of costs. If a case settles for $10,000, and the attorney has paid $1,000 in costs, those costs are deducted from the $10,000, leaving $9,000. The attorney fee would be a third of the $9,000, or $3,000; your share would be $6,000.

Attorney's Expenses

In addition to attorney fees, you'll have to pay for the things the law office wouldn't do if it weren't for your case, like make copies or send documents by an overnight service. This is something to negotiate with your attorney as part of your representation agreement. Some clients would rather not see a charge for $5.37 in copies on their monthly bill; they want those kinds of charges folded into the attorney fee. Expect to pay a higher fee if that's your preference. Other clients want to manage costs to the penny, and that's something to discuss up front with the attorney as well. Common nonfee costs include the following.

- Copies

- Messenger fees

- Long-distance phone calls

- Postage and delivery

- Mileage

- Transcript costs

- Court reporter fees

- Private investigator fees

What Happens to the Money You Pay

Money you pay for work already completed belongs to the attorney and can go straight to her bank account. Any money you pay the lawyer before work is started doesn't really belong to the lawyer until the work is done. Because it technically belongs to you, the lawyer cannot put it in her own bank account. The solution is to put it in something called a client trust account. This keeps your money completely separate from the lawyer's money and the law office's money.

The lawyer is responsible for setting up the client trust account with a bank, and it's usually the same bank he has his business account with. Lawyers are only required to have one client trust account to serve all their clients. You will pay no fees for the set-up or maintenance of the account, but you won't get any interest on the money you put in, either. (Neither does the lawyer, by the way.) Most banks provide the account as a public service; the lawyer's only expenses are having checks printed for the account and accounting services from his CPA.

JUST THE FACTS

The interest on the money in the client trust account, a.k.a. Interest on Lawyers Trust Account (IOLTA), by law usually goes to funding programs like Legal Aid for the poor. If there is a huge amount of interest (tens of thousands of dollars), that may go back to the client, but it depends on the particular state's law.

The state requires that the lawyer keep all unearned client money in the client trust account to keep that money separate from the lawyer's. Failure to keep client money separate from the lawyer's money is called commingling funds, and it's a major ethical violation. Lawyers have lost their licenses for not keeping client money in the separate client trust account.

Money you win in a lawsuit generally is paid directly to the lawyer, rather than to you. When the lawyer receives the money, it is put directly into the client trust account. If the lawyer is owed any money, for example from litigation costs she advanced, she'll be paid from that sum first. The remainder of the money will be paid to you in accordance with your agreement, usually by a check drawn on the client trust account.

Making the Most of Your Money

We've spent an entire chapter talking about your paying out money for all kinds of things. How can you make sure you get your money's worth? How can you reduce your costs? You can take some simple steps to make your lawsuit go more smoothly and more efficiently.

Preparing Documents and Information

If it's at all possible, supply important documents for your attorney so she doesn't have to find them herself. This saves the attorney's and support staff's time, and therefore saves you money. Another big money-saver is organizing the documents in some logical fashion, so the lawyer or his secretary or paralegal doesn't have to spend time trying to figure it out. Again, their time is your money.

Making a list of the documents will give your legal team an easy guide. Make your own copies of the documents you're giving the lawyer before you turn them over. First, it is always a good idea to have backup copies in case something is lost. Second, making your own copies of important documents for your attorney is cheaper than having her office do it.

You can also save time and money by writing out a summary of your story before you meet with the lawyer. While the lawyer is going to want to interview you as well as read your summary, writing out the facts will help you focus on what the real issues are, and help you to remember what to bring up with the lawyer when you meet. This simple step can save many billable hours and a lot of your money.

Phone Calls and E-Mails

Before you call your attorney, write out what you want to ask or talk about. That way, you're more likely to hit the important points, and you'll save time by not making multiple phone calls or extending the time for each call. If the lawyer's not available, be willing to tell the lawyer's staff what your questions are. That way, when the attorney does call you back, he'll be prepared to answer your questions efficiently. Don't be offended if the lawyer has her staff call you back with the answers. That's another time- and money-saver for you. Last, be aware that after-hours calls may be billed at a higher rate. Discuss that with your attorney when you negotiate your agreement.

> **PITFALLS**
>
> Don't pay for phone tag! Will your lawyer charge you for leaving a message on your voice-mail? What about for listening to a message you've left on his voice-mail? Negotiate! You don't want to pay the minimum billable period for a 30-second "call me" message. Don't be shy about negotiating these points; the lawyer won't be shy about billing for them!

E-mail has been shown to be a good alternative to the phone call. It enables you to put your thoughts down and look at them, as opposed to just talking and "thinking out loud." There is no time limit to send e-mails, so you don't have to feel bad about sending an e-mail at 9 at night. The attorney can answer e-mails at his convenience. Many attorneys have BlackBerrys or netbooks, and as they sit in court, waiting for their turn before the judge, they can return e-mails. E-mail also creates a record of all conversations as you go. E-mails are billed out the same way any time spent on your case is billed.

Working With Paralegals and Legal Secretaries

Lawyers, like doctors, have professionals working to support them. Doctors have nurses; lawyers have paralegals, also called legal assistants. See Chapter 6 for a discussion of what paralegals do and their position on your legal team. The more use you can make of their services, the less expensive your overall attorney costs will be.

Get It in Writing

Once you've decided to hire an attorney, you should get a written agreement that clearly states what you can expect. This agreement might be called an engagement letter, retainer, or contract, or might not have any title at all. Most states say that attorneys have an ethical obligation to put this agreement in writing, to protect both you and the lawyer. Most attorneys will want this signed before they begin work on any case. Look for things like:

- What services the lawyer or firm will provide

- Which lawyer or paraprofessional will provide the services

- Whether you'll pay a different rate depending on who provides the services

- How and when you're expected to pay

- What happens to the money you pay

- What happens to the money you may win

- What happens if you don't win any money

- What happens to your papers and files

- How the relationship will end

Be wary of lawyers who promise specific results, like "You will definitely win this suit," or "No one will ever challenge this trust document." As frustrating as it is, even the best lawyers can't guarantee that nothing will go wrong. In fact, any lawyer worth his salt will never make such a guarantee. It's like predicting who will win a football game: you can make an educated guess, but injuries, bad calls by the referees, and unexpected plays can change everything. The only people who can guarantee the outcome of a football game have cheated by fixing it in advance. The same is true of the law. The only lawyer who can guarantee your win is the one who's bribed the judge and jury. Regardless of what you see on TV, there aren't that many bribable judges and juries, or that many dishonest lawyers.

Free Legal Services

The last option for paying for a lawyer's services is not to pay at all. Not skipping out on your bill, but getting an agreement up front that the lawyer will not charge at all for her services. This is a form of public service, formally known as *pro bono publico*, which in Latin means "for the public good." It's also a form of charity. Most states have a voluntary requirement that attorneys provide some form of service to the public annually, either by donating their services to a particular case, or by paying money to allow legal service groups to provide free services. It's up to the attorney to decide how he's going to fulfill this duty, and with whom. Most lawyers get many more requests for free services than they could possibly provide, even if they did nothing but free legal work all year. There is no requirement that an attorney take a particular case pro bono, no matter how huge the injustice.

Court Costs

Remember "how much justice can you afford?" Well, another expense of pursuing a lawsuit is court costs. The court system charges the parties filing a suit for several reasons. One is to help pay for the court's overhead. Taxes don't cover all of the expenses. Another is accountability. Costs help ensure that people are serious about using the court's services to resolve the problems they face.

Court fees get paid to the court clerk's office. By law, lawyers aren't allowed to pay for their clients' court fees. They may advance the fees for the client, but the client must pay the attorney back. What this means is that the lawyer can pay the court from his own bank account, but the lawyer is then ethically obligated not only to bill the client for the court fee, but to require that the client pay the fee back. Lawyers are not permitted to charge a service fee for paying court fees out of their own accounts. They are permitted to charge interest for past-due payments, which could include court fees that the client hasn't yet paid.

IN THE KNOW

As a society, we believe that poverty shouldn't prevent someone from getting access to the courts. If you are at or below the poverty level, or have special circumstances, the court will allow you to file your case without paying court costs. Before you file your case, you make a special request to file in *forma pauperis,* which is Latin for "in the poor person's way." If your request succeeds, you won't have to pay court costs.

The first fee you'll pay is called a filing fee, money paid to begin the case in court. The amount of the fee depends on the state and the kind of court you're going to. You can expect to pay anywhere from $50 to $750 as an initial filing fee. This fee, like all court fees, is nonrefundable.

The next fee you'll pay is a service fee, or process fee. Although this isn't technically a court fee, it's closely related to the filing fee. As discussed in Chapter 1, every individual has a constitutional right to know that she's being sued, the right to due process of law. To fulfill that right, the defendant must get notice that a suit has been filed against her in court. This notice includes getting hard copies of the filing papers. Typically, only the plaintiff pays this first service or process fee. The defendant doesn't have to pay a fee to get notice of the lawsuit.

The papers must be handed to the defendant by an adult not associated with the lawsuit, or a process server. Most servers are paid a flat fee, sometimes plus mileage. The flat fee can run from $20 to $50; the mileage fee is usually set at whatever the IRS rate is. If the defendant is difficult to serve, the flat fee might go out the window, and the price will go up.

The jury fee is the fee that helps defray the cost of assembling a jury. Civil cases don't require a jury, but if the plaintiff or defendant chooses to have one, this fee will be levied. The fee can run from $75 to $250, depending on the jurisdiction. The party that chooses to have a jury pays the fee. The other side doesn't have to pay anything.

The motion fee is the cost of requesting to the court to make a decision on a specific part of your overall case. Motion fees are generally fairly low, ranging from $20 to $200, depending on the court and the kind of motion. For example, a trial court may charge $20 to hear an ordinary motion, but charge $175 to hear a child-support motion. An appeals court might charge $200 per motion regardless of the topic. State court motion fees are usually lower than federal court motion fees. The party making the motion has to pay the fee. The party responding to the motion doesn't have to pay anything, just like with a jury fee.

There are other fees as well. Most courts charge a per-page fee for copies of documents, usually around 50¢ to $1 per page. The fee goes up if you want the copy certified, meaning stamped as official, and can be anywhere from $2.50 to $10 per page. There are fees for appeals ranging from $100 to $200; fees for filing documents, which can be charged by the page (25¢–$10 per page) or by the document ($1–$50); fees for court-ordered mediation services that often run around $250; and fees for garnishment orders running around $20 to $50. In short, every time you deal with the court, you will pay a fee.

JUST THE FACTS

Keep in mind that the court fees generally have to be paid in cash. Many courts now take credit cards but might charge a service fee for their use. Courts typically won't accept personal or business checks, except from attorneys. The attorney will then charge back these fees to the clients or deduct it from the retainer.

Your Nonmonetary Costs

We've talked about the actual financial costs of using a lawyer and going through a lawsuit. Those comprise the proverbial tip of the iceberg when it comes to what a lawsuit might cost you. The most important costs to consider are your time, your energy, and your stress levels.

Your Time

You'll be paying the lawyer for his time, but your time is worth money, too. Because courts operate during business hours, you're likely to miss work as a result of the lawsuit and lose income. It will also take time to prepare your arguments or prepare papers for your attorney. Whether you're the plaintiff or the defendant, let your boss know what's going on, and work as far in advance as you can to make arrangements to reduce the impact on your job.

Your Energy

Lawsuits take mental and physical energy. You'll be physically moving things around, looking for documents, making copies, trying to find evidence to support your case. You'll also be doing some mental heavy lifting trying to remember just how things happened and putting your story in order. Be prepared to be more tired than usual during a lawsuit, and try to manage your energy as best you can. Try to arrange your schedule to allow for adequate sleep, and do what you can to keep your energy levels up. That includes eating regular meals and doing all those things you know are good for you.

Most important, until you know how much time the lawsuit is going to take, be careful of committing your time to things outside your lawsuit. You can easily end up overcommitted and exhausted. Consider your energy an asset to be spent as wisely as you spend your money.

Your Emotional Strain

Lawsuits are emotional events, even when they're "just" about money. Let's face it: lawsuits are never "just" about money. They're about fairness. Money, or custody, or anything else you're arguing about, is the measure of how fair or unfair the world is being toward you. The fact that you're involved in a lawsuit is enough to make you feel unfairly used, which means you'll feel resentful, angry, unhappy, and just generally cranky, and that's if everything's going your way. Stress levels naturally go way up the minute the conflict begins, and the confrontational nature of a lawsuit isn't designed to soothe that stress away.

While everyone deals with stress differently, it's important to recognize the stress from the outset, and do what you can to reduce that stress. Learning about how lawsuits work is one way of reducing stress and uncertainty, and you're doing it right now! Of course, there's more you can do: you know about the standard stress-relievers like mild exercise or a glass of warm milk before bedtime. Don't be surprised if you need more than that during your lawsuit. Even the strongest person has a breaking point, and the idea is to avoid reaching yours. Seek out support groups and professional therapists; your lawyer can probably recommend a few. Take advantage of the help that's out there for you, and reduce the cost of stress in your lawsuit.

The Least You Need to Know

- There are several methods to pay an attorney.
- Negotiate your fee structure and get it in writing.
- Courts charge a variety of fees for legal actions.
- You can keep costs down by being prepared and working with the lawyer's staff.

The Cast of Characters in a Lawsuit

In This Chapter

- Who's suing and who's being sued
- The law office team
- The staff at the courthouse
- The jury

Most people already have a general idea of who's who in a lawsuit—the people suing and the people being sued as well as lawyers and judges. Let's get into more detail about who does what, how, and why.

The Parties

Only two kinds of people are referred to as "parties" in a lawsuit: plaintiffs and defendants.

Plaintiff

Every lawsuit starts with a person or company with a problem they want the courts to solve. Whatever entity starts the lawsuit with the court is called the plaintiff. The plaintiff may also be called "the complainant" or "the complaining party," because the document that begins the lawsuit is called "the complaint."

JUST THE FACTS

The parties' last names are used to make up the case name or case title for the lawsuit. For example, a case is referred to as "*Jones v. Smith,*" not "*Mary and John Jones v. Sam Smith.*" The plaintiff's name always comes first.

The old-fashioned legalese that insists on calling people "the party of the first part" is no longer used. Most attorneys now use plain English, referring to people by their names or roles. It's still easier to refer to the plaintiff and defendant together as "the parties," so you'll hear people talking about "parties" all the time.

Plaintiffs must satisfy the following three conditions:

- They must be legal entities.

- They must have standing.

- They must be legally competent.

Legal Entities

In the eyes of the law, only human beings, corporations, partnerships, limited liability companies, governments, or government agencies can be legal entities.

If more than one person or entity's rights are affected, there can be more than one plaintiff. In those cases, the first plaintiff's name is used in the case name. That first plaintiff is also called the name plaintiff. In a class action lawsuit, the plaintiff who's suing on behalf of the entire group of plaintiffs is called the lead plaintiff. (See Chapter 2 for a discussion of class action lawsuits.)

Standing

Standing is the ability to claim a potential loss of rights. Think of it as the "Whose business is it, anyway?" question. Only the person who is actually affected by the incident can file a lawsuit. For instance, if Bob is hurt in an auto accident, Dave cannot sue for Bob's injuries because Dave wasn't the one who was hurt. Because Dave wasn't the one who was hurt, the injury is none of his business in the eyes of the law. Dave has no standing in this case. Only Bob has standing to sue.

Legal Competence

The final requirement a plaintiff must satisfy is the legal ability to file suit, which is known as legal competence or simply competence. This isn't about how skilled a person is at a task, and it's not completely about sanity, either. Instead, legal competence has to do with whether the law considers a person able to handle her own affairs. Generally, once a person is 18 years old, she's considered legally competent. Among other things, legally competent adults can file a lawsuit in their own name.

The opposite of being legally competent is being "legally incompetent." Children are legally incompetent, even if they're very mature for their age. If a child has a lawsuit to file, someone else has to file it on his behalf. The same is true of adults who have been judged incompetent by the courts. In these cases, a separate court action is needed to name a conservator, guardian, or "next friend" to file the suit.

However, just because you think someone's not competent doesn't mean you can go ahead and file suit on his behalf. The person needs to have been declared incompetent by the court first, and the court must name you as conservator, guardian, or next friend. If not, you have no standing to sue. This is not a minor technicality. Without standing, no one can successfully begin and maintain a lawsuit.

Here's the kicker: As mentioned in Chapter 1, starting a lawsuit is a simple matter of filing a claim with the courts. If a suit is filed by someone who is not a legal entity, doesn't have standing, or is legally incompetent, it's up to the other side—the defendant—to prove this and get the case kicked out of court.

IN THE KNOW

People who aren't U.S. citizens can file suit. Because they're not citizens, they may be forced to go to federal court rather than state court under some circumstances. It's a complicated situation, so you're best off checking with an attorney before you begin.

Defendant

The person or entity being sued is the defendant, so named because they're called to defend themselves against the charges in the lawsuit. Because the defendant responds to the lawsuit, they are sometimes also called the respondent. There aren't very many criteria that need to be met to be a defendant; all you need is to be a legal entity. The legal competency requirement (being over 18 and being sane) can be dealt with by suing the person through their parent or guardian.

As with plaintiffs, there can be more than one defendant in a lawsuit. The first defendant listed is known as the name defendant. Some people call that defendant the lead defendant, even if the case isn't a class action suit.

Other fictitious names used are Coe and Roe. In fact, in the now-famous Supreme Court case *Roe v. Wade,* the plaintiff used Roe as her name to protect her privacy.

If the plaintiff doesn't know the name of the defendant, they can refer to the defendant using a fictional name, such as John Doe. If there is more than one unknown defendant, they are listed as John Doe 1, John Doe 2, John Doe 3, and so on. This convention enables plaintiffs to sue within the *statute of limitations.* When the actual defendant is discovered, their name takes the place of the fictional name on the case.

DEFINITION

Statute of limitations is the time limit on suits that starts from the date of the injury and stops at a specific time listed in a statute.

Cross-Plaintiff and Cross-Defendant

When there is more than one defendant, the defendants might have a dispute among themselves about who is responsible for what in the lawsuit. In that case, one of the defendants sues the other, becoming the cross-plaintiff. That entity is still a defendant, too, so they're known as "defendant/cross-plaintiff." The defendant being sued by his fellow defendant becomes "defendant/cross-defendant."

A subset of cross-parties is third-party plaintiffs and third-party defendants. Often, additional people or entities who are not part of an original lawsuit filing may want to participate in the lawsuit. In other situations, additional people or entities who are not part of a lawsuit may be, in the eyes of the defendant, the true responsible party. Therefore, they are added to the lawsuit as third-party plaintiffs or defendants.

Counter-Plaintiff and Counter-Defendant

If the defendant believes he should be the plaintiff, he can turn around and counter-sue the plaintiff. The defendant remains the defendant and must defend himself against the plaintiff's claims, but is now defendant/counter-plaintiff. No surprise, the plaintiff now becomes plaintiff/counter-defendant.

Counsel

Lawyers are called counselors or counsel, because they advise clients as to what is best to do. In addition to giving advice, attorneys also represent the plaintiff or the defendant as their agent in court. To protect the public, only licensed attorneys are allowed to give legal advice or represent other people in court. Even though regular people give each other legal advice all the time, it's actually prohibited by law. It's unusual for someone who gave casual advice to be prosecuted for it, but it can happen. There's no requirement that a person use an attorney in court or get advice from a lawyer about a legal situation. People are free to use their own judgment about how to proceed in any situation, including a conflict under the law.

Because the law is so complex, society wants to make sure that any advice citizens are given about the law is at least basically competent. Society also wants to be sure that if the representation and advice are completely off-base, there's a way to eliminate the incompetent adviser to protect others. Licensing also offers people some reassurance that the money and trust they put in their lawyers' hands are guarded by the law. You can sue a lawyer for malpractice, but there is no such recourse for nonlawyers. Plus, many state bars have a fund to reimburse clients who've had money improperly taken by their attorney. Without licensing, those safeguards wouldn't exist.

One of the results of requiring licensing for lawyers is that it gives lawyers a monopoly on the market for providing legal advice. While that can result in higher costs, there is enough competition among lawyers that you should be able to find an attorney willing to work with you on the cost of her fees.

PITFALLS

Because lawyers' services can be costly, people sometimes want to hire one attorney to represent both the plaintiff and the defendant in the same case. This is very common in divorce cases where people start out believing that they will have a friendly split.

Some states allow one attorney to represent both parties in a divorce only if both parties are told of the dangers and both give their knowing consent. Realistically, there is still a conflict of interest.

When an attorney represents both sides, she can't advocate strongly for either side. A better solution is for the parties to start with a mediation service to work through the details and help them come to an agreement. Each party should then hire their own attorney, who can review agreement for fairness and "legality." Costs stay lower, and each side is still protected.

Lawyer for the Plaintiff

Plaintiff's lawyers start a case in court. Any licensed attorney can start a case in court; no separate educational requirement or licensing is required. The plaintiff may hire the attorney, use a legal services attorney, or get free legal services. See Chapter 4 for advice on selecting a lawyer to start or defend your case.

IN THE KNOW

If you hear an attorney referred to as a "plaintiff's lawyer," that usually means they start personal injury cases, like medical malpractice and auto injuries.

Lawyer for the Defendant

Just as any lawyer can help a plaintiff start a lawsuit, any attorney can help a defendant respond to a lawsuit. Again, the defendant may hire the attorney, use a legal services attorney, or get free legal services.

A good lawyer focuses on the client's needs and can represent the client as a plaintiff or defendant.

Associate Attorney

A lawyer who is an employee of another lawyer, rather than a partner of that lawyer, is called an associate attorney. Most law school graduates start out as associate attorneys because it's an excellent way to learn the ropes while still having some supervision. Some lawyers prefer to remain associates, because it frees them from having to attend to things like hiring, billing, and so on.

Of Counsel

Sometimes an attorney will hire another attorney as a sort of subcontractor because of the other attorney's expertise in that particular kind of case. The subcontracted lawyer is called "of counsel," or sometimes a "third-party lawyer." When a lawyer brings on a third-party attorney to assist in a case, it doesn't mean that the original attorney is incompetent; it means that she's trying to bring on board the best available person for the case.

Some semi-retired attorneys are often listed as "of counsel" with the law firm they practiced with before retirement. They're available to give advice to the younger attorneys and to take cases that are of special interest to them.

Paralegal or Legal Assistant

As doctors have nurses to provide some medical services to patients, lawyers have aides called paralegals or legal assistants to provide some legal services to clients. The terms paralegal and legal assistant are interchangeable, but some prefer one title over the other. Paralegals work under the supervision and direction of attorneys. They do legal research and writing, fill out forms, and meet with clients to get information the attorney needs for the case. The lawyer is ultimately responsible for everything the paralegal does. Paralegals are not licensed as attorneys are, and they cannot give legal advice.

Some paralegals set up to serve the general public. Be aware that public paralegal services cannot be used to start or maintain a lawsuit. Paralegal service businesses are legally limited to acting as a scrivener, which means they can only fill out forms at your direction. They cannot select the forms or suggest how they should best be filled out, because that counts as giving legal advice. Sometimes a scrivener service is helpful if you don't have access to a computer and printer, or if you are too stressed to deal with a form that you know you have to fill out.

 PITFALLS

Unscrupulous or ignorant public paralegal service providers will try to convince you to use their service as a substitute for an attorney, promising big money savings. This strategy can backfire and cost you more money in the long run to fix mistakes.

Law Clerk

There are two kinds of clerks: one works for the court or a judge, and the other works for a law office. Law clerks in law offices tend to be law students who work part time during the school year while also going to school. They may perform many of the duties of a paralegal but are less likely to be allowed to interview clients or have any client contact at all. You shouldn't be billed for a law clerk's time—that should be included in the attorney fee—just as you shouldn't be billed for the receptionist's time.

The Court

Although all courts in the United States are generally structured the same way and have the same kinds of personnel, there are some differences from court to court.

> **IN THE KNOW**
>
> Regardless of the position of the person you are dealing with in the court system, they have a great deal of power. It's in your best interest to be polite to them no matter how frustrating the situation may be. Courtesy will go a long way to making your case run smoothly. Not only that, certain rules require politeness and collegiality in the court. By remaining calm and polite, you won't run the risk of being held in contempt of court, which can lead to fines and jail time.

Judges: From Magistrates to Justices

In almost every state and in federal courts, judges must be attorneys before they can become judges. They may be appointed, as in the federal system, or elected, as many states do. There are different kinds of judges, depending on the kind of court they preside over.

Magistrates

The lowest level of judge is usually a magistrate. Magistrates can specialize in an area of law, as in federal courts, where there are bankruptcy magistrates. In some courts, magistrates preside over small claims courts or administrative law hearings. Regardless of where you encounter a magistrate, address him or her as "your honor." There are always a few people who address the magistrate as "your majesty," but this is not the correct usage.

> **JUST THE FACTS**
>
> You and your attorney have no control over deciding which judge will hear your case. Judges are assigned randomly, usually by computer. In the good old days, some courts had decks of index cards with the judges' names on them. They'd shuffle them up and deal them out like a hand of poker. You almost literally had to play the hand you were dealt!

Trial Judges

Like magistrates, trial judges decide cases. They are in federal and state courtrooms, sometimes working alongside or above magistrates. Judges are addressed as "judge" or "your honor." Sometimes trial judges can also act as appellate judges, when they review cases decided by magistrates who work under them.

Justices

Appellate court judges are called justices, and are called "your honor," or "Mister Justice" or "Madam Justice." The only exception is the Chief Justice of the Supreme Court of the United States, who can also be addressed as "Mister Chief Justice" (or, someday, as "Madam Chief Justice").

Judge's Clerk

The judge's clerk fills either of two roles. One type of clerk researches the cases that the judge will hear and helps the judge manage his caseload. The second kind of clerk is more of a secretary to the judge and handles the calendar, the judge's correspondence, and general administrative work.

Both kinds of clerks are very important people, as they can control the dates and times your case is heard, along with having a say in the information the judge sees and hears before the case. They're both good people to contact to confirm dates and times for your case, as well as to be sure the judge has everything that's needed for the case.

Court Clerk

The court clerk is an administrator for the entire courthouse. Again, the court clerk is an important person, with a lot of power over how judges and the court as a whole deal with each case. If you have any interaction with the court clerk or any court personnel, be very polite to them. You'll stand out from the crowd and get treated better in return. Depending on the size of the courthouse, the court clerk may or may not be the best person to contact for confirmation of dates and receipt of documents. The clerk is a good place to start, though, as she can direct you to the best place to get your questions answered.

Court Reporter

In a court of record, everything that is said in the court is preserved or recorded. Courts of record are usually trial courts. Everything that happens is recorded so that the application of law can be reviewed at the appeals level.

The standard way to record the proceedings in a court of record is to use a court reporter or court stenographer. This person is paid by the court to take down, word-for-word, everything that is said by every party, witness, attorney, and the judge. They do this with a special typewriting machine (a "steno machine") that enables the stenographer to take notes in shorthand. A copy of what happened in court at a particular time can be transcribed into English from the shorthand notes and presented as a transcript. Anyone who wants a copy can buy one from the court reporter for a per-page fee.

Because it is so difficult to learn the steno machine, there is a shortage of qualified court reporters. This is one reason more and more courts are turning to videography. The court may hire a videographer to set up and maintain the video recorders and records. However, if a transcript is needed, a court reporter usually has to watch the video, take down everything with the steno machine, and then transcribe it.

Bailiff

The court has an officer whose duty it is to enforce the judge's orders about behavior in the court. If a judge has forbidden cell phones in the courtroom (a common ruling) and someone's cell phone rings, the bailiff is the one who confiscates the cell phone. The bailiff works closely with the judge, the clerks, and the various police or sheriff's officers to ensure the physical safety of the court as well.

Jury

Juries consist of 6 to 12 people called jurors. The number depends on the kind of case and the local statutes. The jury decides the facts and how the law, as interpreted by the judge, should be applied to the facts.

When Is a Jury Needed?

Not all trials must be decided by a judge with a jury. In fact, a jury is not mandatory in civil suits. However, if the plaintiff or defendant chooses, a jury can be used, but only to decide the facts of the case. The judge still makes decisions about how to interpret the law.

People choose to use juries when they believe that their case has emotional appeal. The hope is that jurors will be more sympathetic than a judge alone. In reality, there's no guarantee that a jury will feel more kindly toward any one plaintiff, or that a judge will be heartless. However, the bias toward juries for emotionally appealing cases is deep, and often turns out to be true.

Jury Foreperson

The jurors themselves vote on who among them will serve as the foreperson (or foreman or forewoman). The foreperson is the juror who helps keep the jury on track during their discussions, called deliberations. The foreperson also calls for votes on the charges and delivers the verdict, or final decision, to the judge in the courtroom.

The Least You Need to Know

- Plaintiffs must be legal entities, have legal standing, and be legally competent.
- Plaintiffs can be counter-sued by the defendants in the same lawsuit.
- You can save time and money by working with the lawyer's staff.
- Be as polite as possible to everyone who works in the courthouse; it can't hurt and it might help.

The Legal Environment

You probably have a good, basic knowledge of how our justice system works. The more technical aspects of the legal world are discussed in this part, where you'll learn about the rules that govern the courts. You'll also see how one kind of court, the small claims court, points out the differences and similarities all courts have.

Background Basics

In This Chapter

- Making sense of the court system
- Why the courts can make and enforce their decisions
- Federal versus state level cases
- An overview of the trial process

To understand how a lawsuit works, you have to know a bit more than what you learned in your high school civics class. It's still based on the same principles, but you need more detail. Although there are differences in detail from state to state and even from county to county, the basics remain the same throughout the United States.

The Court System

You know that there are three branches to the United States government—the Legislative, the Executive, and the Judiciary. You're probably more familiar with their common names—Congress, the President, and the judicial system. Most states have a similar structure, in which the courts are a separate branch of government.

Different courts have different jobs. In most lawsuits, you'll begin in a trial court, which has the power to hear and decide your case. Trial courts are further classified by the type of problem they handle, like bankruptcy courts, probate courts, and courts of "general jurisdiction," which pretty much handle the bulk of the lawsuits that are filed.

Within the general court system, different courts hear different cases based on the amount of money involved. If the case is worth a relatively small amount of money— usually anywhere from $3,000 to $15,000—it will go to a general court such as a small claims court.

If a case involves more money than the small claims court can hear, it goes to a second level of courts that can hear those claims. Depending on where you live, these might be called district courts, municipal courts, or some other local name. Usually, these courts are your "local" courts.

If a case involves more money than the local courts can handle, then there is a third level of courts, usually at the county level. These courts can hear cases of an unlimited value. Again, depending on where you live, these courts might have different names, such as "circuit courts," "court of common pleas," "superior court," or the like.

The federal court system doesn't have a small claims court. There is only the trial court, called the district court. To have your case decided by federal court, it's not enough to ask. The federal court has to have jurisdiction, which we'll talk about a little later in this section.

Once your case has been decided by the trial court, whether it was a federal or state trial (and it has to be one or the other; it can't be both), the loser can ask for a review of the way the law was applied in the trial. This is called an appeal, and each state and the federal system has an appeals court (usually called the court of appeals) where the trial can be reviewed. It's important to understand that the appeals court usually reviews only the way the law was applied, not the facts; nor do appeals courts hold new hearings to redecide the facts. Once the jury or trial court has decided which witnesses to believe and what the facts are, that decision is final. Getting the facts changed is so rare that when it does happen, as in a criminal case where new evidence is found, it makes the news.

JUST THE FACTS

Appeals courts typically only review and make decisions about the law and how it was applied, not the facts, because the judges of the appeals court weren't there to evaluate the witnesses and the evidence themselves.

Once the intermediate appeal has been decided, there is one more level of appeal available, to a supreme court. Both the state and federal system have these final courts of appeal. You can appeal from the state supreme court to the Supreme Court of the United States, but you cannot appeal from the Supreme Court of the United States to a state court. There isn't an international court that you can appeal to that is higher than the U.S. Supreme Court.

JUST THE FACTS

If you ever see something referred to as SCOTUS, they're referring to the Supreme Court of the United States. Some lawyers also call the Justices of the Supreme Court "The Supremes," as a nod to the Motown group.

The U.S. Supreme Court and state supreme courts do not have to "take" or hear the appeal for civil cases. The main reason they will hear an appeal is if there is a new legal issue involved that needs to be cleared up. Each year more than 10,000 cases are proposed to the U.S. Supreme Court. They actually hear 100 or fewer of those cases. As you can see, your chance of having your case heard by the U.S. Supreme Court is very slim. You are more likely to have a state court case heard by your state supreme court, although state supreme courts have the same power to decide whether or not to hear your appeal that the U.S. Supreme Court has.

The Constitution

The courts get their power from the U.S. Constitution and the state constitutions. The Constitution gives the courts the power to hear and decide "cases and controversies," meaning things that are current problems. The courts make these decisions by looking at the Constitution, laws that are validly passed under the Constitution, and previous cases that have similar facts and questions of law. The courts have the power to decide whether a law is valid under the Constitution, too.

Jurisdiction

The important thing to know about jurisdiction is that unless the court has it, the court cannot make a decision that the parties must obey. That's why jurisdiction is so important and why it's the first thing that attorneys should decide about a case.

Jurisdiction is another way of talking about the court's power to hear and decide a case. Jurisdiction isn't about geography, although geography has something to do with it. County lines, state borders, and so on are the points where it's been agreed that the court's power begins and ends. The power doesn't come from the earth or from the imaginary lines drawn to create boundaries. It comes from the Constitution and from laws and rules created under the Constitution.

There are many kinds of jurisdiction, and they can be categorized by how the court gets its power to make a decision. The first way that courts get their power is based on where the parties were located when the problem came up, and where they are now. This kind of jurisdiction is called personal jurisdiction. State courts are limited to personal jurisdiction over people who were in that state when the controversy began.

Federal courts don't have personal jurisdiction, except in criminal cases when the crime occurred on federal lands or property, or when the crime is a federal one. For civil cases, federal courts have something called diversity jurisdiction, which requires that the parties be from two or more different states. There's an additional requirement that stops many cases that have parties from two or more states from being heard: the case has to be worth more than $75,000, not including costs.

The next way courts get their power is based on the topic of the lawsuit. This is called subject matter jurisdiction. There are two kinds of subject matter jurisdiction: general, which covers topics that can go to any trial court, and limited jurisdiction, which covers special topics that have to go to a particular kind of court that can hear the case. Limited jurisdiction deals with things like divorce, bankruptcy, or wills and trusts. Only the federal bankruptcy court has power to decide bankruptcy cases. Only the probate court has power to decide cases involving wills and trusts.

Subject matter jurisdiction is also divided into federal and state; if the subject matter is covered by state law, the case goes to state court. If the topic "arises under" or is covered by a federal law, the case goes to federal court.

Last, within the subject matter jurisdiction in state courts you'll find a monetary jurisdictional limit for the different trial courts. This is the sort of issue that was discussed earlier. For example, in some states, any claim for under $15,000 must be heard in small claims court. This is because the jurisdiction, or the power of that particular court, is limited to hearing and deciding cases worth less than $15,000.

Venue

Once you've decided which kind of court has power to decide the question, you need to decide which court within the group of those courts to go to. This is a question of venue, which means place. For example, you may have decided that the state's main trial courts have the power to hear and decide your case, but should you go to the one where you live, or the one where the incident took place? This is a decision that really boils down to convenience, and which place has more of an interest in the incident. If both you and the defendant live nearer one courthouse, then that's the one you would probably pick. However, there may be a court rule that says you must pick the place where the acts took place; if that's the case, that's where you'll go. You may think that a bigger city courthouse would be more sympathetic to your case, so you might pick that venue. Because all of the courts in the group have the same power, you can consider issues of fairness and convenience when making your decision.

Federal vs. State: Is Federal Better?

You might have heard the saying, "Don't make a federal case out of it," implying that someone's making a big deal out of nothing. There's a sense that going to federal court is somehow a bigger deal than going to state court. Maybe it's because of the jurisdictional requirements—you know that to have a federal case, it either has to be a case that comes up under federal law, or it has to have two people from different states and a value of over $75,000. That's a lot of money, and that financial require-ment may be why people think of federal cases as a big deal.

Some people believe that federal judges are less biased because they are appointed rather than elected. Then, too, federal trial cases are reported and published in sum-mary form for lawyers and anyone who's interested in reading them; state trial cases are not. Neither of those facts makes federal courts better or worse than state courts. Federal and state courts are pretty much equal; they just have different topics they cover and different jurisdictional requirements. If your case is best handled by a state court, that doesn't make it less important or less significant than if it were something a federal court would deal with.

How a Case Moves Through the System

All cases are different, but under our system, they must all be treated the same way and follow the same procedures. This is actually a constitutional requirement called due process of law, and it comes up frequently throughout a lawsuit, for everything from giving proper notice to each side of what's happening to following the rules of court in every step of the way.

Pretrial

Pretrial has two meanings: one is in the sense of everything that happens before you actually get to the trial. This includes attempts to negotiate and solve the problem so you don't have to go to court. The other meaning is more specific: it's the phase of a lawsuit when the attorneys meet with the judge and set the schedule for the lawsuit, deciding when the deadlines will be for finding evidence, submitting witness lists, and when the trial will actually take place. This type of pretrial actually takes place shortly after the lawsuit is formally opened, or filed, with the court. All these dates might be determined at a pretrial hearing in court. More and more, though, pretrial hearings are done by phone, and sometimes the dates are simply set by the court and sent to the parties. You don't need to attend the pretrial hearing unless you really want to; your lawyer can take care of this for you. This is discussed in greater detail in Chapter 10.

Discovery

Discovery is the part of the trial process in which both sides try to find out as many facts from the other side as possible to develop evidence to bring before the court during the trial. Discovery happens in a variety of ways, but the two most common are as follows:

- **Interrogatories**   Written questions that only go to the plaintiff and defendant

- **Depositions**   Mini-hearings to get witness testimony, held without the judge present

Other methods of discovery can be loosely grouped under the heading of requests. These are things like requests for production of documents and requests for examination by a doctor.

As a party in a lawsuit, whether plaintiff or defendant, you are likely to have to participate in all of these methods of discovery. It can be a time-consuming, frustrating process. A favorite tactic is to "bury" the other side with discovery requests and lengthy interrogatories, hoping they'll get so discouraged that they're ready to end the lawsuit rather than continue on through trial.

Interrogatories can only be given to the plaintiff and defendant, and I'm really not sure what the rationale is behind that. Your attorney might hand a stack of papers to you and ask you to do your best to answer the questions first, and then go through them with you. Other attorneys will go through them with you from the start or have their paralegal work with you. You'll be signing your name to the finished product, and swearing that it is the truth as best you know it, so it's very important that you answer the questions honestly. The truth is always easier to remember than a lie, and the other side's lawyers will be using your answers to try to trip you up later in the process.

Depositions are mini-hearings, often held in a lawyer's office or even at your own place of work, wherever the parties feel it is most convenient. The lawyers from both sides are there; you don't have to appear unless you are the witness being questioned, or deposed. Before the deposition begins, the witness is asked to swear or affirm that she will tell the truth. Usually, the person who "swears in" the witness is the court reporter who attends the deposition to record every word that is said. The court reporter is paid to attend the deposition by the side that scheduled it. She often charges between $25 and $50 per hour, or has a per-deposition fee of $100 to $200 to cover her time in case no one buys the transcript, as discussed below.

At the deposition, the court reporter takes down the witness's testimony and questions from the lawyers with a specialized shorthand machine and then translates what the machine writes into English. The resulting transcript can be purchased by either side for a per-page charge and used to prove what a person swore to under oath, just as if the person were in court. The cost of a court reporter isn't a whole lot of money; the transcript, however, usually runs between $150 and $1,000, depending on the length of the deposition.

When you're the witness at a deposition, remember that you're in charge. You can take a break if you want, and you can stop to think about your answer before you say anything—it's your show, and you're the star. The most important thing is to be consistent and tell the truth.

 PITFALLS

One of the ways lawyers try to trap witnesses at depositions for later use is to ask whether they've told absolutely everything about a topic. For example, "What kind of music do you like?" "Well, I like jazz and blues." "Anything else?" "I like hip-hop, too." "Anything else?" "No, that's it." That's the wrong answer! The right answer is, "That's all I can think of right now." Never let yourself be maneuvered into saying something is completely final.

Motions

A motion is a formal request to the court, asking the court to order something to be done—or to order that something not be done. Depositions and interrogatories can breed motions like mosquitoes in a swamp; the lawyers want to force a witness to answer a question, or they've discovered an asset they want to be sure the witness doesn't sell or give away, and they make a motion asking the court to do just that.

Depending on the motion, you may want to be present in court with your attorney. Some motions don't require your presence, like motions to force the other side to answer an interrogatory. Others require that you be present to testify as to a fact or situation. Motions are made throughout the trial process, from beginning to end and even after the trial is finished. There is a fee associated with each motion that you bring up, usually anywhere from $20 to $200, but no charge to respond to or answer the motion. It's important to respond to every motion, no matter how stupid it seems, because you might otherwise lose by default. Your attorney should give you copies of all motions filed on your behalf, along with the responses made and the ultimate court decision or disposition on the motion.

Trial

Most cases don't actually reach the point of trial. They're settled by negotiation between the parties at some time before the trial, sometimes on the courthouse steps just before the trial is to begin.

IN THE KNOW

If the case settles before trial, it's often a good idea to get a judgment entered, meaning that the court officially recognizes the settlement as a win for one side. This means you can enforce it more easily if the other side fails to pay up.

Everything up to the point of the trial is like a dress rehearsal for a play. The trial itself is opening night, and like opening night, there should be no surprises. All the facts have been discovered through discovery, you know what the witnesses will say, and you've got an excellent idea of what the other side's arguments are. However, like opening night, not everything goes as planned. In fact, the trial is more like a professional sports game, with a referee making calls as the event takes place. As many times as the players practice a throw, the day of the game they might miss.

The referee can make a surprising call, or a poor performer suddenly has the game of his life. See Part 4 for a more thorough discussion of the trial itself.

After the Trial

After the trial is over, the judge will enter an order, called a judgment, stating who won and who lost, and who has to do what. The parties can make motions asking for changes to the judgment, and motions asking for a new trial. The party who won can begin the process of collecting on the judgment, which may be simple and straight-forward if the loser is cooperative, or may include further motions and court hearings to force payment.

Appeals

If the losing party believes that the law was improperly applied at some point during the case, he can appeal to the intermediate appeals court. An appeal can be made in the middle of a trial if the point is important enough. This is called an *interlocutory appeal*. In special circumstances, which are very unusual, he can appeal directly to the state supreme court or the Supreme Court of the United States. It is more usual to appeal to an intermediate appellate court first.

DEFINITION

An **interlocutory appeal** is an appeal made to a higher court before the end of a trial.

The only points an appeals court will consider are legal points, not factual. Once a fact has been decided by the trial court, whether by the judge or a jury, it's considered closed. That's why it's so important to do the discovery portion of the trial process well, and why it's important to practice feeling comfortable being questioned by a hostile person. The impression you make on the judge or jury is going to affect whether they believe you or not, and they're not only entitled to, they're commanded to decide who to believe. People often dismiss a case as impossible to decide because it's a "he said–she said" situation, where one side must be believed and the other disbelieved. This is not a problem for the courts. They routinely decide to disbelieve one party and believe another.

The Least You Need to Know

- Power and place are two different issues to consider when picking a court to hear your case.
- Without the power of jurisdiction, the court has no power to decide your case.
- Constitutional requirements of due process govern everything that happens during the trial.
- The process of discovery is the basis for everything that happens at trial, so it's important to make sure that you follow all the rules and requirements in a timely fashion.

Court Rules and Civil Procedure

In This Chapter

- Rules about time
- Rules about notification
- The rules that trip people up
- Figuring out deadlines and due dates

Because of the constitutional requirement, known as due process, to treat everyone equally in lawsuits, the legal system has been forced to come up with rules that it can easily apply to all people in all cases. The rules are published in statutes and gathered in special handbooks (called something like "Rules of Court" or "Rules of Civil Procedure") that you can find in law libraries. It's still difficult to find these rules online for all states and all levels of court, but it's getting easier. See Appendix B for a list of helpful websites that have some of these rules available online.

Time Is Always Critical

The most important set of rules you'll be dealing with concern time. Although lawsuits can take years to work their way through the system, rules are in place to keep them moving along. One of the most frustrating aspects of lawsuits is that you'll be doing a lot of "hurry up and wait" throughout the process.

One of the first things a lawyer does when she gets a new case is to check the court rules to find out when everything's due. Some lawyers have special computer programs that help them figure out deadlines and schedule them directly onto their calendars, with warnings a few days or weeks ahead of time put on the calendar, too. This ensures that nothing falls through the cracks and that all deadlines are met. Attorneys can do the same thing without the computer program, just by counting out the days and marking them on whatever calendar they use, computerized or not.

> **JUST THE FACTS**
>
> Americans might be frustrated with the speed (or lack of it) of the U.S. legal system, but residents of the United States are actually pretty lucky. In India, there are lawsuits that are still going on decades after they began. People inherit the lawsuits from family members and keep them going.

Deadlines Are Critical

It's difficult to overemphasize the importance of deadlines in lawsuits. Although it's possible to get more time by asking the opposing side for a favor or the judge for a continuance, it's best not to put yourself into a position where you need to do that. While it's considered a professional courtesy to grant the first request from the other side for an extension of time, it's not a requirement.

Under some circumstances, denying the request for extra time can result in a forced loss or a disadvantage to the other side. Therefore, there are times when the request won't be granted by the opposing side, and you have to go to the court for permission to extend the deadline. The court isn't required to grant an extension, either. If the case has been dragging on, or the party or his attorney has a reputation for not meeting deadlines, the extension won't be granted. If the extension is not granted, you're stuck with the consequences, and they can be very bad.

Because deadlines are published in the court rules, and because the parties themselves help set the deadlines during the pretrial process, discussed in Chapter 10, the courts are very particular about meeting the deadlines. The phrase "a day late and a dollar short," meaning "you're too late and you couldn't have done it anyway," might have been invented by lawyers for just these situations.

Statute of Limitations

The first major deadline is called the statute of limitations. This is an actual law or statute that says how much time you have to sue from the date of the injury or problem. The amount of time is different for every kind of problem. It's also different from state to state, and the federal system has different statutes of limitation from any of the states. Whether you're in a state or federal court, you need to know when to begin counting time for the statute of limitations. This is called "finding out when the statute begins to run." Usually, the statute starts to run from the date of injury or the date that the problem started, but it can sometimes run from the date you discover the injury or the problem.

You must sue within the statute's time limit or you cannot sue at all. This can lead to injustice, but there are two very good reasons for this rule. First, people's memories fade as time goes by, and evidence is harder to find. Getting testimony and evidence as fresh as possible is important to getting a fair resolution to the case. Second, the law doesn't want people to "sit on their rights." If it's that good a case, pursue it. The law wants people to get on with their lives, not wait for a possible lawsuit that may never come.

If you don't sue within the time limit given by the statute, you're said to "blow" the statute of limitations. When you blow the statute, you've lost your chance to sue forever. When you see the attorney for the first time, be sure to let her know when the incident occurred. Ask how much time you have left to sue, and don't be surprised if the attorney needs time to research the question. The attorney should let you know how long you've got to sue, and whether she believes it's worth pursuing the case. If she doesn't think it's worth pursuing, she should tell you so in writing, and include in the letter she sends you how much longer you have to find another attorney if you want to go forward with the lawsuit.

PITFALLS

If you've seen an attorney, and the attorney doesn't tell you how long you've got left on the statute, ask. If the time is running out, and the attorney isn't moving forward, find out why. If you're not satisfied with the answer, find another attorney fast. You may have a malpractice case against an attorney who misses the deadline set by the statute of limitations.

Very rarely, though, even if the case is past the statute of limitations, there may be an exception that applies to the case that extends the time you have to file suit. For example, if a child is injured, he or she usually has until turning 19 years old to file suit, regardless of when the injury occurred. In cases like that, the statute of limitations is stopped or "tolled." Ask your attorney if your case falls into one of the exceptions, but don't be surprised if it doesn't. The reasons the exceptions exist are generally to protect people, like children, who were absolutely unable to act on their own in time.

There's a Rule for Everything

One of the reasons people find going to court intimidating is the large number of rules on every conceivable topic. The courts really do have a different rule for everything, and it's important to follow all the rules. Some of the rules seem extremely petty and small-minded, but they must be followed regardless. Having your documents refused for filing because of a seemingly minor court rule infraction can ruin your case. You won't be given any extra time to fix the problem, which means you could miss the deadline and lose on a technicality.

Federal and State Rules Are Different

Even though the rules are similar in all courts, they're not identical. Each state has its own rules, and each level of court within the state, trial and appellate, has different rules, too. On top of that, the federal courts have an entirely different set of rules altogether. Most states base their rules to some extent on the federal rules, so if you're aware of a rule topic in the federal courts, you'll know to look for it in the state courts.

There are also "local rules," which can be set by each individual court. These local rules exist for every kind of court at both the federal and state levels. Often these rules cover things like how many copies of a document the court wants you to turn in, or what kind of clothing is acceptable in that courthouse. The local rules are a way to adjust for local needs without making everyone else follow a rule that's not necessary everywhere. Some courts don't bother with a rule on bringing food into the courthouse because they haven't had any problems with food and drink. Other courts need a rule telling people where and when they can have food and drink within the building. A local rule can be created, stating where and when food and drink are allowed, without adding to any other court's enforcement issues. The theory is that there are enough rules as it is; local rules are there to address local problems.

Rules to Be Aware Of

Your attorney is the expert in the court rules and, for the most part, you don't need to be aware of too many of them. However, so you understand what's going on around you, and so you know what you should be doing at various points, you should be aware of rules that fall under the following general categories:

- **Timing rules**   As discussed earlier in this chapter, remember to ask about due dates and deadlines for everything, and to work with your attorney to meet or beat them.

- **Codes of conduct**   Everyone involved in a court case must behave in a polite, collegial, and cordial manner. Of course, this is a rule that's broken all the time, but when it's broken in a particularly outstanding manner, the violator can be found in contempt of court. That can mean monetary fines and even jail time.

- **Due process**   This group of rules deals with making sure the parties' constitutional right to know what they're being sued over is met. Many other rules deal with things like making sure things are run efficiently by the court and the parties, making sure that the correct court and correct level of court are being used, and so on.

You've Been Served

Your constitutional right to know you're being sued is assured by court rules surrounding "notice," or notification. The first time you'll deal with the rules about notice is through the procedure by which the plaintiff officially tells the defendant he is being sued. This is called "service of process." Service of process also refers to giving any official notice having to do with the lawsuit. You'll have to serve the other side with copies of all the papers you officially give to or file with the court.

Movies like *Serving Sara*, in which people go to crazy lengths to give the defendant notice that she's being sued, are fun to watch, but they miss a major piece of reality. Avoiding service of process does not cancel out the lawsuit. In fact, avoiding being served can actually hurt you in the long run. The court doesn't see this as you avoiding the crazy nutcase who's come up with some stupid, baseless case against you. The court sees it as you avoiding the authority of the court, and sees it as disrespectful to the court.

Rather than letting you get away with disrespect to the court and avoiding the court's power, the court can do something called "ordering alternate service." This means you no longer have to get a copy of the lawsuit in your hand to be served; the papers can be mailed to you, or posted on the wall of the courthouse. They can even be posted in a regular newspaper or the local legal newspaper. Sometimes just the fact that you're being sued might be posted in the newspaper.

If you've been avoiding service, you're likely to throw out the first-class mail from the law firm handling the case, and refuse to sign for the certified mail they'll send as a backup. Most people, even if they aren't avoiding service, don't read the legal newspapers, or go to the courthouse to read the postings on the wall. It doesn't matter. The whole point of alternate service is that it provides official notification of a lawsuit. Whether it's actually effective is up to the defendant, not the court. The court orders alternate service when it has seen a pattern of the defendant actively avoiding notice, which the plaintiff was trying to give in a fair and timely manner.

Once the plaintiff has fulfilled the alternate service requirements, the defendant is considered to have notice that he's being sued. This notice might not actually be received, but the defendant is treated as if he's received it. This is called getting "constructive notice." Even though it doesn't give the defendant personal, in-hand delivery, it's considered as good as delivery because he had every opportunity to take delivery but refused it.

If the defendant does actually find out about the lawsuit, for example by opening his mail, he now has "actual notice," which is the opposite of constructive notice.

If the defendant doesn't respond for whatever reason, the judge will likely enter a default judgment. Any time one side does not show up to fight the lawsuit, that side automatically loses the fight. A final court order, called a "judgment," can be issued. In cases like this, the judgment will state that the other side won by default and gives the winner everything she asked for.

The process is straightforward. When people avoid service and end up with alternate service and constructive notice, they don't know when the hearings are to be held, so they don't show up. When they don't show up, the other side can ask for everything it wants. Because the person who avoided service is not there to object to any of it, the other side gets everything it wants, and wins by default.

IN THE KNOW

If you act fast enough and have a good enough reason, you might be able to get a default judgment "set aside," meaning cancelled or thrown out. Most courts allow about a month, and won't cancel the default judgment if it was entered because of avoiding service.

Showing Up in Court

No matter how ridiculous you think the lawsuit is, you absolutely must defend your-self against it. You will lose by default if you don't. A similar thing can happen to the plaintiff if she doesn't show up for hearings; the defendant can ask that the case be dismissed, and very possibly can also win by default.

From the discussion about service of process, you can see that being aware of what's going on and just showing up are incredibly important. Missing a court date is a big deal. The courts have heard of so many deaths in the family that they'll actually ask for a death notice before accepting that as a valid excuse. By the way, attending a funeral isn't considered a valid excuse, because you generally have enough notice before the funeral that you could contact the court and the other side and arrange for a continuance.

If courts aren't impressed by death, they're really uninterested in excuses like "my car didn't start" or "I couldn't find a baby-sitter." The solution isn't to bring your children with you. Many courts won't allow children in the courtroom, no matter how well behaved, unless they are part of the suit. Make sure you have a backup plan for transportation, childcare, and work. As a practical matter, have a backup for your backup.

The minute you know you're going to have a problem, contact your attorney. If you don't have an attorney, or can't get hold of your attorney, contact the court. The sooner you know you've got a problem, and the faster you work to let people know, the better able you'll be to solve it without negatively affecting your case.

"Filing" Papers

When you submit a document to the court for consideration, you "file the papers." Papers can be filed in person, by mail, and electronically. Not all courts are equipped to handle electronic or e-filing, but every court has a procedure for accepting papers from litigants.

With a traditional filing, the lawyer or someone hired by the lawyer will go to the courthouse with money and several copies of the papers to be filed, or mail the papers with a self-addressed stamped envelope for return of the documents. Depending on the court, you might have to pay first, or pay after the papers are filed. The cost depends on the type of papers being filed; remember from Chapter 5 that filing fees can range from free to $300.

Multiple copies of the papers are necessary to make sure everyone who needs an official copy gets one. Each copy is stamped by the court clerk, often with a machine that works exactly like a time clock used by hourly workers who punch in and out. This proves when the document was filed with the court. One copy goes to the court's own file; another copy goes to the other side; another copy goes back to the attorney's file; and sometimes yet another copy is requested for the judge.

The person filing the papers is responsible for making sure the other side gets an official stamped copy of the document within the time specified in the court rules. You should make sure your attorney sends you copies of all documents filed with the court as your case progresses. That way, you will be kept up-to-date on what's going on and can maintain your own file. If something happens to the attorney or to your relationship with the attorney, you'll be able to move ahead quickly and smoothly by giving the relevant documents to the new attorney.

If you file electronically, you'll get some sort of receipt from the court, either via e-mail or by checking the court's website to see whether the document's been entered into the system. You're still responsible for making sure the other side gets the documents before the deadline.

The court may accept payment by credit card for e-filings but will likely charge a processing fee for the service. This is because the credit card company charges the court for the use of the system. Statutes establish how much parties will pay for filing fees, and by law 100 percent of the fee must go to the courts. If the credit card processing fee is 2 percent per transaction, and the court doesn't charge for the processing fee, the court only gets 98 percent of the required amount, and the law is violated. To avoid that, you pay the processing fee because you're the one using the special service. As time goes on and e-filing becomes the norm, the statutes may change to incorporate the cost of the credit card processing in the filing fee. For now, it seems fairer for only the people using credit cards to pay the extra, "hidden" fee.

IN THE KNOW

Most courts don't allow electronic service of process on the other side for the initial papers in a lawsuit. You'll still have to have hard copies made specifically for that purpose.

Rules for Document Formatting

As discussed previously, there's a rule for everything, and many of the rules strike people as unnecessarily detail-oriented. A good example of one of those detail-oriented rules is the rule regarding paper size. Most court rules now forbid the use of legal-size paper (the 8.5×14 stuff). It seems petty, but if you present your documents on anything other than regular 8.5×11 paper, your documents will be refused. Courts decided to save physical filing space, which at 3 inches per filing cabinet adds up, and insisted that everyone switch to ordinary paper. There's no place to put your paper if it's the wrong size. Plus, many courts now scan documents into their computer systems, and scanners can't handle oversize documents.

Other rules you should be aware of include using easy-to-read fonts like Arial, Courier, or Times New Roman in a minimum size of 12 points; printing on only one side of the paper; and using the proper heading on every document you turn in. The heading, also known as the caption, gives information about the case, such as which court is hearing the case, who the plaintiff and defendant are, who the assigned judge is, and the court's case or file number.

That being said, there are allowable stylistic differences that attorneys even in the same region disagree about. For example, some bold the plaintiff and defendant's names on all documents; others put the plaintiff and defendant in all capital letters, and continue to do that throughout the document. If you are filing without an attorney, you might be given more leeway in the style of what's accepted in your documents, but it's not a license to do whatever you want. You still have to follow the appropriate court rules.

Figuring Out Deadlines and Due Dates

The court rules will tell you how many days you have to do a specific action or respond to the other side. The big deal is properly counting out the days and making sure you have the right due date. There are two times the count can start: the day the paper was filed, or the day after the paper was filed. Most court systems begin the count the day after the paper was filed; the court rules will specify exactly how to begin counting.

The next thing to find out is whether your court figures deadlines by calendar days or by working days. If the court uses calendar days, then every day, including weekends and holidays, counts. The working-day system counts only days that the court is open, which excludes weekends and holidays.

It works like this: If you have 14 days to respond to a motion filed on November 2, then start counting with November 3 as day 1. If it's a calendar-day system, then the due date is November 14, by the time the court closes. If it's a working-day system, you still start counting on November 3, but your due date is by the time the court closes on November 20.

If you're working with an attorney, the attorney will figure out the dates for you. If you're not working with an attorney, double-check with the court clerk and aim for filing your papers at least two business days before the due date you've calculated.

The Least You Need to Know

- Always show up for every court date.
- Don't try to avoid getting "served."
- Give proper notice to the other side at all times.
- Ask if you're unsure of anything.

Small Claims Court

In This Chapter

- Why small claims court may be right for you
- Requirements for small claims courts
- When to avoid small claims court
- Collecting on your judgment

Lawyers often call small claims courts the courts of small claims and large principles. The amount of money involved is never very large, but the litigants say over and over, "It's the principle of the thing." These are the cases people swear they'll take all the way to the United States Supreme Court. In reality, the United States Supreme Court isn't likely to be interested in hearing the case; see Chapter 15 for a discussion of how you get a case to the Supreme Court.

That being said, small claims courts are real courts, and there are real consequences if you decide to sue—or are sued—in small claims court.

What Makes Small Claims Courts Different?

Small claims courts are different from regular trial courts because everything about them is smaller. The fees are smaller, the timeline is shorter, the cases are worth less money, and the courts tend to be less formal. Don't let that fool you. Small claims court is still a court, and must be treated with the seriousness and respect due to all courts.

In a nutshell, small claims courts typically …

- Have a "top end" in terms of the amount of money in controversy.
- May not allow attorneys to appear to represent the parties.
- Do not follow strict rules of evidence.

Separate rules typically govern small claims courts. Check with the court clerk at the small claims division to find out where to get those rules, and read them. If you don't follow those rules, you could lose your case on a technicality. In addition, following the rules shows respect for the court and prevents you from making basic mistakes like missing deadlines.

When Should I Use Small Claims Court?

Ask yourself the following questions to see whether small claims court is the right place for you to go:

- Have you tried to settle the dispute?
- Is it not worth it to you to hire an attorney?
- Are you willing to go it alone without an attorney?
- Are you willing to limit any monetary recovery to the amount allowed by your local small claims court?

If you answered "yes" to those questions, next check to see what the monetary limit is in your state (see Appendix B for a list). Small claims courts tend to have monetary limits from a few thousand dollars to $25,000 or more. As long as your conflict is for less than that amount, and doesn't involve something that's only handled by a special court like divorce, bankruptcy, or will contests, small claims court is the place to go.

Before you do head to small claims court, contact the other side and ask for what you want. Keep written track of your requests, including whom you've talked to and what you talked about. Be willing to negotiate; see Chapter 18 for a discussion of negotiation techniques that may help you. Make sure you get any agreement in writing for two reasons: First, writing it out helps ensure that there's less confusion about what you agreed to do. Second, it helps prove what you agreed to do if you do have to go to court to enforce your agreement.

The Kinds of Cases Heard in Small Claims Courts

Small claims courts hear disputes between two or more parties. These disputes usually fall into one of two categories. The first is when someone breaks a promise he made in an agreement (a contract) to do or not do something specific. The amount that's being argued about has to be within the limits specified for small claims courts. Because of this, there are lots of small claims cases for unpaid phone bills, unshoveled driveways, and improperly fixed plumbing.

The second type of commonly heard disputes in small claims courts are based on an incident of some sort, other than a breach of contract, that caused damage. The damage might have been the result of an accident (called negligence) or the result of an intentional act. This kind of injury is called a tort.

JUST THE FACTS

When you see ads on TV asking if you've been involved in an automobile accident, dog bite, or slip and fall, you're seeing ads for lawyers who do tort cases.

Small claims cases are often between friends, neighbors, and acquaintances, which makes them more explosive and emotional than a bare reading of the facts would suggest.

It's All Based on Monetary Value

Whatever the problem facing the parties, the small claims court is hearing it because the amount of money in dispute is within the small claims limits. That means it is under the *jurisdictional amount*, or the amount the small claims court is permitted to deal with. (See Chapters 7 and 8 for a fuller discussion of jurisdiction, or the power of a court to hear and decide a case.) Small claims courts have been specifically separated from regular trial courts to keep cases that are smaller, and so theoretically faster to solve, from being slowed down by the larger cases heard in the regular courts. The idea is that the smaller the amount of money involved, the less complicated the case will be, and the faster it will be to resolve.

DEFINITION

The **jurisdictional amount** is the limit to the amount of money in question in a case that a particular court can hear.

Accidents

Cases involving accidents, or tort cases, can be heard in small claims courts. These accidents can involve cars, people (usually minor physical injuries), or physical objects. For example, in suburban areas, there are frequent small claims lawsuits involving mailboxes and lawn services. There must be something about a riding mower and a mailbox that makes them irresistible to each other, because riding mowers are forever knocking mailboxes down. Depending on how fancy the mailbox is, the owner is out anywhere from $50 to $300. The mailbox owner goes to small claims court and sues the lawn service or his neighbor, whoever knocked the box over, to get the money he's going to spend replacing the box. Ordinarily, the person who knocked the box over is willing to pay to replace it but believes the amount quoted is ridiculously high. That's where the court comes in.

Other common accident claims are for dings and scratches to cars or motorcycles, or a request for reimbursement for the deductible on the car insurance after a larger accident. People also go to small claims court to get the deductible from their health insurance paid after a minor accident that resulted in the need for medical treatment.

Debts

Unpaid bills from your lawn service, your dentist, or a debt you owe a friend can all end up in small claims court for resolution. Again, the amount has to be within the jurisdictional amount for small claims court, but this is a very efficient way to collect on a debt. It's always best to have something in writing, but even oral contracts may be enforceable under some circumstances. In some states, unpaid rent can be sued for in small claims court as a regular debt, but typically evictions cannot be handled in small claims. Once you have a judgment, you can collect the debt using the court's power to garnish or seize assets.

The Kinds of Cases *Not* Heard in Small Claims Courts

Even though the monetary amount is right, some cases can't be heard in small claims courts because other courts have jurisdiction, or power, over the specific topic. Before you decide to go with small claims, check to be sure that another kind of court isn't the more appropriate place to go.

In particular, if your case grows out of a previous lawsuit, check to be sure that you aren't supposed to go back to the original judge and court that the lawsuit was decided in.

Remember the Monetary Value

Again, the first thing to check is the value of the debt or loss, not including the fees you'll have to pay the court. One way to try to get to a higher trial court is to include the value of things you lost because of consequential damages (discussed in Chapter 3). Some courts will not permit this; others will.

Although they don't count for purposes of establishing which court to go to, you are entitled to be reimbursed for your provable costs in filing suit. Include receipts showing the exact amount you paid for things, such as the filing fee, the cost for service of process, and the interest you lost because you weren't able to bank or invest that money.

IN THE KNOW

To calculate the lost interest, use what's called the "judgment interest rate" or "statutory interest rate," which you can usually find by going to the highest state court's website. It's normally the prime rate (the interest rate used by the government when it lends money to banks) as of a specific date plus a few percentage points. The statutory interest rate or judgment interest rate changes as the prime rate changes, and is the rate that the courts allow or impose on their final judgments.

However, if the person you want to sue has declared bankruptcy, the monetary value becomes unimportant. You'll have to go to the bankruptcy court and get listed as a creditor in the bankruptcy proceedings. You should get notice as a potential creditor when the person you would otherwise sue in small claims decides to file for bankruptcy. If you don't, you may be able to convince the bankruptcy court that you should be paid in full. Otherwise, you're likely to be treated like all the other creditors, and get paid a portion—or even none—of what you're owed.

Family Law

Most states require that anything having to do with family law, including collecting back child support, spousal support, or alimony, be done through the family courts. There are a few states that do allow collection of small amounts of money owed because of a family law issue to be pursued in small claims court, but they're unusual. For the most part, even with smaller amounts of money, the court that was first to deal with the parties is the court the parties always go to for anything that happens afterward that's connected with the original conflict.

In particular, for family law issues like child support, entire bureaucracies are in place to collect and process payments. Going outside of that system is not a great idea. For one thing, the system exists to protect both parties—the payer and the payee—by documenting that payment was made. If payment is made outside the system, it's not properly documented. If it's not properly documented, it won't be properly credited. It's always best to make payments as the court orders so that you get credit for the payment. Any other payment, even one made directly to the payee, and even with an official-looking receipt, doesn't count without a great deal of extra work on your part.

Evictions and Other Landlord-Tenant Issues

Landlord-tenant matters deal with land rights, not just with money, so they're ordinarily state court issues. Many states don't allow any landlord-tenant issues to be handled by the small claims court, even if the amount of money involved seems like a small claims amount. Major metropolitan areas often have a separate landlord-tenant court that handles evictions, rent withholding, and other related issues. It's more common for states to handle landlord-tenant cases through their regular trial courts, whether at the municipal or county level.

Costs Associated with Small Claims Court

As discussed in Chapter 1, every individual has a constitutional right to know she's being sued. To fulfill that right, the defendant must get notice that a suit has been filed against her in court. This notice includes getting hard copies of the filing papers.

As noted in Chapter 1, the papers must be handed to the defendant by an adult not associated with the lawsuit, or a process server. Depending on the court rules, the process server may be a court officer, like a bailiff, or a service hired by the plaintiff. Most servers are paid a flat fee, sometimes plus mileage. The flat fee can run from $20 to $50; the mileage fee is usually set at whatever the IRS rate may be. If the defendant is difficult to serve, the flat fee may go out the window, and the price will go up.

IN THE KNOW

To learn the current IRS mileage rate, go to www.irs.gov. In the search box, type "mileage rate" and the year for which you want to know the rate. Several documents will come up, at least one of which will have the rate announcement for that year.

The fee you pay the process server is called a service fee, or process fee. Although this isn't technically a court fee, it's closely related to the filing fee, and in some small claims court cases is even paid directly to the court.

Why Can't I Have a Lawyer?

One of the goals of small claims courts is to keep everything as small, informal, and inexpensive as possible while still maintaining the seriousness and respect due to the courts. Many states have decided that allowing attorneys to represent the parties in small claims court adds an unnecessary layer of complexity to what should be a simple process. Other states allow attorneys on the theory that the presence of an attorney simplifies things for people who are in the middle of a conflict. Still other states make it a requirement that corporations and LLCs (limited liability companies) be represented by an attorney, but not ordinary individuals.

JUST THE FACTS

Corporations and limited liability companies generally have to be represented by an attorney in any legal action because they're considered "persons" separate from the real people who own them. Real people can represent themselves in court. Corporations have to be represented by an agent, and the only agents allowed to represent anyone in court are attorneys.

Why Can't I Have a Jury?

For the same reason that many states don't allow attorneys in small claims court, many states also don't allow jury trials in small claims court. Jury trials take more time and more court resources than trials presided over by a judge or magistrate. Because courts have limited resources, they're charged with using them as wisely as possible. For small claims cases, jury trials aren't seen as the best use of those resources. The decision has been made that, in general, it's better to try to solve a small claims dispute with a hearing by a judge or magistrate, or even mediation.

Small Claims Mediation

Frequently, small claims courts have mandatory mediation. Local attorneys often act as volunteer mediators. If the mediation is successful and the parties agree to a solution to their problem, the solution can be written up as a consent judgment. (See Chapter 13 for a discussion of consent judgments.) Because, as stated earlier, this is the court of small claims and large principles, mediation is often a long, drawn-out process. More often than not, mediation does result in a good solution for the parties. Small claims courts were one of the first places mandatory mediation in the courts was tried, and the success shown at this level made it very attractive for higher-level trial courts as well.

Enforcing a Small Claims Judgment

As part of the judgment handed down by the court, you should ask that a deadline be included for when the action the court orders has to be completed by. Once you have your judgment in hand, you can make a request to the other side that they fulfill their obligations under the judgment. Often, that's all you have to do. You can ask verbally at the time the judgment is granted, and follow up with writing a letter asking that the other side pay up.

PITFALLS

Be sure to ask for a time limit in meeting the requirements of the small claims court's judgment. That way, it'll be clear when the other side is not following the court's order, and it'll be much easier for you to get further action from the court to enforce the judgment.

As with all aspects of any lawsuit, keep track of what you've done and what the other side did in response. This is particularly important when you're trying to get the judgment enforced, as the court will probably want to hear about what happened— or didn't happen—in more detail than a flat "they didn't pay."

When you go back to the court because the other side didn't live up to the judgment, you have two main options: garnishment or asking for further "equitable relief" or enforcement. Which option you use depends on what you got in the judgment.

Garnishment

If you were awarded money, and the other side hasn't paid, you can ask the court for permission to garnish the money owed to you. You can take money the other side's employer owes them, or that the IRS owes them, or that a bank is holding for them. The key is to find these people or institutions who owe the other side money so you can garnish it. Garnishment also requires that you fill out a court form and get an order from the court telling the person holding money for the other side to pay you instead of them. You'll have to pay the court for the motion for garnishment, and you'll have to pay someone to serve notice of the motion and hearing. Fortunately, you can add the cost of the motion and serving it to what the other side owes you. Don't forget to add interest at the statutory rate, as discussed previously!

Equitable Enforcement

When the judgment has the other side doing or not doing something specific, other than paying money (called "injunctive relief"), there's a different option used when the other side hasn't lived up to or "satisfied" the judgment. For example, a defendant might be ordered to remove a fence that was wrongfully placed on your property. If the order provides that the defendant is to remove it within a certain time period, and the defendant never does it, what do you do? You go for further equitable relief. In that circumstance, you may ask the court for permission to take down the fence yourself, and charge your costs to the defendant. In these situations, you need to be creative. Can you come up with a solution that gets you what you want and gives you control over how it is done? Make sure you understand the limits of your particular small claims court. The court might not have the ability to grant you certain forms of relief. You don't want to find yourself in a position where you got a judgment that the court can't enforce. Again, this is another reason why you might want to have the help of an attorney.

Removing a Case from Small Claims Court

Just because a case starts in small claims court doesn't mean it has to stay there. The defendant may have the option of moving the case to the regular trial court. When you take a case from one court with the power to hear and decide the case (that court is said to have "proper jurisdiction") and move it to another court, which also has power to hear and decide the case, you're "removing" the case, not just moving it. Your ability to remove the case depends on the law and your reasons for wanting to remove the case to a higher court. Removal isn't usually automatically granted, so check the court rules and see what circumstances allow you to remove the case.

There are some advantages to removing the case from small claims court to a higher court. The first is that you can't have a jury trial in small claims court, but you can in higher courts. Whether that's really an advantage depends on whether you believe that a jury will give you a better result than the magistrate in charge of the small claims court.

The second advantage has to do with whether or not you can be represented by an attorney. In some states, lawyers are not permitted to represent people in small claims court. If yours is one of those states, removing your case to a higher court will allow you to put your problem in an attorney's hands.

The disadvantages to removing a case are strongly related to the advantages. If you have a jury trial, it's likely to take longer and therefore cost more. Having an attorney represent you reduces the burden on you in some ways, but it increases your financial burden. If you want a speedy, relatively inexpensive conclusion to your dispute, you may want to stay with the small claims court.

The Least You Need to Know

- If the amount of money you're after fits the requirements, use small claims court.
- Keep written track of everything that happens with your case.
- Small claims court can be faster and cheaper than regular trial court.
- Your case isn't over until the judgment is completely paid off or satisfied.

The Trial Process

The trial process is the meat and potatoes of lawsuits. This part covers everything about the trial itself. It starts at the very beginning, preparing for trial and establishing evidence. The process continues with a real-life discussion of what to expect at the trial and how the decision for one side and against the other is made. Once the trial is over, you'll need to make decisions about appeals and moving on with your life. Finally, you may need to decide whether or not you have a case against your attorney for legal malpractice.

Pretrial

Chapter 10

In This Chapter

- Settlements
- Scheduling
- Getting evidence through discovery
- Pretrial motions

There are two ways of thinking about the pretrial period. One is the way most people think of it: as the time before you start the lawsuit. The other is the way lawyers think of it: as the time after you've started the lawsuit, but before the actual trial takes place. This book is going to take the lawyer's definition, because that's the one you'll be working with in your lawsuit. The issue of ending the conflict through negotiation, called a settlement, is one that comes up under both definitions of the pretrial period, but it's often easier to settle once both sides know there are serious consequences for not settling.

Should You Settle?

People often ask themselves how they got to the point where they're involved in a lawsuit in the first place. At the very beginning of the process, there doesn't seem to be any reason to settle, because you've probably already tried talking to the other side to solve the problem without success. There's also a sense that you have to fight this through, that settling is giving in, and that you should only settle if there's no chance of winning.

While those are legitimate feelings, settlement might be the best solution. Settling can give you the best of all possible worlds: a quick conclusion to an unpleasant situation, with minimal money and time spent on the problem. Remember the costs discussion in Chapter 5. Your time, your emotion, your stress, and your money are going to be flowing freely throughout the litigation process. Settlement is an opportunity to cut those all off at the knees.

Only you can answer the question of whether or not to settle. Take into account the costs, take into account your attorney's prediction of the likelihood of success, and take into account the effect the lawsuit will have on your business and your life, whether you win or lose. Be particularly clear with yourself about what will happen if you lose the suit. Often, people are so sure of their own case that they never consider the possibility of losing. Remember that there are two sides to every story. In the event that you lose, can you deal with the consequences?

Another issue is publicity. The more interesting (or scandalous) the case, the more likely it is to be watched by the public, who are free to come into the courtroom to observe any case. If you would prefer to avoid the public eye, settlement can be an excellent solution, because then no one has to know your business. "Nondisclosure clauses," discussed later in this chapter, help keep things private.

It's often economically wiser to settle—even if you're 100 percent right—than it is to fight on to win far less than you spent. If your attorney advises settlement, ask why. Ask whether your attorney has (preserving your confidentiality, of course) discussed your situation with other attorneys to confer about your case. Really listen to the answer. This is the person you're paying to give you advice; if you're not happy with the advice you're getting, go somewhere else. It's a difficult decision, but it's ultimately yours.

Negotiating Settlements

You've probably been negotiating with the other side since before the lawsuit was filed. Now it's time to step back and let the lawyers do the talking. In fact, once the other side has a lawyer, you shouldn't communicate with the other side except through the lawyer. If you have a lawyer, too, then don't communicate except through both lawyers. For one thing, it's what you're paying them for; for another, it keeps a record of what's been going on and makes it difficult for the other side to make a false claim as to what was said. It's your responsibility to let the lawyer know what you can afford and what you're interested in getting from the settlement, and let the lawyer go from there. The lawyer has a responsibility to tell you about any settlement offer the other side makes.

JUST THE FACTS

If the lawyer conceals settlement offers from you (most likely because the lawyer really wants to go to trial), she can lose her license to practice law. Accepting or declining a settlement offer is always up to you, the client.

How Is This Different from Any Negotiation?

Negotiating a settlement is different from other negotiations because there is the knowledge that if you cannot come to an agreement, the court will make a decision for you. Professional negotiators call what you'll do if the negotiations fail your "fall-back position." If going to court is your fall-back position, it's not a bad one, as long as you believe you have a strong case.

The other difference between settlement negotiations and regular negotiations is that at the end of this, the parties can agree upon something called a *consent judgment*. This basically takes the points you agreed upon in the negotiation and turns it into a final court order that both sides must live up to. If one side doesn't live up to the agreement, the other can go back to court and ask that the judgment be enforced by the court. It's a much stronger assurance that you'll get what you agreed to than the usual contract that is the result of ordinary negotiations.

DEFINITION

A **consent judgment** is an order ending a lawsuit according to the agreement (or consent) of both parties.

Nondisclosure Agreements

Trials are public events, unless the court believes there is some strong reason to close the courtroom to observers. Ordinarily, anyone can sit in a courtroom and watch what's going on. Also, people can go through the court files, see all the documents that have been filed with the court, and even get copies of them. In the courtroom itself, you'll find lawyers waiting for their case to be heard, other litigants and their friends and families, reporters from newspapers and TV, and students sitting in a courtroom at any given time. The juicier the case, the more people will come to see it and the more publicity it will get. Details about your business or private life will be exposed.

To avoid all that, you might want to settle, since one of the advantages of settlement is that it avoids a public trial. To make sure that no private details get out, you can have a *nondisclosure agreement* as part of the settlement and even as part of the consent judgment. Nondisclosure agreements usually state that the parties and their attorneys cannot discuss details of the case. If a party does discuss the details, the other side can go to court and get an order stopping that party from talking any more. Because that's about as effective as the old "closing the barn door after the horse gets out," most nondisclosure agreements also have major financial penalties for breaking the agreement. The court will enforce that part of the agreement or consent judgment as long as that agreement or consent judgment is seen as fair.

> **DEFINITION**
>
> A **nondisclosure agreement** is a contract agreeing that aspects of your dispute that led to the case being filed will remain confidential, and providing financial and legal penalties for breaking the agreement.

Court Proceedings

Some of the court proceedings in the pretrial phase are aimed at getting you to settle the case without a trial. The majority of pretrial court proceedings have to do with scheduling and getting all of the information needed for the trial together. Your attorney will let you know whether or not you need to be there for these proceedings. If you don't have an attorney, you absolutely must be there for all of the proceedings or you might lose your case on a technicality.

When Will Your Case Be Heard by the Court?

The court will hear parts of your case as they come up, but the trial isn't likely to happen for a minimum of three to six months, and probably closer to a year. This is because it takes time to collect all of the information and evidence needed for the trial to go forward. It's also because your trial needs to be fitted into the court's schedule, which is usually packed full of cases. Once you see the events on the schedule the court sets for you, and once you see how long it takes to perform each of the required tasks, the wait won't seem quite as unreasonable.

If your case is time-sensitive or somehow urgent, you can request that the court hear it more quickly. You need to have a very good reason for this, like needing to make an immediate decision about health care for a relative who's ill. Otherwise, you'll be put on the court's *docket* like everyone else.

DEFINITION

The **docket** is the court's schedule or calendar. Many attorneys refer to their own schedule or calendar as their docket, too.

Setting the Schedule

The court has a list of things that have to be accomplished before the trial can begin. One of the first proceedings is a pretrial hearing or a scheduling conference, in which the judge typically asks if the parties have come to a settlement; if the answer is no, he will start setting dates for each of the phases of the trial. This hearing might be held by telephone in some courts, to save everyone's time. If you don't have an attorney, be sure to find out when this takes place and be present for it. It's critical for the rest of the trial process to know when things will happen. If you do have an attorney, it's unlikely that you'll need to be present for this.

Discovery

The trial, while it is a fact-finding event, isn't a fishing trip. Believe it or not, by the time a case goes to trial, both sides pretty much know what the other side is going to argue, and what facts and evidence the other side has. This is because of something called "discovery." Discovery is exactly what it sounds like—each side to a lawsuit literally "discovers" all the facts and evidence that the other side has.

What the courts mean by fact-finding is deciding which of two conflicting facts is actually true. Before the trial, you must find, or discover, the facts to present to the court. Parties can discover the facts of the case in several ways, but all essentially involve asking the other side for information that you can't get any other way. The court requires that when asked a question, you answer it truthfully or not answer at all. The only way to get out of answering a question is by claiming that it's *privileged* or that the information is not relevant to the case. It's particularly hard to prove that a question is not relevant, because any question that could bear on the case is considered relevant. The question has to be far outside the realm of the case to be considered irrelevant enough not to answer.

> **DEFINITION**
>
> **Privileged** information is legally protected because of the kind of relationship it came from. For example, information you give to your doctor for the purpose of treatment is privileged because society wants to protect the doctor-patient relationship.

Interrogatories

Interrogatories are written questions that are given only to the parties in the case. They can run to hundreds of pages, even without the required space put in for the answer to be written in. Any question can be asked if it could lead to information that may be important to the lawsuit. Interrogatories usually start with questions aimed at identifying the parties and move on to questions having to do with the case. They can go into tremendous detail.

> **DEFINITION**
>
> **Interrogatories** are questions given in writing to the plaintiff or defendant in the case. Interrogatories cannot be given to anyone who is not a direct party to the suit.

Usually there is only one set of interrogatories sent per trial, but there can be follow-up questions sent based on the answers in the original interrogatories. Some questions might seem to be completely irrelevant. That usually doesn't matter; there is a difference between questions and information that can be asked at a trial, and those that can be asked in discovery. In discovery, there is much more room to ask questions to see where they might go than there is at trial.

Depositions

Anyone who's connected with the case, whether as a party or just as someone who has relevant information about the case, can be summoned to an out-of-court hearing to obtain his testimony. This hearing is called a deposition, and the person who is giving his testimony is called the deponent. The attorneys from both sides are present, and can ask any questions they like, just like in interrogatories. There's an opportunity to ask questions directly and, in the case of the parties, to compare the answers to those given in the interrogatories. When the witness is questioned, he is being deposed.

IN THE KNOW

Keep a copy of the deposition and the answers you give in the interrogatory and read them over to refresh your memory as you get closer to the trial.

As a party with an attorney, unless you're being deposed yourself, you don't need to attend the depositions, but you are usually allowed to be there. Depositions can last for hours, or even days, with bathroom and lunch breaks. The witness is in charge at the deposition; it's her story, and it's her time to tell it. If you're the witness and you need a break, say so, and you'll get it.

There are some basic guidelines that attorneys generally tell their clients when preparing for depositions. These are as follows:

- Do not answer any question that you don't understand; tell the attorney that you don't understand his question, so he can rephrase the question.

- Answer only the question that is asked.

- Do not guess or speculate as to any of your answers.

- Do not volunteer information.

- For anything that can be exact—like a time, date, distance, speed, amount of money—say "approximately" or "about" unless you know the *exact* amount.

- If you don't remember, say you don't remember. If you never knew the answer, say "I don't know."

- Always tell the truth. You are better off telling the truth, even if you think it's bad for the case, than lying; if you are caught lying, you might lose the case and, more important, you may be charged with the crime of perjury.

One of the tricks attorneys use in depositions is getting you to make a definite, final statement. This trick is called "closing the door." Here's an example. You are asked to list all the music you like. You say "Pop, country, and jazz." He then asks "Is there anything else?" and you say "No." You've just closed the door.

You will be asked that same question at trial. If you answer "Pop, country, jazz, and opera," you've changed your answer. The attorney will say "Which time were you lying? Did you lie at your deposition, or are you lying to the court now?"

If you are being asked to list as much as you know about something, the attorney is trying to get you to close the door. Don't close the door! End your answers with "That's all I can remember now," not "Yes, that's everything."

Document Requests

Another way to get information from the opposing side is to ask for documents that you suspect might have the facts you need in them. Like questions in depositions and interrogatories, unless the information contained in the document is protected by law or is completely irrelevant, if you're asked for it, you must give up the documents requested. You don't need to hand over the originals, and you may, if the documents requested are large enough, charge for your copying costs. You may even require that the other side make the copy themselves, at your location, during regular business hours.

Request for Admission

Sometimes the parties are willing to admit that certain things are true. It saves time and effort when neither side has to argue that the weather was sunny the day of the accident. To get at those kinds of facts, the parties can send each other requests for admission of specific information. Before answering any of these, check with your attorney. Often, one side will slip in a request that you admit you're entirely wrong. Read the requests carefully; you aren't required to admit to anything, but you must answer one way or the other.

Electronic Discovery: Give Me Your Hard Drive!

With computers affecting every aspect of our lives, evidence related to lawsuits is often found on them. E-mail messages, instant messages, Facebook and other social-site postings, and computer-driven calendars can hold important information. Courts have decided that information on your hard drive and online can be requested and must be turned over in the discovery process. There's an entire subspecialty in finding information on people's hard drives and servers. You might end up hiring one of these specialists, who often charge between $100 and $300 per hour.

Court-Ordered Mandatory Mediation

The entire trial process is an attempt to solve the problem the parties have. If the court can help the parties come to a resolution without going all the way through a trial, everybody saves time and money. Courts have experimented with mediation, a form of negotiation with a third party acting as a go-between, and found that many cases were resolved quickly. Because of this, many trial courts now have rules requiring that the parties in civil cases go through mediation before they can actually go to trial. Neither party is required to accept a suggested resolution, but there might be penalties for refusing the solution and then losing at the trial. The penalties often include having to pay all of the attorney fees for the other side, so there's tremendous incentive to accept a reasonable mediated settlement. Having to pay your own attorney fees is bad enough, but having to pay both sides' attorneys fees is twice as bad. If only one side accepts the solution, then the case will go to trial as planned.

Some courts, rather than using mediation, have something called case evaluation, in which a panel of experts (usually lawyers with experience in the kind of case in question) look at the facts of the case and decide how much they think a jury would award at the end of the case. The parties can accept the evaluation, which ends the case via a settlement that formalizes the evaluation. If one party accepts the evaluation and the other party declines it, the case goes to trial. Again, there are usually penalties like having to pay the other side's attorney fees if you refuse to go along with the evaluation and end up losing at trial.

What Is a Motion?

When you want a court to do something, you must ask the court. If all the parties agree, then more often than not, the court will follow along. If, however, one side wants the court to do something, and the other doesn't, you have to file a *motion*.

DEFINITION

A **motion** is a plaintiff or defendant's formal demand that the court take a specific action and order that something be done.

There are pretrial motions, which have to be scheduled for the court to hear, and motions that are made during trial, which are made right then in the middle of another hearing. With formal motions, the court rules will tell you how far ahead you must schedule the motion in order to give proper notice to the other side. You will have to file the motion in the same way you file any other formal paperwork with the court, pay a motion fee of anywhere from $20 to $300, and provide the other side with both a copy of the motion and a notice telling them when the motion will be heard.

Different trial courts have different ways of dealing with motions. Because a motion is the main way to get things done in terms of moving a trial along, hundreds or thousands of motions are made each week in the larger courts. Some courts have a particular day each week called "Motion Day," when all motions must be scheduled and heard. Unless it's an emergency, you'll have to wait until Motion Day for your request to be heard and decided. Because of notice requirements, you might have to wait an additional week or more so that the other side gets its notice and enough time to prepare.

Attorneys know that the motions made before, during, and after the trial are critical to the success or failure of a lawsuit. If an attorney is successful in her motions, she might be in a better position to negotiate a settlement with the other side. Doing motions is so important that attorneys actually have a name for the process—motion practice—to distinguish it from actual trial work. Like many other aspects of the trial, if you have an attorney, you might not need to appear at the motion hearing unless you yourself are a witness and need to testify. If you don't have an attorney, you'll need to be present for every motion or you'll lose it by default.

Motions Before Trial

Several common motions are made during the pretrial phase of the lawsuit. They usually have to do with evidence or with eliminating the lawsuit entirely. Sometimes these motions are made simply to cover all bases, even if they're not likely to win or get the result asked for in the motion.

Motion to Dismiss

Both sides can do a version of a motion to dismiss the case before trial. The plaintiff's version says that the defendant didn't make any recognizable legal defense. The defendant's version argues that the plaintiff didn't make a claim that the law recognizes or for which it provides a solution. This is a little different from making a claim that the lawsuit is frivolous, which can also be a basis for asking that the case be dismissed. This is just saying that the other side tried to file a lawsuit, but didn't meet the standards the law requires.

If the case is dismissed, it can be *dismissed with prejudice* or *dismissed without prejudice*. If a case is dismissed with prejudice, it has been "prejudged" already, and cannot come back to court to be judged again, ever. If the case is dismissed without prejudice, the plaintiff can fix the mistakes that caused it to be thrown out and try again.

> **DEFINITION**
>
> A case **dismissed with prejudice** can never be brought back to any trial court to be litigated again. A **case dismissed without prejudice** can be started over fresh, as if they had never been brought before any court.

Motion to Get Information from the Other Side

One of the major motions made during the pretrial phase is to force the other side to answer the questions in interrogatories, requests for documents, and depositions. All of these kinds of requests are *motions to compel discovery*. Remember that unless the information is protected by law or is not reasonably calculated to lead to relevant evidence, it must be revealed if asked for. The court does not generally look kindly on parties who try to conceal evidence; then again, the court isn't too fond of parties who abuse the discovery process. The best solution is to be fair and reasonable in what you ask for, and fair and reasonable in what you provide in response to a request.

Motion to Limit Evidence

The last major pretrial motion is made to limit the evidence that can be used in the trial. This kind of motion is called a *motion in limine*. A motion in limine is made when one side wants to keep out evidence it believes is irrelevant, or is protected by law, or is less likely to help get at the truth than it is to prejudice the jury against one side or the other. This is a key strategic motion; winning it can mean the difference between winning and losing at trial.

> **DEFINITION**
>
> A **motion to compel discovery** is a request to the court to require the other side to answer questions or produce documents. A **motion in limine** is a request to the court to limit the evidence that can be used to decide the case at trial.

The Least You Need to Know

- Settlement may be a good option; don't dismiss it.
- Keep close track of all due dates and court hearings.
- Answer all questions honestly, but don't answer anything that wasn't asked.
- Use motions wisely to try to control the litigation process.

Proving Your Case: Evidence

In This Chapter

- What counts as evidence
- What makes evidence acceptable to the court
- Types of evidence
- Preparing evidence for an appeal

Anything that tends to prove (or disprove) a fact is considered evidence. For the evidence to be taken into account by the court, it has to be connected to a fact that's called into doubt, one that the parties are actually fighting over. That makes the evidence relevant. When the courts say "anything," they mean anything—statements under oath from witnesses, photographs, test results, physical objects. One of the most important steps to winning your case is producing enough believable evidence to convince the judge and jury that you're telling the truth. When you combine the believable evidence with laws that are interpreted in your favor, you've got a winning case.

If They Don't Ask, Why Tell?

In civil cases, there is no duty to produce evidence that was not directly requested by the other side in discovery (see Chapter 7 for more on discovery). It really is a civilian version of "don't ask, don't tell." This is unlike criminal cases, where the government in particular must provide any evidence they find to the defendant, especially if it tends to show the defendant's innocence.

Parties often run into two problems in avoiding disclosure of facts. The first is that unless the information was very clearly not asked for, the other side can legitimately complain that you were withholding requested evidence. This can lead to problems with the judge, who may impose a monetary fine or even hold you in contempt of court if she sees a pattern of noncooperation. The second problem is that just because you don't supply the information doesn't mean the other side can't get hold of it. People who assume the other side is missing information don't plan for its introduction at trial and get caught short. Make sure you've got a plan in place to deal with information you didn't give to the other side.

Types of Evidence

Evidence is classified in several different ways, but the most basic way is by how it's presented in court. The four ways evidence is presented in court are through …

- Witness or expert testimony.
- Documents.
- Objects.
- Interactive presentations.

Regardless of how evidence is classified, the same basic rules apply. The information has to help prove or disprove a fact, and the fact has to be connected to something the parties are actually arguing about. The following sections look more closely at each type of evidence.

Testimony

Facts that are in a person's memory or mind are presented through testimony, or testimonial evidence, in which a person is sworn to speak the truth. Often, people believe that if the evidence is just someone's word or statement, it's not worth very much. In fact, this isn't true at all. Testimonial evidence is as valuable as any other kind of evidence. Its worth rests on how believable, or *credible*, the witness and the testimony he gives appear to be to the judge and jury. The finder of fact, whether judge or jury, has to decide how believable the testimonial evidence is.

DEFINITION

Credible evidence is trustworthy and believable by the finder of fact, which may be the judge or the jury.

Documentary

Evidence can be presented through documents that show something is true or not true. Today, the documents aren't limited to paper; documents can be electronic, computer generated, and live only on someone's hard drive, too. There is a rule called the "best evidence" rule, which states that the best, most acceptable evidence is the original document, if it's available. There are all kinds of exceptions made for unavailability, but the court prefers to work with a document that isn't likely to have been altered.

Documents can include things like contracts, diaries or journals, appointment books, employee files, computer documents, or anything else that holds written information.

Physical

Actual objects, like a defective artificial joint, can be introduced as evidence. Questions about the object, like how it became defective, may be answered by other forms of evidence, like testimony, but the object itself is important proof of what actually happened. As with all other forms of evidence, credibility is important, so proving that the item is original and hasn't been tampered with is critical to its acceptance as evidence.

Demonstrative

The last kind of evidence, demonstrative, shows how things worked, didn't work, or should have worked. Using the defective artificial joint as an example, a party might bring in a good artificial joint to show just how the defective joint differs. Demonstrative evidence is like physical evidence because it's often a physical object. The big difference is that demonstrative evidence isn't the actual thing that was involved in the incident that brought you to court. Demonstrative evidence can be a map of the intersection of the accident, with toy cars playing the parts of the cars involved in the accident. It can be a photograph of a building or area, used by the witnesses to point out where something happened. Demonstrative evidence can be anything that helps a witness tell his story more clearly and accurately.

Like other forms of evidence, the demonstrative evidence has to be relevant, helping decide a question the parties are arguing over, and it has to be accurate, so that it's credible and believable.

Preserving Evidence Before the Case Begins

Because the "best evidence" rule requires original documents and items whenever possible, you need to make sure the originals are kept in their unchanged, original state. Make a list of all the evidence you plan to bring to court, and make copies of the originals. As best as you can remember, give a history of where the document or item was before you pulled it out to use in your trial. List the people who handled it and might have had an opportunity to access it. Keep a copy of the list, and give another copy to your lawyer.

If you give the original documents or items to your attorney, ask how they will be preserved until trial and what will happen to them after trial. Most law offices have a log book that, together with the client file, lists where the evidence is and who has handled it. You need to do the same sort of thing. Your goal is to show that no one could have changed or altered the items you're bringing to court. You don't have to present this entire list to the court, but it's helpful to have when you're asked questions about the item while the court considers that item for entry as evidence.

How to Get Facts Considered by the Court

The court doesn't just let any piece of information float in for use as evidence. The party *proffering* the information or item as evidence must show that it meets the following two main requirements before it can be considered:

- The evidence is relevant to the proceedings.
- The evidence is reliable. This is done by "laying a foundation."

 DEFINITION

Proffering is producing and offering something to the court, like a piece of evidence or a motion.

Relevance

It's not enough that information can help to prove or disprove a fact. The fact that the information is intended to prove or disprove has to have a direct bearing on the argument the parties are having. This is known as *relevance*. The formal way of describing relevant evidence is to say, "the fact must relate to an issue in question." "Issues in question" are topics the parties are actually in conflict about.

DEFINITION

Relevance is the state of having a direct relationship to the matter at hand.

Evidence must somehow relate to a fact in question. Regardless of how true the evidence is, it won't be considered by the court if it isn't relevant. This is the first major hurdle you must jump with any facts you want to present to the court. Relevance seems fairly obvious; unless we're arguing about how old you are, evidence about your birth date is not relevant.

Despite the seemingly obvious nature of relevance, attorneys are always trying to slip in evidence that isn't entirely relevant in the hope that it will help sway the jury. If you can find some way to claim that the evidence will help the jury answer a question between the parties, the evidence can be considered. Otherwise, the evidence must stay out.

Foundation

Showing that evidence is believable or credible starts with showing that the person testifying has direct knowledge of what she's testifying to, or that an object is what you claim it is. This is called laying a foundation. Law school classes often use a "brick-by-brick" analogy to teach law students how to lay a foundation. Each brick is a fact about the evidence that shows why the witness is qualified to testify about the evidence. The bricks are things like the questions you hear on TV: "Where were you on the night of October 23rd?" "Could you see what was happening?"

These question bricks get at whether the witness was there and could experience what was going on. Every question helps strengthen the foundation of credibility that the court wants to see before allowing evidence to be considered. If the answer to "Could you see what was happening?" is no, why should the witness be allowed to testify? Look for other bricks; maybe the witness couldn't see, but could hear. During discovery, discussed in Chapter 7, the attorneys will develop information that can be used in court to lay the foundation before the witness testifies.

Foundations are laid for documentary evidence, too. The attorney usually needs a witness to testify that a document is something specific, and to testify as to its whereabouts before the trial, to show that it hasn't been altered. For demonstrative evidence, the foundation is laid by testimony agreeing that the item or photograph or map is an accurate depiction of the actual original evidence. To lay a foundation for physical evidence, again, you get testimony, this time showing that the evidence is the original, when it was retrieved and by whom, and where and how it was kept before the trial.

All evidence requires that a foundation be laid, and all foundations show that the evidence is what it claims to be, that it's possible for this to be true, and that the evidence isn't changed from its original state.

Problems with Evidence

Just because you have information that you believe will help the court come to a decision regarding the facts of your case doesn't mean you're home free and clear. Even the most truthful information can have a variety of problems that may keep it from being presented at trial. It's up to the judge—not the jury, and certainly not the attorneys or parties—to decide whether a piece of evidence can be presented at trial.

Irrelevance

The first problem goes back to the first hurdle all evidence must clear: relevance. You might believe very strongly that your information not only helps prove or disprove a fact, but that the fact is also critical to your case. The other side might disagree just as strongly. This is frequently the case when one side wants to introduce evidence of their good character to prove their good conduct—or to introduce evidence of the other side's bad reputation to prove bad conduct. Character is generally considered irrelevant, except under special circumstances, because even a liar can tell the truth every now and then. It's left up to the judge or jury to decide whom to believe based on what they're saying and doing now, not what they did in the past.

More Prejudicial Than Probative

If something is prejudicial, it makes people prejudge something or someone without hearing all the facts. Probative means to prove the truth. When a piece of evidence is called more prejudicial than probative, the evidence isn't going to help prove the truth as much as it will make the jury prejudge the witness or the evidence. Gory pictures of an accident scene are often relevant, and a good foundation can be laid for them, but they might be so vivid that the jury immediately decides the defendant was wrong to have caused these injuries. The photos don't show the defendant causing the injuries; they're just so intense that the jury skips the middle step of waiting for more evidence to decide the truth. For that reason, if evidence is more likely to make a jury prejudge rather than continue to look for the truth, then that evidence has to stay out of court.

Hearsay

Hearsay is literally someone testifying that they heard someone else say something, trying to get the judge or jury to believe that what was said is true. Hearsay isn't accepted as evidence because it's vital to be able to question the person who made the original statement in court under oath, to get more information on the topic, not to mention that the person who heard it said might not have heard it correctly, and certainly doesn't know whether or not the speaker was telling the truth. The only witness whose truthfulness the jury can evaluate is the one sitting in front of them, and the original speaker might not be as truthful as the witness.

JUST THE FACTS

The formal definition of hearsay is "an out-of-court statement offered to prove the truth of the matter asserted." How's that for saying "your word is no good for what someone else claimed is true"?

There are some exceptions to the block or bar on hearsay evidence, but they're very specific. Most of them allow the hearsay evidence in because there's something about that evidence that makes us believe the speaker was telling the truth. For example, if someone makes a statement that's against her own best interest, like admitting she caused an accident, it's not likely that she's lying. Why would she admit to causing an accident when she knows it would get her into trouble, unless it were true? The person who heard that statement is allowed to repeat it in court, even though it's hearsay. Another situation involves going to the doctor to get treatment. It's assumed you're going to tell the doctor the truth because you want to get better, so the doctor is allowed to testify as to what you said, again, even though it's technically hearsay.

Preserving an Issue for Appeal

The trial is the point at which the evidence gets evaluated and one version of the evidence is accepted as fact. The way the evidence is evaluated can be challenged later on appeal, as can the way the law was applied. But in order to make that challenge on appeal, you have to do what's called "preserving the issue for appeal." This is done by making statements during the trial, pointing out that there's a problem with the way the law is being applied or the way the evidence is being evaluated. This is to give the trial court a chance to make corrections on its own and possibly avoid the appeal altogether. There are three main components of preserving an issue for appeal: making an objection, making a timely objection, and ensuring that the timely objection is on the record.

Objections

One of the few accurate things in TV trials is the attorney jumping up and shouting "Objection!" An objection is a formal statement to the court that a mistake has been made. Ordinarily, it's not enough to just say "Objection!" The party making the objection has to give a reason for the objection, too. The better TV court shows have the attorneys saying things like "Objection! Calls for a conclusion," rather than just "Objection!"

IN THE KNOW

When addressing the court, you must stand as a show of respect. Most judges wouldn't tolerate a TV lawyer–style seated objection. In fact, attorneys who can't rise because of a broken leg or something usually ask the court's permission not to stand; otherwise, they get up, broken leg and all.

Once one side makes an objection, the other side gets an opportunity to respond. It's extremely helpful to have a thorough knowledge of the rules of evidence and civil procedure so that you can make the proper objections and counter the ones the other side makes. With good trial preparation and discovery, you can get a pretty good idea of the kinds of evidence the other side will try to introduce, and you can plan your objections before the trial even starts.

Once both sides have been heard, the judge will make a ruling on whether the evidence can be entered or the questioning continued. If the judge agrees with the party who made the objection, she *sustains* the objection. This means that the other side cannot continue with that line of questioning or introduce that piece of evidence. If the judge doesn't agree with the party who made the objection, she will *overrule* the objection, meaning the questioning can continue or the evidence can be entered.

DEFINITION

A judge's decision to **sustain** an objection means that he agrees with the objection. A judge's decision to **overrule** an objection means the judge disagrees.

Done properly, objections preserve the issue for appeal, and the appeals court can review whether the judge's decision was correct based on the law. There are two more elements that need to be taken into account to ensure the objection is done properly: timeliness and the record.

Timeliness

Objections must be made in a timely fashion or they're worthless. There's an entire body of law that discusses what exactly makes an objection "timely." It's enough to know that the objection should be made as soon as possible after the offending question is asked or the offending evidence is offered. If you wait too long to object, the judge will overrule the objection as not timely. Worse than that, the information you didn't want to have entered into evidence will have already been presented to the jury, or the question you didn't want even to have asked will have been answered. Once the information is out, it's hard for the jury to ignore, despite any orders the judge might make telling the jury not to consider that particular bit of evidence. By the way, it's enough for the judge to order the jury not to consider a piece of evidence; you're unlikely to win an appeal when improper evidence was presented and then withdrawn, as long as the jury was properly instructed to ignore the evidence.

The Record

The last element of making a proper objection is ensuring that the objection appears on the official record of the trial. Complaining about evidence during a break in the action of the trial does exactly nothing. Objecting to the judge in a *sidebar* does nothing, too. Neither of these are times when the court recorder or video recorder is taking down the proceedings. The objection needs to be done when the court reporter or video recorder is working, and should be done loudly and clearly enough that it can be easily heard and understood. Otherwise, the best and most accurate objection in the world isn't preserved on the record. The record is the transcript that's made of every word that was said at the trial, and it's the only thing the appeals courts look at when making a decision about whether the law was correctly applied and whether the evidence was properly admitted.

DEFINITION

A **sidebar** is any discussion held next to the judge's bench or desk, usually out of the hearing of the jury, and not recorded by the court reporter.

The Least You Need to Know

- Evidence is anything that proves or disproves a fact.
- Evidence must be relevant to be accepted by the court.
- Evidence has to have a foundation laid for it before it's accepted by the court.
- To be preserved for appeal, objections to the admission of evidence have to be timely and on the record.

The Trial Itself

In This Chapter

- How real life is different from TV
- How to behave and what to wear
- What not to bring with you
- The layout of the courtroom
- How the trial is run

If you've gotten to the point of actually having the trial, it means you haven't been able to come to an agreement with the other side. By now, you should have gotten everything you need in terms of information from the other side through the discovery process. If you have an attorney, he should be able to anticipate just about everything that may come up, based on what was found during discovery. There may still be surprises, but for the most part, the trial ought to feel somewhat anticlimactic. Nothing really new (except for surprises) will happen. Witnesses should more or less repeat what they said in depositions, and the evidence you've found should be all set for the judge and jury to consider. What makes the trial exciting is the same thing that makes any kind of sports match exciting: there's no way to absolutely predict the outcome.

What You See on TV Isn't Always What You Get

Most people who watch any TV in the United States are familiar with trials. You'll see them on situation comedies, in reality shows, and in dramas. Because trials are based on conflict, they make good watching. The trials on TV, though, are dramatized quite a bit to make good watching great. For example, the slow parts of a trial, like repeating the same question over and over for a witness who doesn't understand what he's been asked, get left out.

Then too, there are techniques used on TV and in movies that really don't happen in real life. On TV it's not unusual to see an attorney stay seated while snarling "Objection!" to show how comfortable (or disdainful) he is. On TV female lawyers wear micro-mini skirts, and lawyers jump up and down, scream at witnesses, yell back at the judge, make dramatic side speeches, and just generally make themselves the center of attention.

The reality is that lawyers can't do big TV or movie drama. The court rules in every court—federal or state—require that attorneys behave respectfully throughout the proceedings. Telling the judge "No, you're out of order!" will land the lawyer in jail for contempt of court, not get her an Oscar. Lawyers cannot yell at the other side's witness, no matter how much the witness lies or how badly the witness behaves.

It's up to the judge to reprimand the witness, and maybe even charge or cite her with contempt of court. As far as micro-mini skirts go, lawyers are subject to the same rules of dress that everyone appearing in court is, but more so. Many courts have specific rules requiring that attorneys dress in business clothing when appearing before the court. The only time that rule is relaxed is when an attorney has a temporary disability like a broken arm or leg, which has to be accommodated with nonbusiness clothing like sliced-up sweatpants. Even then, the attorney has to notify the court in advance and request permission to appear that way. If the attorney has a permanent disability, she is expected to get business-appropriate clothing that accommodates her disability. See "What to Wear to Court" on the next page for a discussion of appropriate clothing for participants like you.

How to Behave in Court

The most important thing about your behavior in court is that it must be respectful of the court at all times. No matter how angry you get, it's considered highly disrespectful to the court to yell, even if it's not at the judge. Swearing, even mildly, is also considered disrespectful. If you're quoting someone else, it's okay, but even then, you should make it clear that it's a quote.

Don't eat, drink, or chew gum in the courtroom, and absolutely do not smoke or chew tobacco in the courtroom. Don't talk or whisper while someone else's matter is being heard. As dull as it may get, you cannot read books or newspapers or magazines while court is in session. Don't bring signs or buttons or anything that advocates a position on a matter before the court. You need special permission to do that, and it's not likely to be given.

Do not text or play with any of your electronic gear, and make sure the ringer or anything that makes noise is completely off, not just on vibrate. If you're not sure how to do that, leave the phone in your car or at home. It's extremely disruptive when electronic gadgets go off in the courtroom, and judges have been known not only to confiscate the gadget when it goes off, but fine and send the offender to jail for contempt of court.

Stay calm as best you can. This is a stressful situation, but you are expected to act like a very polite adult throughout the trial. This means that, yes, you have to sit there and listen to people lie on the stand. You won't convince the judge or jury that a witness is lying by popping up and screaming "LIAR!" Let the evidence speak for itself, and when it's your turn to speak as a witness, concentrate on telling your story as clearly and convincingly as you can.

What to Wear to Court

The theme for everything you do in court is respect. Dress respectfully. Don't use what people wear to religious services or funerals as a guide, because people wear all kinds of casual clothes these days. If you have a suit, wear it. Gentlemen should try for, at the least, a long-sleeved collared shirt and tie. Don't wear anything ripped (no matter how artistically it's ripped) and certainly don't wear anything dirty. Stay away from jeans, sweats or exercise clothes, and camouflage gear. Don't wear anything on your head, unless it's for religious reasons. This means no caps, hats, hoods in the "up" position, or "do-rags" in the courtroom.

In particular, avoid anything that you might wear out to a bar or a club. For ladies, this means no short skirts or short shorts, no halter tops or tube tops, no sequins or other bling, and nothing tight or form-fitting. Some women believe that the sexier they dress, the more likely they are to win their case. This isn't true. First of all, not everyone involved in making the decision is going to let sex appeal override their decision-making abilities. Second, even people who might find you attractive may find sexy clothing offensive in a courtroom setting. This is particularly true of judges, male and female, who are more likely to see sexiness as out of place and disrespectful rather than as attractive. Dress conservatively and you and your case will get more respect.

For both men and women, no leather outfits, and no matter what the weather, keep your arms and belly covered. No one should be able to see what is conventionally referred to as underwear, meaning panties, boxer shorts, bras, bra straps, or the tops of your hose or socks. If you have tattoos, try to keep them covered. It's a generational thing, but judges tend to be of the generation that sees tattoos as evidence of a party personality. You're trying to look as serious as possible.

Try to wear shoes that cover your toes and heels. Avoid flip-flops, sandals, and super-high heels.

> **IN THE KNOW**
>
> If you have a disability and don't have appropriately respectful clothing to wear, contact the court ahead of time and talk to the judge's clerk. They will appreciate your concern and are likely to give you permission to wear whatever is comfortable and as respectful as possible.

What Not to Bring with You

Over the years, courts have found that some things people bring with them to court are disruptive to the judicial process and others are downright dangerous. Most courts have rules that state what is and isn't allowed in the courtroom. The general rule of thumb is that any kind of weapon is not allowed in a court building, even if you have a government permit for it. The only people who can go armed in court are police and sheriffs. This doesn't just go for guns; pepper spray and tasers are not allowed, either. Martial arts weapons are also forbidden.

The rule against weapons is carried to an extreme. Here's a list of common things considered weapons that cannot be brought to court:

- Knives of any size, including little Swiss army knives or penknives you might have on your keychain
- Leatherman-style multi-tools
- Screwdrivers of any size, including the little ones used for fixing eyeglasses
- Perfume; it can be used like pepper spray
- Anything in a glass container
- Nail polish

- Metal or glass nail files
- Nail clippers
- Scissors of any size
- Cuticle trimmers
- Single-bladed paper cutters
- Razors, even safety-bladed ones

You may be thinking MacGuyver-esque thoughts about how to use other ordinary items as weapons, and wondering why those items aren't forbidden, too. Don't share your curiosity or ideas with the people running security at the courthouse. They have absolutely no sense of humor about this sort of thing. Rather than appreciating your point, they're more likely to prevent you from entering the courthouse.

Other common items you might carry with you that are forbidden in courtrooms include:

- Cameras
- Camera phones
- Video cameras
- Any kind of recording device (the only record that can be made is the official court record)
- Video game players
- Personal DVD players

JUST THE FACTS

Cameras and camera phones are forbidden in part because there have been cases where people used them to take pictures of witnesses, which they sent to their associates outside the courtroom. The associates then found and beat or even killed the witness.

Who Sits Where

When you enter the courtroom, the judge's seat, called the bench, is usually at the opposite end of the room from the public entry door. There are entrances near the bench for the judge and her staff to use; those typically lead to the judge's office, or chambers. There's a public door to the judge's chambers, too, but that's usually outside the courtroom. To one side of the judge's bench is a place for a witness to sit while testifying. Some courtrooms have a spot on the other side for the judge's clerk, while others have the judge's clerk sit in front of the bench. The court reporter may be seated in front of the bench or may have a special spot next to the judge or next to the jury.

There is no rule about which side of the room the jury will be placed. The jury sits in an area called the jury box, and it's often near one of the private entry doors to the courtroom. It might be the same door that criminal defendants enter through. Whichever side of the room the jury box is on, it will be at a right angle to the judge's bench.

There are usually two tables in front of the judge's bench, placed parallel in front of the bench and at a right angle to the jury box. The plaintiff always gets the table closest to the jury box. The defendant gets the other table. Immediately behind the tables for the parties is usually a half-wall with a gate for people to go through to get to the tables and the judge's bench and clerk. General seating fills the rest of the courtroom.

When you arrive for your hearing or trial, your attorney will check in with the clerk at the front of the courtroom to let him know you're present and ready to go. You will take a seat in the general seating area of the courtroom and wait for your case to be called. Your attorney might have more than one hearing in the same courthouse at the same time; she'll let the clerk know which other courtroom she has to be in, and generally the clerk will accommodate her. In that case, the attorney might leave you in the courtroom and go to another courtroom to check in. When the judge is ready to hear your matter, the clerk, the bailiff, or even the judge will announce "Calling Case Number [Case number here], Jones versus Smith." If this happens while your attorney is out of the room, stand up and say "We're ready, your Honor, but my attorney is in Judge X's courtroom." If your attorney is there and everything is set, your attorney will say "Ready, your Honor," and you and your attorney will move toward the appropriate table.

Timing

As always, timing is everything in legal matters. Be on time for your hearing, and a little early if at all possible. If necessary, do a dry run a few days before to be sure you can find the courthouse and parking. Be ready for parking to be difficult, especially on a Motion Day. (See Chapter 10 for a discussion of Motion Days.) Parking is also likely to cost money in urban areas, so be sure to have cash—including quarters to feed the meters—available.

When Does Everything Begin?

Courts schedule everyone's hearing for the same time. You are not the only one who's been told to appear at 8 A.M.! Judges generally pick their own starting times and make their own schedules. It's common for judges to have general hearings in the morning starting between 8 and 10 A.M., and to reserve the afternoon for full trials. Ask your attorney or the judge's clerk what the judge assigned to your case prefers. You'll be told anyway on the notice that comes to you or your attorney from the court.

PITFALLS

It's impossible to overemphasize the importance of opening all the mail that comes from your attorney's office or from the courts. Mark every date and time down on a calendar, and check the calendar daily. Missing or being late for a court date is not an easily excusable thing.

The judge won't be in the courtroom for the check-in and settling-in part of the morning. The judge will enter once all of that is taken care of. She'll be announced by the bailiff or the clerk, who will tell everyone to stand up ("All rise!") and state the name of the judge. The bailiff or clerk will wait until the judge is all settled, and then will tell everyone they can sit down—"You may be seated."

How Long Will This Take?

Because everyone's hearing is scheduled for the same time, you are not likely to be heard immediately. One of the reasons it's a good idea to arrive early is that courts often take cases in the order in which the attorneys signed in. If your case is set for 8:30 A.M., you might well be sitting in the courtroom until 11 A.M., or even have to come back after lunch if the court is particularly busy.

If you're just in court for a hearing, the hearing itself might take anywhere from five minutes to an hour or more. It depends on the complexity of the issue and how much argument both sides can come up with.

It's really difficult to predict how long a trial will take. Some are over with in just a few hours. Others can take days, weeks, or even months. Your attorney should be able to give you a vague estimate of how long the trial will take, but he can't make any guarantees. One reason is that there will be interruptions to your trial when emergencies come up that the court must deal with, like people needing protective orders. These interruptions will slow your trial, and there's nothing you can do to prevent them. Remember the importance of remaining calm and polite under all circumstances in court, no matter how frustrating the situation. Delays and interruptions happen during almost every trial.

Breaks in the Action

As discussed previously, there will be breaks in the action of your trial because other people have problems that need to be dealt with immediately. Other breaks will be due to regularly scheduled times to hear motions and other requests. You and your attorney can request breaks when you need to take a rest or when you need time to react to a surprise that came up in court. The other side can make the same kinds of requests, and the judge can make a decision on her own to take a break. These breaks are called recesses. Typically, your case will not be heard past 4:30 or 5:00 P.M., because the courthouse closes around then. If your trial isn't over when the courthouse is ready to close, the court will decide that it's in recess until a specific date and time. For example, the judge may say, "This court is in recess until 1:30 P.M. tomorrow, Wednesday the 28th." You are expected to show up again tomorrow at the same courtroom at 1:30 P.M., but of course, you'll show up a little bit earlier.

Opening Statements

Just like on TV, your trial begins with opening statements. This is the part of the trial when the judge and jury are introduced to the problem that brought you to court, and how your side believes it should be solved. It's sort of like story time, because it should make even the most complicated case sound like a straightforward story, with a beginning, a middle, and an end. Before the trial goes any further, both sides give their opening statements. The plaintiff goes first; if there's more than one plaintiff, they go in the order that they're listed in the pleadings. If there's more than one defendant, they also go in the order that they're listed in the pleadings.

There are two major differences between reality and what you see on TV: during the opening, your lawyer can't create a dramatic, heart-thumping, foot-stomping speech, and your attorney can't give testimony.

Your Attorney Can't Do Big Drama

In movies and on TV, the opening statement is often a really exciting event. The attorney doesn't just tell a story; he acts it out, with gusto. The attorney calls the other side names, exaggerates the problem, and goes all out to show how horrible the other side is and how innocent and pure his client is. Unfortunately for reality, lawyers don't get to do that in real life. Name-calling is not allowed, and exaggerating the problem leads to worse problems later on when it comes time to support the story told in the opening with facts and evidence. TV attorneys violate the concept of respect toward the court and even toward the other side all the time; in real courtrooms, judges don't stand for such behavior.

Telling the Story Without Testifying

The attorney isn't a witness to anything that happened, so he's only qualified to give a summary of the story. Attorneys get around this by saying things like, "You'll hear this witness testify that she saw ...." If the attorney doesn't step carefully, he can be stopped by the judge and possibly punished, formally known as sanctioned. That can mean a charge of contempt of court, complete with a fine or jail time if the testifying is really obvious.

Plaintiff's Case

Once both sides have given their opening statements, the plaintiff can start bringing forward witnesses, examining them, and trying to get pieces of evidence entered so the judge and jury can consider them. This is called starting the plaintiff's case, or stating the case. The attorney should have a plan for which witnesses get called in what order, and what questions to ask. The attorney also should know what sorts of physical, documentary, and demonstrative evidence she plans on using, and have them ready for use without too much fumbling.

Calling Witnesses

The plaintiff begins by "calling" the first witness. Calling a witness means that the witness's name is called out by the attorney or the bailiff so that the witness comes to the front of the courtroom. Witnesses are usually kept out of the courtroom, or *sequestered*, so that they don't hear other witnesses' testimony and consciously or unconsciously change their own testimony because of it. Witnesses may be sequestered by waiting in the hallway, or they may be asked to wait in a room in or near the judge's chambers.

When the witness comes forward, he is usually not allowed to sit in the witness box or witness stand immediately. Instead, he stands in front of the spot where he'll be testifying, and gets "sworn in." Swearing in is a process where the witness swears or affirms that he will tell the truth. It's designed to remind the witness of the importance of telling the truth on the stand. It doesn't prevent lying on the stand, but it's impressive how difficult it is for most people to lie on the stand once they've promised to tell the truth. After the witness has made his oath or affirmation, the judge or bailiff tells him he may be seated. For anyone in a courtroom while the judge is there, even a witness, it's a good idea not to sit until you're told to do so.

Direct and Cross-Examination

After the witness has been sworn in, the party that called the witness (in this case, the plaintiff) will start questioning her. This is called direct examination or direct, because the questions are asked directly of the witness. Direct examination is treated as a method of introducing evidence, so it starts with laying a foundation, as discussed in Chapter 11. The foundation for a witness includes asking the witness her name, and sometimes age and address, along with questions about how the witness knows about the events at issue.

Once the foundation is laid and the attorney has established that the witness has reason to know about the events she's going to testify to, the attorney will start asking questions. The questions asked on direct examination cannot suggest the answer; they're supposed to get the witness to tell the story in her own words. Questions that suggest the answer are called leading questions. They tend to have phrases like, "Isn't it true that …" and often end with "didn't you?"

When the plaintiff's attorney is finished with his questions, it's the defendant's attorney's turn. His questions to the witness are called cross-examination, or just cross. As far as the defense is concerned, witnesses brought forward by the plaintiff are enemies of the defendant, and are called hostile witnesses. Hostile witnesses can be asked leading questions, because it's assumed that whatever answer is suggested by the question, the witness isn't going to take it as a hint about where the right answer is.

The defendant's attorney is limited to asking questions about the topics that were covered on direct. A careful plaintiff's attorney won't ask questions that could open a can of worms on cross.

PITFALLS

If you're not completely honest with your attorney in pretrial preparations, she won't know where the wormy cans are, and can't avoid questions that might open the cans up on cross.

When cross-examination is over, the plaintiff's attorney can question the witness one last time on redirect examination. This is an opportunity to literally redirect attention away from points the plaintiff didn't want emphasized, and to clarify points that got muddied up on cross.

The defense has one more opportunity for recross, and then that's it. The next witness is called by the plaintiff. When it's the defendant's turn to present his case, the same process applies, except that the defendant does direct examination and the plaintiff does cross-examination.

Entry of Evidence

To enter evidence like documents, physical objects, or demonstrative evidence, the plaintiff needs a witness to help him lay a foundation for the evidence. First, the attorney asks permission to approach the bench to show the judge the proposed evidence. When the judge has seen it, the attorney then shows it to the other side, giving them a chance to object to its entry. If there is no objection, the attorney then asks the witness if she recognizes the object or the document, or if the map or photo or other demonstrative evidence is a fair representation of the original.

If the witness agrees that the object is what the attorney claims it is, the attorney asks that the item be officially recognized by being "entered into evidence." The attorney will give the item to the court reporter for labeling and give the item a name like "Plaintiff's Exhibit Number 1" or "Plaintiff's Exhibit A." The numbering or lettering is usually up to the attorney, but some courts have one side use letters and the other side use numbers to avoid confusion—are we talking about Plaintiff's Exhibit A or Defendant's Exhibit A?

Once the evidence has had a proper foundation laid and has been properly labeled and entered by the court reporter, the attorney can ask the witness questions about the evidence to bring out the facts that the attorney believes will most help his case.

Motions During Trial

Several types of motions, or formal requests to the court, are made during trials. Mostly they tend to have to do with evidence and trying to end the trial early. When motions are successful, the judge will say the motion is sustained. When the motion fails, the judge will announce that the motion is overruled. Just as with pretrial motions, it's important to make these kinds of motions so that there is a record of the legal issue being brought forward. As you'll recall from Chapter 11, that's called preserving the issue for appeal. If the issue isn't preserved for appeal, there isn't a decision for the appeals court to review. With nothing to review, there's no decision to change, and the lower court's rulings remain.

Motion Limiting Evidence

A motion limiting the evidence that can be brought before the court is a motion in limine and is the same motion that is brought before the trial (see Chapter 11). The difference here is that when it's done during trial, it's a more spur-of-the-moment kind of thing. It usually happens when evidence that wasn't available during discovery is presented at trial, or when the pretrial motion in limine failed. It never hurts to try again!

Motion to End Jury Trial Before Evidence Is Heard

In a jury trial, after the opening statements, but before the plaintiff begins her case, most attorneys will make a motion to end the trial. The idea behind this motion is that there is no real conflict about the facts, and that there is only one correct way to interpret the law. As a result, there's nothing for the jury to consider, and only one way that the case can be resolved—the way the party making the motion (the moving party) wants it to be resolved. There are three names for this kind of request: a motion for summary judgment, a motion for summary disposition, or a motion for a directed verdict.

A motion for summary judgment or summary disposition is usually only done at the beginning of the trial, while a motion for a directed verdict can be made both at the beginning of the trial and at the end of the presentation of the evidence. A motion for directed verdict basically asks the court to resolve the case by telling, or directing, the jury to agree that the facts are as stated by the moving party. It also asks the court to enter a judgment in favor of the moving party. When successful, this ends the trial completely.

Motion to Remove Evidence

When evidence has already been admitted, whether or not an objection was made or raised beforehand, a party can ask that the evidence be removed from consideration by the judge or jury. This kind of motion is called a motion to strike. If the judge grants or sustains the motion, the evidence in question must be ignored by the judge and jury.

Motion to End Trial Because There Is No Dispute

Related to the motion for directed verdict is a motion that claims the plaintiff didn't actually make a claim that the law can resolve, or that the defendant didn't make a valid defense. This is called a motion for summary disposition or summary judgment, depending on the court. If the plaintiff doesn't have a claim that the law can resolve, there's no dispute; the defendant wins. If the defendant can't make a valid defense, then everything the plaintiff claims must be true, and the plaintiff wins.

Other reasons for a motion for summary disposition or summary judgment to be granted tend to be what people think of as technicalities, like a lack of jurisdiction (see Chapter 7), improper service or delivery of notice (see Chapter 8), or some other legal reason that prevents the claim from being heard.

Defendant's Case

When the plaintiff has finished calling its witnesses and introducing its evidence, it's the defendant's turn. The defendant puts on his case exactly the same way the plaintiff did. The defendant calls witnesses and does direct examination; the plaintiff cross-examines those witnesses, and the defendant can do a redirect examination if he chooses. When he's done bringing forth his witnesses and evidence, he, like the plaintiff, is finished and announces that he "rests his case."

Witnesses: Expert and "Lay"

We've talked about witnesses and the evidence they present to the court, but we haven't talked about what qualifies someone to be a witness. To be a witness in a trial, a person must qualify as either an expert witness or a lay witness.

The most common kind of witness is a lay or eye witness. This is a witness who has direct experience of what she's going to testify about. She was there; she heard, saw, touched, smelled, or felt something that will help the judge and jury make a decision about the facts in question. Some legal experts think the term "eye witness" should be replaced by the term "sense witness," because the witness may not have actually seen anything. The fact that she was there and experienced something relevant is what qualifies her as a witness.

Expert witnesses were not present at the actual event that's in question, so they can't qualify as an ordinary lay or eye witness. But they do have information that will help the judge and jury make a decision about the facts in question, so we want to get them in to testify. The kind of information an expert witness has must be something that helps the judge and jury understand the evidence presented by lay or eye witnesses. Expert witnesses qualify by showing why they have more information on a particular topic than the average person, and that their information is from a respected source. Experts can qualify by education or training, or by years of experience in a particular field. Ordinarily, expert witnesses are used to help the judge and jury understand medical testimony or technological testimony, or to show how something works or should have worked.

Closing Statements

When both the plaintiff and the defendant have rested their cases, they summarize their side of the story by giving closing statements. These parallel the opening statements, but because the evidence has already been given, it's an opportunity to emphasize the positive and explain away the negative. It's the last opportunity each side has to influence the judge or jury to see the evidence their way. As usual, the plaintiff goes first. Once both sides have given their closing statements, the active part of the trial is over, and the final decision-making process begins.

The Least You Need to Know

- Whatever you do, be respectful of the court and the system.
- If you're not sure whether something is appropriate to wear in court, ask your attorney or call the court.
- Don't bring weapons or anything that might be used as a weapon.
- The trial runs like you see on TV, but with less drama.

Coming to a Decision

In This Chapter

- Who decides the law for the case
- Who decides the facts for the case
- How the law is applied to the facts
- Why the law is always applied the same way to the same kinds of facts

At the end of every trial, a decision is made either for the plaintiff or for the defendant. Sometimes the process of coming to that decision seems mysterious, almost as if it took place inside a black box that no one can see into. While it's true that, in a sense, jury decisions happen inside the black box of the jury room, and the judge's decisions happen inside the black box of the judge's brain, there is a logic and procedure that must be followed. Because of that, you can actually get a very good idea of how decisions are made in legal cases.

How Are the Facts Decided?

Each trial has a "finder of fact." The finder of fact has the following responsibilities:

- Decides what facts are true or false.
- Decides whom to believe or whom not to believe.
- Applies the law to the facts.

In a nonjury trial, the finder of fact is the judge. In a jury trial, the finder of fact is the jury.

Nonjury Trial

In a *bench trial*, there is no jury. In addition to deciding which laws should apply and how, the judge in a nonjury trial has the additional task of considering the evidence presented and deciding—or making a "finding" of—what the facts are based on the evidence presented. (Sometimes a judge will make a decision about something in the case, even when there is a jury present. That doesn't change the case from a jury to a nonjury trial; that is the judge handling a legal or procedural issue, and not one of fact-finding.)

> **DEFINITION**
>
> A **bench trial** is a trial held without a jury, where a judge decides both what facts are true and how the law applies to those facts.

Jury Trial

In a jury trial, the jury's role is to be the "finder of fact," and then apply the law that the judge gives them to those facts. The jury doesn't get to decide which law should apply; that's always the judge's job. The jury is supposed to consider the evidence that's been presented throughout the trial, and, using only the evidence presented, make a decision about what evidence to believe and what not to believe. Once the jury has made that decision, they're said to have made a finding of fact.

Criteria or Standard of Proof

You may have heard two legal expressions involving proof: the term "burden of proof" refers to *who* has to prove something to the fact finder; the term "standard of proof" refers to *how much* they have to prove something.

The standards of proof used to make a finding of fact constitute the measuring stick that has to be used by the finder of fact in evaluating the evidence. The standard of proof that applies in a case depends on what the case is about. Surprisingly, only a few standards of proof are typically used, and the one thing they all have in common is a fuzzy, unclear definition. Because of their lack of clarity, people frequently appeal cases on the grounds that the wrong standard was used, or that the standard wasn't properly followed, because the explanation given to the jury for the standard wasn't quite right.

The most famous standard of proof is reserved for criminal cases. The evidence has to be believed "beyond a reasonable doubt." It's the highest standard or level of belief in the justice system, and the toughest standard to meet. This high standard is used because people's physical liberty is at stake. It means that there's no reasonable, believable story that shows the defendant is not guilty. Some people try to explain this standard as being "99 percent sure" about the facts in the case, but the law doesn't say that it has to be a specific percentage.

At the other end of the scale is the standard used in most civil cases—"preponderance of the evidence." This means the finder of fact has to believe that one side's evidence is more likely than not to be true. Some people try to explain it as the evidence must be 51 percent likely to be true, but there's no actual percentage of belief required by law.

In the middle is another standard of proof, called "clear and convincing" evidence. Some civil cases involving important rights need a higher standard than the preponderance of the evidence. Sometimes, the allegations made in a case border on criminal cases. These kinds of cases tend to be things like termination of parental rights, fraud, or civil rights cases. Although the rights are central to people's lives, the end result of their loss won't be jail time, so the standard of beyond a reasonable doubt can't be used. This is the fuzziest and least clear of the standards. The best anyone's been able to do is say that it's less than beyond a reasonable doubt, but more than the preponderance of the evidence. If you were playing the "percentage" game, you might say that the fact-finder has to be 75 percent sure of the facts, but again, the law doesn't say that it has to be a specific percentage.

Credibility

All of these standards of proof deal with how believable the evidence is to the finder of fact. That believability is known as "credibility." Believable evidence is credible evidence.

Credibility has two parts. The first part is whether or not the witness or the evidence should even be allowed at the trial. It's a decision about whether the witness or evidence meets the bare minimum of what can be considered believable or credible. Think of it like this: if the issue is whether or not a doctor committed malpractice, who has more knowledge and authority to testify about what should have happened—a real doctor, or some guy who saw a TV show about a doctor? Why waste the finder of fact's time with Mr. TV Guide? Because he has no basic credibility, he's unlikely to be believed anyway. More than that, he shouldn't be believed. That's why the question of whether a witness or evidence should be allowed in is one part of credibility.

The judge makes this decision of basic credibility before the trial reaches the presentation of testimony and evidence to the jury. The judge merely decides whether the person or item has characteristics that make it possible that they will help the finder of fact determine the truth. It doesn't mean that the person or item has to be believed by the finder of fact.

The second part of credibility is the most important: Is the evidence believable enough to meet the standard of proof required by the kind of case in question? When the evidence is presented, when the witness testifies, how believable do they seem? It's up to the finder of fact to decide whether or not to believe the evidence presented, by deciding how credible the evidence is.

For example, suppose that each side to a lawsuit has a doctor as an expert witness. If the plaintiff's doctor has performed a surgery 100 times, but the defense doctor has only done it once or twice, the plaintiff's doctor may be more credible. However, if the plaintiff's doctor has been an expert witness in over 100 cases, all for plaintiffs, and makes a substantial amount of money as an expert witness, he may lose some credibility.

Ultimately, believability is in the eye of the beholder. As mentioned elsewhere, because only the people at the trial actually see the witness and his behavior on the stand, they're the only ones who can legitimately decide whether or not to believe him.

Appeals judges won't second-guess the finder of fact on issues of fact because they weren't there to see what happened. Your parents may have told you to "look someone in the eye" when you talk to him. Did the witness do that? Did the witness seem convincing in her testimony? Or did the witness mutter, look down, or act as if she was uncomfortable being questioned about her story? These are all things that come into play when dealing with credibility.

The transcript that's made during the trial is helpful for getting information about decisions that were made and who said what, but it's not always helpful in evaluating witnesses' credibility. Think about reading the words, "No, I did not." You may have emphasized the word "no" when you read it. The meaning changes if you emphasize the word "I" instead. "No, *I* did not" implies that someone other than "I" did it. Knowing that the tone of voice, inflections, and facial expressions add so much to the judgment people make about whether to believe a witness's statement or not, it's hard to require that someone who wasn't there make a judgment as to the believability of a witness.

If you will be testifying at trial, or if you will be sitting at the table with your lawyer throughout the trial, consider how you can make yourself and your case seem more credible to the other people there. One way is to dress respectfully and professionally when you are in court. Another is to know your side of the story so well that you can answer any question you're asked clearly and confidently. Sit up straight and make eye contact with the judge and the jury as you speak.

PITFALLS

Try not to roll your eyes or laugh when the other side puts on their evidence; it may be tempting, but it's very disrespectful to the court. Not only that, but it may make you look immature and therefore less believable!

How Is the Law Decided?

The American legal system relies on two kinds of laws to come to a decision in trials. The first kind of law is what people generally think of when they think of the law: statutes passed by Congress or some governmental body. The second kind of law interprets the statutes, and is called "case law" or "common law." It's law that's made by judges as they decide individual cases that come before the courts for solutions. The difference between the law created by the legislature and the law created by the courts is that the legislature creates general rules, and the courts create specific interpretations and applications of the legislature's rules based on the facts of cases that come before the courts.

JUST THE FACTS

The American legal system is based on the British legal system, which gave us case law working with statutory law. This is true for 49 states and the federal system. The odd-duck state is Louisiana. Because of their French heritage, they follow a statutes-only system for state cases, but still follow the American system at the federal level.

You've probably heard people say that it's wrong for judges to make laws and it's the job of the legislature alone to make laws. It's true that only the legislature has the power to create statutes under the Constitution. But the Constitution also gives the courts power to interpret the statutes passed by the legislature, and the power to decide whether those statutes fit the requirements of the Constitution. In order for the court's decisions about statutes to have any effect, they have to have the same force of law that the statutes do. That's why judges can and do create law—case law—that is every bit as important and binding as statutes and has to be followed the same way statutes have to be followed. The difference between the power to create statutory law and the power to create case law is that case law is limited to the topics that come before the court. Statutory law can be created on any topic the legislature wants to address.

Same Law, Same Facts, Same Outcome

So how is case law applied to your case? The judge will tell the jury which case law to apply; the jury doesn't get to choose which case law to use. Case law is followed by comparing your case to a previous case. If your set of facts is similar to the facts of a previous case, and the statute you need to apply is the same or very close, you have to follow the logic of the previous case. Following the same logic usually means your case will have the same result as the previous case. This is called "following precedent," and the case you're following is itself called "precedent."

For example, suppose the issue is whether or not a consumer can return a product to the manufacturer for a refund, because the manufacturer breached its warranty. If you could say "in the case of *Smith v. Jones*, the warranty was the same, the product was the same, the acts that resulted in a breach of warranty were the same, and the court in *Smith v. Jones* said that the product could be returned to the manufacturer," you would be "citing precedent" to the court. The court could then say, "I will follow the case of *Smith v. Jones*, and because the facts are so similar between the two cases, I believe that a refund is warranted."

Following precedent ensures one element of fairness, by ensuring that everyone is treated the same way by the courts. As just described, precedent requires that people who are using the same statute and have similar facts will end up with the same outcome as anyone else in that situation. By limiting the courts to interpreting statutes and precedent, it's much more difficult for the courts to overstep their power and create law on new topics.

Because the courts use precedent to solve cases, you would think it would be easy to predict the outcome of any given case. In reality, it's very difficult to predict outcomes. This is because it's almost impossible to have a case that has the exact same facts with the exact same questions of law as a previous case. The best you'll find is a set of facts that are similar to precedent, or a question about a statute that's similar to precedent. The art of a skilled lawyer lies in her ability to take a client's facts and use them to persuade the court that they're so similar to precedent that the client has to win. No matter how skilled the lawyer is, she still has to deal with the reality that a client's case is always different from precedents. Those differences are why lawyers can't really predict or guarantee an outcome in any case.

What Happens When There's No Precedent to Follow?

It's even harder to predict or guarantee an outcome in a case in which there's no precedent to follow. This happens when there are new statutes, under which no one has had a conflict yet. It also happens when there is a situation that's very different from what has come before, like when new technology comes along and changes a situation that everyone thought was unchangeable. These kinds of cases are called "cases of first impression," because they're the first of their kind, and they'll make an impression on the rest of the cases that follow them.

Although in a case of first impression there aren't any cases of precedent to look at, the court isn't free to make whatever decision it wants. The court first has to look at any relevant statutes to see if and how they apply. The court will also look at the discussions the legislature had about the statute, to see what the reasoning was for passing the statute. This is called looking at "legislative intent." The court has to do its best to make sure that the legislative intent is followed in interpreting the statute and applying it to the facts of the case.

The next thing the court looks at for cases of first impression is other, similar cases. Because it's a case of first impression, the cases of precedent out there will have facts that are too different from the current case's facts, or follow a different statute, to make those cases genuine precedent. However, there will be cases that are comparable in some ways to the one the court is trying to decide. The facts might be related but not the same, or the statute might have some parallel to the one in question in the current case. The court can use those close but nonprecedent cases as an example for the logic that it can use in deciding the current case.

Sometimes courts in one state have never handled the issue before, but courts in another state have. In those cases, courts may look at how those other jurisdictions have handled the question. The federal courts, for example, aren't required to follow a state court's precedent, but the federal court can examine the logic the state court used and decide it works well with federal law, too. It also works from state to state. For example, Hawaii doesn't have to follow the case law of the New York state courts, but Hawaii's courts can use the New York court precedent as a persuasive example that they can choose to follow.

A perfect example is the Internet. This is a new technology that has its own set of problems that have never been dealt with before. For example, we know that it's illegal to record a phone conversation where you are not a participant; however, is it illegal to receive or access someone else's e-mails? That would be a case of first impression in many states, but there may be a state that's already dealt with that question.

How Is the Law Applied?

Once the court has decided which statutes and precedents apply to the case in front of it, and the finder of fact has decided what the facts are, the statutes and precedents have to be applied to the facts. This is done step by step, and is actually pretty straightforward.

Every statute and every rule of law in a case can be broken down into its most basic parts or steps, which are called "elements." For example, if someone were being sued for negligently causing a car accident, the plaintiff would have to prove each of the following elements of the rule of law for negligence:

- Duty

- Breach (or violation of the duty)

- Causation

- Injury

The fact-finder applies the rule to the facts of the situation by incorporating the elements with the facts, like this:

- The defendant had a "duty" to drive his car carefully.

- The defendant "breached his duty" because he did not drive his car carefully.

- The defendant's careless driving was the "cause" of his car hitting the plaintiff's car.

- When the defendant carelessly hit the plaintiff's car, he caused "injury" or damage.

At each element, the facts must fit the statement of the element. If one element doesn't fit the facts, the plaintiff loses. For example, the fact-finder may find that the defendant did have a duty to drive his car carefully, so the first element is "satisfied" or "met." The fact-finder then turns to the second element, whether the defendant breached or violated the duty to drive carefully. If the finder of fact decided that the driver was careless, then the court must find that the second element is satisfied. But if the finder of fact decides that the defendant did, in fact, drive carefully, the court must find that the second element is not satisfied, and the plaintiff loses.

The same thing happens with the third element. Was the defendant's careless driving the cause of his car hitting the plaintiff's car? If it was, then the third element is satisfied. If it wasn't, then the third element isn't met, and the plaintiff loses. At each point, if even one of the elements isn't met or satisfied, the plaintiff loses his case.

The last element, injury, has to mesh with the facts, too. If the defendant …

- Had a duty to drive carefully;

- Did not drive carefully;

- And caused his car to hit the plaintiff's car;

- BUT didn't cause any damage or injury

… then the plaintiff loses his case. The two-part decision about whether injury was caused, and whether the defendant's actions were the cause of the injury, is a question of fact that's up to the finder of fact. In cases where the jury is the finder of fact, the judge's only legal role is to decide that the rule for negligence is the one to apply to the facts.

There are several reasons that this part of the decision-making process seems so much like a black box. First, most people don't know all the elements of the rule of law going in. That's why they hire a lawyer—to find out what law is likely to apply to a particular problem. Second, if the law in question is complex, and especially if the facts are complicated, too, keeping all the elements straight and figuring out how they'll apply is very difficult, even for experts. Most of all, no one knows what the finder of fact has decided is true about the evidence until after the decision is given by the court. Going in, you don't know the facts as decided by the finder of fact. You only know that your side of the facts is the one that should be believed. Again, and unfortunately, nothing can guarantee that your side will be believed.

Not knowing what the facts "really" are according to the finder of fact makes it seem that the process of applying the law is very mysterious. However, if you come at it backward, once the decision is made, and accept (even if only for the sake of argument) that the findings of fact are the basis for the decision, it's usually very simple to see how the law was applied.

Take each fact as found by the finder of fact, and match it to the element of the rule of law that it supports. If you can't make a good match, that means the law was improperly applied, and you've got a good issue on which to appeal the case. See Chapter 14 for more on appeals.

Consistency from Case to Case

One of the most important factors in coming to a decision in any case is making sure the decision is consistent with precedent. Judges can move away from precedent legitimately if they can show that the facts in the case before the court are too different from the case claimed as precedent for the same rule to apply in the same way. However, if the facts aren't that different, or if it's not logical to use a particular precedent in deciding the case, as stated previously, there's a good issue for appeal.

Trial judges are notorious for disliking appeals, and in particular for disliking being told by the appeals court that they were wrong. This gives them real motivation to apply the law correctly to the facts the first time around, so that they aren't embarrassed in front of the entire legal community by a successful appeal. Consistency from case to case in applying the rule of law from precedents and statutes is critical to a trial judge's success rate. Every trial judge has his decisions changed or overturned now and then; it's only when a large percentage of the judge's cases are overturned that the judge starts to look incompetent.

Making the Final Decision

There is no way to predict how long it will take for the final decision to be made, or "come down." Part of the prediction depends on how complicated the case is. The more complicated the case is, the more likely it is to take a long time to decide. Essentially, the more argument there is about what version of facts should be believed, the longer it will take the finder of fact to come to a decision.

Jury Instructions and Verdict Form

If the decision is to be made by the jury, the judge will inform the jurors of the elements of the rules that apply in the case and what facts have to be true to meet the elements. These are called "jury instructions."

With those instructions is something called a "verdict form." This is an actual document upon which the jury's decision is written.

Jury instructions also usually include telling the jurors what the final result will be if each element is or isn't met. In most courts, both the plaintiff and defendant have the opportunity to submit suggested jury instructions and verdict forms to the judge. The judge can use the instructions provided by one side or the other, a combination of both sides' instructions, or neither side's instructions. There are standardized jury instructions for most common kinds of cases, and judges frequently like to use them as the basis for the instructions they give to the jury.

How Is the Final Decision Actually Made?

Whether the final decision is made by a judge or a jury, the same process is used. The judge calls a "recess," where everyone can leave the courtroom temporarily. The judge leaves to go to his office or "chambers," and the jury leaves to go to the jury room. Once there, the first step is for the finder of fact to decide what the facts are. This is often what takes juries the longest time, particularly if there are many versions of the facts to consider. Next, if there's a jury, the jurors consult the jury instructions to make sure they're properly applying each element of the rule of law to the facts. If there's no jury, the judge just applies each element of the rule of law to the facts according to the statute or case that's being followed.

If a decision cannot be made quickly, the jurors may be held, or "sequestered," in a hotel overnight to be sure that they're not influenced by any outside information. In other cases, jurors are permitted to return home after each day's deliberations.

Once the facts have been matched up with the rules, the judge or jury looks to see whether there are any elements of the rules that haven't been met. If there are elements that haven't been met, then the plaintiff loses. If all the elements have been met, the plaintiff wins. The jury fills out a jury report stating what their decision was and why, and then calls the bailiff to tell the judge that a decision has been reached. In a nonjury bench trial, the judge may write a sort of essay called an "opinion," stating who won or lost and why.

The Announcement of the Decision

Once the decision has been reached by the judge or the jury, the plaintiff and defendant are notified that it's time to return to the courtroom to hear the decision, or verdict. The parties enter the room first and wait for the judge (and jury, if there is one). The announcement of the verdict is very much like what you've probably seen on TV.

IN THE KNOW

It's a good idea to take notes as the decision is announced. That way you can make sure that any subsequent paperwork is in line with what the court ordered.

In a jury case, the judge asks the jury if it has reached a verdict. If it has, the head juror—called the "foreman," "forewoman," or "foreperson"—usually responds by saying, "We have, your honor." The less usual response is "We were unable to reach a decision." If the jury wasn't able to reach a decision, the judge will ask the foreperson if the group has tried everything it can to come to a decision. The judge may even ask each juror if he or she believes the group can come to a decision. If the jury cannot, they are dismissed and a "mistrial" is declared. This means the parties can try to run through the lawsuit again.

If the more usual response is made, and the jury has come to a decision, the foreperson hands the jury form to the bailiff, who then hands it to the judge. The judge reads it, usually for the first time, and then hands it back to the bailiff who gives it back to the foreperson. The judge then asks the foreperson what the verdict is. There are at least two possible responses.

The response can be stated as "for one side and against the other," which is common, mostly because that way it's clear who won and who lost. However, because there's usually more than one question—called a count—to be answered, the more usual response is to state the number of the count and describe it, and then say which side won and which side lost. This ends up sounding something like, "For count one, negligence in the operation of a motor vehicle, for the plaintiff and against the defendant."

Once the foreperson has read the findings out loud, the jury's job is basically done. Before the jury is dismissed, though, the plaintiff and defendant can request that each individual juror be asked how he or she voted. This is called "polling the jury." Because civil jury verdicts don't have to be unanimous, the parties want to see how close they came to winning or losing. Most of all, though, it's done so that the parties can be sure the reported verdict is the true verdict.

The Least You Need to Know

- The finder of fact can be the judge or the jury.
- The judge alone decides what law should apply to the case.
- Each individual element of the law must match with an element of the facts in order for the law to be said to apply.
- Fairness requires that the same logic and law be used in cases that have similar facts.

After the Trial

In This Chapter

- How you can try to change the outcome of your case
- What to do with all that paper
- Taxes and your judgment
- Collecting on your judgment

After the verdict is delivered, the trial is officially through. However, the case is far from over. There are requests to be made of the court for help in clarifying things, paperwork to fill out and get to the right people, tax questions to answer, and of course, paying your legal fees.

What Does a Verdict Mean?

A verdict is the decision, which may be read out loud by the judge or by the foreperson of the jury. Sometimes, if the judge is trying the case (a bench trial), the judge may send you her decision in the mail.

The most important thing to know about a verdict is that it's the decision of the court, but there's more that needs to be done to make it effective.

There's an old saying, "The court speaks through its orders." What the court says is one thing; what the court actually puts down in writing in an order is quite another. Basically, if the court says something, and it's not in an order, no one can act on it. Therefore, once the verdict is rendered, an order of judgment must be prepared in conformity with that verdict.

Depending on the case, if the judge issues a written opinion, the judge's written opinion may also serve as the order. Each case is different, and you have to read the document from the court to see if the opinion is the order.

Motions After Trial

After the verdict or decision is announced, and even after a judgment is entered, you can still make requests of the court that can change the outcome of the case. Some motions might have to be made while you're still in the courtroom, and some can be made well after the trial is over, depending on the court rules. This is a technical area, and each state, and sometimes each judge, is different. This is a great reason to consider hiring an attorney.

Motion for a New Trial

A common motion made after the trial is over is a motion for a new trial. It's sometimes referred to as a "motion for trial de novo," which is Latin for "new" or "from the beginning." This is usually based on the argument that there was some major problem with the trial as it just happened. A perfect example would be if it was learned that someone lied while testifying, or that the court made a ruling on a point of law that was clearly wrong.

IN THE KNOW

As noted in Chapter 11, one of the main reasons attorneys object during a trial is to preserve the issue for appeal. Throughout the trial, both sides make motions and objections specifically to preserve the record, so that if the party wants to appeal the decision, there's something for the appellate court to hear and work with.

What happens if a jury comes back with a decision that is clearly wrong? For example, what if every single witness says "Joe hit Sam," and there's a videotape of it, and Joe even admits that he hit Sam, but the jury says "Joe didn't hit Sam"?

You can file a motion called "motion for judgment notwithstanding the verdict," or "motion j.n.o.v." It is typically used when the jury seems to have ignored the evidence or seems not to have followed the law in coming to its decision.

Unfortunately, except as a method of preserving the record, motions for new trial and motions j.n.o.v. rarely work. Judges really dislike overturning jury verdicts, and have very little motivation to overturn their own judgments. However, in order to make sure there's a record for the appeals courts to look at, these motions are made even when the attorney knows there's very little chance of success.

Motion to Change the Amount of the Judgment

When a money judgment is awarded, it's a fair bet that someone isn't going to be happy with it. One side may think it's too low, and the other side is going to think it's too high. To ask for the amount of the judgment to be increased, a "motion for additur" is made. It "adds" money to the judgment if it's successful. To ask for the amount of the judgment to be decreased, a "motion for remittitur" is made. If it's successful, the dollar amount of the judgment goes down.

There has to be a reason to ask for the change in amount of money granted, beyond a gut reaction that the amount is wrong. Typical reasons are that the amount over-compensates or undercompensates for the injury or damage. You'll need to show how, but because you've run the numbers in preparation for the trial, it shouldn't be too difficult to come up with the math that shows you're right. Whether the court agrees with you is a different issue.

Motion for Penalties and Attorney Fees

One of the best things in the American system of justice is that we have full access to the courts—you don't have to be an attorney to represent yourself. For that very reason, most of the time attorney fees aren't available as damages from the losing side.

That doesn't mean, however, that you can never get attorney fees. A lot depends on what your lawsuit was about. Some laws provide that if you break them, the loser pays attorney fees. Some common examples are the Federal Magnusson-Moss Warranty Act, "Lemon Laws," and other consumer protection laws.

Some states have court rules that allow for what are called "offer of judgment" attorney fees. This is almost like making a side bet on the outcome of the case. The easiest way to describe it is that one side makes an offer to have a judgment entered for some amount of money. If the other side rejects the offer, they have to improve upon that number in the final judgment, or they have to pay the other side's attorney fees even if they "win" the case.

There are other sorts of side bets, based on other court rules. Another example would be "case evaluation." Basically, a panel reviews the case, and puts a dollar amount on the case. If everyone accepts, the case settles; if someone rejects and if she doesn't improve on that figure in the final judgment, then she has to pay attorney fees.

IN THE KNOW

Every state and every locality has different rules regarding attorney fees; this is definitely something you should investigate prior to filing suit.

It's pretty rare that a frivolous case goes all the way to trial; most of those cases are dismissed early on. However, when it does happen, a motion can be filed under the rules of the court. These rules often provide penalties including paying attorney fees, but can provide for additional monetary penalties, too.

Regardless of the rule you're using as the basis for the request for penalties and attorney fees, the time to make these motions of the court is immediately after the decision is announced. Like the motion for new trial or motion j.n.o.v., these motions for penalties and attorney fees are sometimes made solely to provide a record for the request and to give the appeals courts an issue to discuss. However, these motions are more likely to succeed than the new trial motions because they're often based on statutes that specifically provide for these payments.

More Paperwork

When the decision is announced, the court issues a judgment, often combined with an order telling the parties what to do. Both sides will provide the court with what's called a "proposed judgment and order," hoping that the court will just go ahead and use that rather than create its own paperwork. Some courts will ask the attorney on the winning side to "write up" the judgment and order and submit it to the court, to save the court's time. When this happens, it's a good idea to check the judgment and order against notes you may have made during the announcement of the decision, to catch any mistakes that might have been made.

Who Gets Copies of What?

Trials generate *a lot* of paper. Hopefully, you've been getting copies of everything as the trial progressed. The last pieces of paperwork are likely to be as follows:

- The verdict form

- Any orders that the court makes as a result of the verdict

- Any orders that the court makes to enforce the judgment

Usually, the winner is responsible for copying the judgment and distributing it to everyone involved.

The first, original document goes to the court clerk. It gets filed exactly the same way all the other documents in the case are filed, with a time stamp at the clerk's office or electronically. (See Chapters 7 and 8 for more details on filing documents with the court.)

The next copies go to the plaintiff's attorney and the defendant's attorney. These should be exact copies of what the court clerk got. If possible, they should be either time-stamped themselves, or proof of the electronic or other filing of the documents should be included with the copies.

You, as the plaintiff or defendant, should get a copy of the judgment from your lawyer. If for some reason you don't get one, you can go to the court clerk's office and ask for a copy yourself. Be sure to have the full case name with you and, if possible, any number the court assigned to your case. The number will make it easier to find your documents, but it's possible to get a copy of the judgment or any other papers without it.

The same kind of distribution list applies to any of the other orders that go along with the judgment or that were made to enforce the judgment. A copy goes to the court, a copy goes to each side's attorney, and a copy should go to you personally.

How Long Should the Records Be Kept?

Don't get too enthusiastic about decluttering after your trial is over. There's no rule that says how long you have to keep your notes and records. Obviously, you're better off keeping documents than getting rid of them. How long you keep the records might depend on whether or not the judgment has been satisfied, which means that whatever the judgment said had to be done, was done.

Here's a nightmare scenario: A person gets a default judgment, because the other side never answered the complaint. The plaintiff, thinking he's got a judgment, gets rid of all the paperwork and evidence that would've helped prove the case. Later, the plaintiff tries to collect the judgment, and the defendant finds out about the lawsuit.

When the defendant says, "I never lived at the address where you sent the papers, and I never had any dealings with the plaintiff in my life," and the court says, "What proof do you have, Mr. Plaintiff, to show he lived there, and that you had dealings with Mr. Defendant?" If Mr. Plaintiff tossed his papers and his evidence, he's got nothing. The court will set aside the judgment, and Mr. Plaintiff will be very sad indeed.

If you've been involved in a divorce or other family law matter, keep your original copy of the judgment with your other important records, like birth certificates and passports. If you were involved in a divorce, there might be an additional piece of paper, sometimes called a "Record of Divorce." You will definitely need to keep that document forever, as it proves that you are no longer married and therefore have different rights. You may even want to keep the judgment (and record of divorce, if you were given one) in a safe-deposit box or a fireproof safe.

You also need to make allowances for appeals; if the case is on appeal, even if you won, you still have work to do, and you'll need all of your papers.

If your judgment is not satisfied, you should keep those records at least until it has been satisfied. Some states provide that judgments are good for 10 years, and can be renewed for 10 more. You'll want to keep those papers, because it's not uncommon for defendants to try to attack the judgment later on down the line.

As a general rule, attorneys keep documents for approximately five to seven years. You may want to follow that same rule.

Before you dispose of the papers, check through them to see if there's anything you should keep. For example, you should probably keep any medical records indefinitely, but other documents, like pleadings, which are on file with the court, might not be so important.

PITFALLS

Many records related to your case will have personal and sensitive information in them, like dates of birth, Social Security numbers, bank account information, and the like. You might not want to dispose of these documents by simply tossing them in the trash. Certain documents are probably best shredded or otherwise locked away.

Is the Win Taxable?

Whether or not a win in court results in taxation is actually a very complicated question. Although the basics are discussed here, it's extremely important that you consult a qualified tax professional when doing your taxes for the year in which you won a judgment. This is especially true because, depending on the topic of your lawsuit, it might change your tax liability for other years, too.

The first thing to know is that the Internal Revenue Service's middle name is "Revenue." As far as the IRS is concerned, any money you get is taxable until proven otherwise. In fact, the most basic rule in the entire field of tax law states that your gross income, which is all the money and benefits you got during the tax year, includes everything regardless of how or where you got it. If you win something in your court case that isn't money but has monetary value, the amount of monetary value assigned to your win gets added to your gross income, too. What all this means to you is that you'll have to declare the money you win in court or the value of the thing you won in court on your income taxes, most likely in the year you win it.

Of course, it's not that simple. Despite the rule that says gross income is everything from any source, there are rules that exclude some things from gross income. So it's not always easy to immediately state what your gross income is. However, once you've figured out your gross income, you now have to look at the various tax rules to determine what you actually pay taxes on.

PITFALLS

The bigger and more complex your court case, the more you'll need expert advice on the taxes and deductions you're allowed.

You may be able to deduct your attorney fees and the costs of the lawsuit. Depending on the topic of the lawsuit, you might not even have to include the judgment as income at all. Judgments that reimburse you for a loss you suffered, for example from an injury, may not be considered taxable income. Judgments that reimburse you for lost wages, on the other hand, are probably taxable income because you would've been taxed on it at the time you should've gotten it.

Punitive damages are another story. Sometimes a statute specifically excludes punitive damages for a specific type of lawsuit from income. Other times punitive damages are seen as pure income, with no deduction allowed. This is why it's so important to check with a tax professional before submitting your taxes for the year of your judgment. There are so many variables that the most it's safe to say about whether you'll pay taxes on your win is "it depends." Find out for sure what your particular situation is by going to a professional. It's well worth the extra money to avoid mistakes that can lead to your having to pay even more money in fines and interest to the IRS.

Is the Loss Deductible?

Once again, the safe answer is "it depends." Some losses are deductible, or at least nontaxable. For example, the amount paid in alimony payments tends not to be considered income for the person making the payments. The payments are taxable income to the person getting alimony, though. Other losses can be considered business expenses and can be deducted that way. Generally, if your loss is due to what a court has decided is your bad behavior, then tax law doesn't allow you to deduct what you have to pay from your gross income.

As with a win, you may also be able to deduct your legal fees from income. Be sure to double-check this, as it varies from case to case. What makes tax law so difficult for many people to deal with isn't the math; it's the fact that there are so many rules that might or might not apply, depending on the situation.

Paying Legal Fees

You might have been paying fees throughout your case on a monthly basis. Or you might have paid a retainer up front and had the fees deducted from that amount as they were earned. You might have had a combination of both, or you might have paid nothing up to this point. See Chapter 5 for a more thorough discussion of what kinds of fees exist and how they're generally paid. This section discusses paying for the other side's legal fees at the end of the trial, and how to deal with paying legal fees when you've had a contingent fee agreement with your attorney.

Court-Ordered Attorney Fees

The loser must pay the winner's attorney fees if there is a statute requiring payment or if the judge decides that the loser should be responsible for paying the winner's attorney fees. There are even some situations, as with divorce, where the party with more money is required to pay for the attorney fees of the party who has less money. These are all legitimate orders the court has the power to make, but they're also orders you can try to appeal. You might not be successful, and you might end up paying interest on the amount of attorney fees you were ordered to pay, but if you can find a good reason that you shouldn't have to pay the other side's attorney fees, it may be worth a shot.

Contingency Payments

From the ads on TV, you know that when you have a contingency fee agreement with your attorney, the usual agreement is that you pay no attorney fees unless you win your case. If you win, the attorney fees will be taken out of the money the other side is ordered to pay you in the judgment. What will happen is the other side will pay the judgment amount directly to your attorney. Your attorney is then responsible for paying you whatever is left after both his fee and the costs of the litigation are taken out of the money paid. You should get an accounting of how much the attorney fee was and how much the litigation costs were, together with the total amount of the judgment that the attorney received from the other side.

Collecting on a Money Judgment

The feeling of victory at the end of a lawsuit is wonderful, but having the cash in your hands can be an even better feeling. The problem is that just because the court orders someone to pay you money doesn't mean that you'll immediately get that money. The person who owes the money, the "judgment debtor," can ask the court for time to pay the judgment, or for permission to pay it off in stages. These are reasonable requests, and they're often granted, despite whatever protests the winner, or "judgment creditor," makes.

A second, related problem is that some judgment debtors simply ignore the judgment and don't make any payments on it at all. Courts do not look kindly on judgment debtors who don't pay at all. Even if the person genuinely doesn't have the cash, not paying the judgment, especially combined with no communication to the court about why there's been no payment, is seen by the court as disrespectful. Up until the mid-1800s, in many parts of Europe, people who didn't pay their debts were put in debtor's prisons. If you couldn't pay, you went away. We don't lock up judgment debtors anymore. Just about the only way you can go to jail for not paying a judgment is if you don't pay a judgment for child support.

There are, however, ways to get the money that's owed to you. One is to sell your judgment to someone who will go through the steps discussed below to collect on the judgment themselves. The purchaser then takes your place as the judgment creditor and gets all the same rights to payment as you had. The purchaser will pay you far less than the value of the judgment, because he's taking the chance that he might not get anything at all. Plus, the purchaser has to pay for the collection attempts he's going to make. After his expenses, he's not going to actually get the entire amount of the judgment, so why should he pay you the full face value of the judgment himself? Regardless, selling your judgment can be a good solution in some situations. For example, if you can afford to take the loss on the amount you'll collect, selling the judgment may be a good idea, particularly if you just want some money in hand and you're tired of dealing with the lawsuit.

JUST THE FACTS

If your judgment provides for annual payments, there are companies that will buy your right to those payments, again for a highly discounted fee. Be careful, though; you might not be entitled to sell your judgment because it was specifically structured to protect your rights.

If the judgment debtor is not paying, the creditor needs to find out what money and other assets the judgment debtor has. You do this is by asking the court to schedule a "creditor's exam." This is an informal, out-of-court hearing, much like a deposition (see Chapter 10 for more on depositions), that focuses on asking the debtor what she owns and where it is. You may be familiar with creditor's exams from bankruptcy proceedings, but they're quite common in ordinary collections cases, too.

The debtor is asked to bring to the hearing bank statements; account numbers; title to cars, boats, and houses; and proof of whatever other assets the attorney can think of. The debtor often claims to have no assets in her name, so that she's judgment-proof. If a debtor makes such a claim, it will cost you more to collect on the judgment, because you're going to have to spend time and money to investigate to see whether the debtor has assets she's hidden or transferred that you can get at, or attach.

Now, remember debtor's prison? Well, there is one other way that a judgment debtor can go to jail—contempt of court. It is one thing not to pay a judgment; it is another not to comply with a court order to appear for a creditor's exam. If this happens, courts can order that a "bench warrant" be issued for the arrest of the debtor. When that person is arrested, assuming that there's no good excuse, the court will allow him to post a bond to stay out of jail. Depending on the amount of money involved in the judgment, the bond may be in the amount of the judgment. If that's the case, and he pays the bond, guess what? Judgment paid!

Once you've established that there are some assets that can be used to pay the judgment, you'll have to go through a few more hoops to get the assets away from the judgment debtor. The two main methods used are the processes of garnishment and liens.

Garnishment

Garnishment is a process that involves an additional set of requests to the court (motions) and new court orders requiring payment to be made to the judgment creditor. What makes garnishment different from the original order to pay the judgment is that an order of garnishment isn't directed at the person who lost at trial, the judgment debtor. Instead, the order of garnishment is made against someone who holds or owes money to the judgment debtor. That person is called the "garnishee." The order tells the garnishee not to pay the money to the judgment debtor, but to pay it directly to the judgment creditor. If the garnishee doesn't obey the order, the garnishee can end up responsible for the entire amount of the judgment, not just the amount of money that he originally owed the judgment debtor.

The two most common orders of garnishment are against employers who owe wages to the judgment debtor, and against banks or credit unions, who hold money belonging to the judgment debtor. Banks and credit unions are very used to dealing with garnishments and are usually very easy to work with in collecting on a garnishment order. Large employers are also used to garnishments and have processes in place to make sure they obey the court's order of garnishment to the letter.

The problems with garnishments tend to come with small employers, who don't know how to deal with the order because they've never had to before, and with individuals who owe money to the judgment debtor, also for the same reason. Of course, another reason it can be hard to collect on a garnishment from the inexperienced is that they don't realize the consequences of not obeying the court's order. They often side with the judgment debtor and don't want to cooperate because they see the order as unjust. In a sense, this isn't really a problem, because by failing to obey the court's order, they may have given you another source of payment for the original judgment!

There are some sources of income you cannot garnish at all. Most of them are a form of government support payment, like Social Security disability or some forms of veteran's benefits. The others tend to be things like child support payments, which are intended to keep children off government support. Before you try to garnish a source of income, check to be sure it is one that is eligible for garnishment.

Liens

Sometimes, rather than money, a judgment debtor will have items that are worth money, like cars, boats, land, and so on. In that case, you can ask the court for a judgment lien "against" the property. This is sort of like having a mortgage on the property, because you now have the same kind of right to foreclose and force a sale as someone who holds a mortgage and doesn't get paid. If the item isn't land, but some other kind of personal property, you can get an order for the item to be seized to pay off the debt. You might choose to auction the item, for example at a sheriff's sale, or you might choose to retain it yourself as payment. It's up to you as the creditor. Judgment creditors have ended up with RVs, fancy cars, and jewelry instead of the cash they were owed through this process.

> **IN THE KNOW**
>
> If you were paying your attorney on a contingent fee basis, you'll probably have to sell any item you were able to get an order to seize so that your attorney can get paid. She's unlikely to want to share a car with you as payment for her services.

The Least You Need to Know

- Before you try an appeal, make sure all the possible motions were made to change the outcome at the end of the trial.
- Don't ever throw away the final judgment papers in a case.
- Get expert tax advice on how to handle your win or loss on your taxes.
- Be prepared to go through hoops to get paid on your judgment.

Appeals

In This Chapter

- Deciding whether to appeal
- What appeals can be based on
- Deciding which lawyer should bring your appeal
- Taking your appeal to the Supreme Court of the United States

The last major step in the litigation process is asking the appellate courts to review the trial for mistakes. It's not a required step, but it's one that everyone who doesn't get what she wanted at trial should consider. Appeals are very different from trials, and they don't always give you exactly what you expect.

Deciding Whether to Appeal

If you're happy with the outcome of the trial, or at least willing to live with it, there's no reason to go to the expense and trouble of appealing the decision. However, if you believe that some major errors caused you to lose something important, you may want to consider appealing.

Your attorney has been preparing for the possibility of an appeal throughout the trial, even if it's not obvious that she's doing so. When she makes sure all the evidence possible is offered to the court, objects when she thinks a mistake has been made, and makes requests of the court in the form of motions to have something done or not done, she's making a record, which will be used as the basis for appeal.

JUST THE FACTS

Most common law, or case law, comes from courts of appeal. That means your case might someday be cited by other attorneys and parties in their cases. Your case could be the next *Roe v. Wade* or *Brown v. Board of Education*.

You should prepare for the possibility of an appeal early on in the trial process, too. If you know what your options are well before the court hands down the final decision, you won't be forced into a hasty or badly considered decision. The things you should consider include …

- The worst possible decision the court could make.

- How you will handle that worst possible decision financially, assuming you have to live with it.

- How you will handle that worst possible decision as part of your day-to-day life, again assuming you have to live with it.

- How you will pay for an appeal, if you or the other side brings one.

- How you will manage the time the *appellate process* will take.

DEFINITION

The **appellate process** is the course a trial case takes after judgment when it goes through the appeals courts. This is when the case is reviewed for errors in the application of the law.

Ultimately, your decision to appeal is going to be based on three things:

- **Whether you think the appeal is worth your time.** Is the likely outcome worth spending more time on this dispute?

- **Whether you think the appeal is worth your money.** Appeals aren't free, and you've probably spent a lot of money up to this point anyway. Is it worth throwing more money at this issue?

- **Whether you can tolerate more legal proceedings.** After all that you've been through with this dispute, how do you feel about continuing to fight?

One other thing you should do is talk to your attorney. Find out what she thinks. There is an old saying in the law, "Bad facts make for bad law." That means that if your case has difficulties like tough facts, appealing it might end up not only with your losing the case, but with bad law being made for other people in the future.

Certain appeals are considered *test cases*, where the facts are just right, so to speak, to perfectly frame an issue for the court. It's hard to say which cases are those perfect test cases, as it depends on the case and the area of law.

Don't Waste Time Deciding!

The most important thing to do is make your decision quickly. The court rules give you a limited amount of time to appeal after the case is over. If you have the ready cash and if you have a reasonable sense that something really went wrong in the trial, file the appeal as soon as you can; the last thing you want to do is miss the deadline to file. The worst that will happen if you file the appeal and change your mind later is you lose some more time and money.

Find out from your attorney what the time limits are on filing an appeal. Don't be surprised if you have something along the lines of 21 days after the final decision of the trial court to file the appeal. The courts' goal is to keep cases moving along as quickly as possible so that as many cases as possible can be heard. For that reason, the courts aren't very easygoing about hearing appeals that are filed after the deadline.

The Facts Have Been Decided

The most difficult thing for people to accept about the appeals process is that usually the only thing that can be reviewed is the way the trial court applied the law to the facts. The facts have already been decided by the finder of fact at the trial. That's why it's so important that your witnesses not only tell the truth but are believable when they do it.

There are very rare circumstances when the appeals court will reconsider whether the facts were properly decided. These are few and far between, and generally only happen in the clearest of circumstances. Even if 100 people said that the traffic light was green when the car went through, if one person said it was red, the jury has every right to believe that one person who said the light was red over the 100 who said it was green.

Appealing How the Law Was Applied

Your appeal is going to be limited to very technical questions that have to do with interpretation of statutes, cases, and court rules. This is where people start snarling about winning or losing on a technicality. The details of how the law was interpreted and applied are critically important. The technicalities are what keep our system fair for everybody, even if that means that every now and then an individual case's outcome seems unfair.

The process of appealing how the law was applied starts with getting a copy of the transcript of the trial. This can be expensive, especially if the trial was long. You'll pay the court reporter a per-page fee for each page of the transcript, and you might also pay a base fee for the production of the transcript. The court reporter might provide you with the actual printed and bound pages, or she might send you an e-mail of an electronic file. Some court reporters provide the transcript on a CD or other storage device, although this is becoming less and less popular as e-mail has become more universal.

The next step is to review the transcript. This can be done by your trial attorney or by an appellate attorney. (See the discussion later in this chapter for finding an appellate attorney.) The review of the transcript is essentially Monday-morning quarterbacking. The idea is to find mistakes and show why they shouldn't have happened. It's much easier to find mistakes after the fact than it is to prevent them! It's also easier to find someone else's mistakes than it is to find your own, so it's often helpful to have a fresh set of eyes looking at the transcript, which an appellate attorney can provide.

For each mistake, the attorney has to show that one of the elements of a specific rule of law wasn't properly applied. See Chapter 13 for a more thorough discussion of application of the law. Basically, though, the attorney finds a spot where he thinks the court should've made a different decision, and then comes up with a statute, case, or court rule that shows why the original decision was wrong. It helps if the trial attorney quoted that statute, case, or court rule at the time the mistake was made, but as long as the trial attorney made some kind of objection, the problem is easy to appeal. As noted in Chapter 11, making the objection or motion is called "preserving the issue for appeal," or "preserving the record."

The attorney takes each mistake that was made and, if possible, tries to put the mistakes into similar groups. Each group or individual mistake then becomes one of the issues for appeal. Each issue gets its own section of the document, called the appellate brief, which is submitted to the appeals court asking for changes to the result of the trial.

The appellate brief is submitted to the appeals court before any actual appearance is made in front of any judges. Appellate briefs are written in paragraph form and often appear to be very scholarly.

It's this scholarly bent that makes an appeal more difficult for a nonlawyer to do on her own than a trial is. Finding and focusing on the legal issues, rather than the factual issues, requires a major shift in thinking. This shift is something that law schools spend a great deal of time drumming into students' heads. Law school exams focus strongly on this skill, called issue-spotting.

Once your attorney has spotted the issues, he compares the way the court dealt with them to the laws that should have been applied to them. What turns this into a scholarly effort is that the appeals court is willing to look at the whether the application of the law to the issue and the facts was in line with the underlying reason for the law. The appeals court looks at the policy reasons and objectives of the statute or case or court rule to see if they were met by the trial court. These reasons are usually set out in things like the history of a statute or the opinion of another appellate case. Finding and interpreting these things is a more in-depth procedure than just finding the law itself for the trial.

The appellate brief spells out the issues, the law, and why the trial court was wrong in applying the law the way it did to come up with its final decision. The brief is therefore usually not brief at all. It's not unusual for briefs to run upward of 100 pages.

Costs of Filing an Appeal

The appellate process isn't cheap. Filing the appeal is not free, unless you can get permission from the appeals court to file *in forma pauperis*, or as a poor person. The initial court cost for filing an appeal often starts at about $250.

Do You Need a Different Lawyer?

There isn't a special appellate license attorneys need to take a case to a state appeals court or to the federal court of appeals. However, some attorneys have a great deal of experience going to appeals courts, and some even specialize in writing appeals for other attorneys or appearing in appellate courts. Appellate courts have different rules from trial courts, and the paperwork filed with them is often complex. Depending on the attorney, some are more or less comfortable dealing with these factors.

Subcontracting to Another Lawyer

It's quite common for an attorney to get another lawyer to write the appellate brief. This kind of subcontracting is usually done because your attorney sees this as the most effective use of time and money. Writing an appellate brief requires significant time that your lawyer might not have. It's also important that all the details required by the appellate court, like the color of the front page, the number of copies required, and so on, are met. Because the appellate attorney is well versed in these kinds of details, they are more likely to do it correctly and efficiently.

Replacing Your Lawyer

If you're not satisfied with how your attorney performed at trial, you should not stay with that attorney for the appeal. Some people believe that they should stay with their trial attorney, as that attorney knows the case best. While it's true that your trial lawyer is most familiar with the case, if you don't like what she did at the trial, you probably won't like what she will do with the appeal.

PITFALLS

Don't blame the dancer for the fiddler's mistakes. Be very careful about evaluating whether the bad result was due to the lawyer's mistakes or the judge's. The lawyer has to dance to the judge's tune!

Some attorneys, knowing that you are dissatisfied, will try to repair the relationship by offering to do the appeal at a reduced rate. The only reason to take an offer like that is if you know deep down that you're not putting your dissatisfaction with the outcome of the case onto the attorney. You need to be comfortable with the idea that the outcome is not because the attorney did something wrong before you decide to stick with the same attorney. If you can't bring yourself to believe that, then you need to find a new attorney for the appeal.

Check your original letter of agreement or "retainer" that you signed when you first hired your lawyer. What was supposed to happen at the end of the trial? Did the attorney agree to do an appeal if you weren't satisfied with the outcome of the trial, or is that left open? Many times appeals are not addressed in the letter of agreement. If appeals are not mentioned, then your association with the lawyer is considered finished at the end of the trial.

Knowing that your time to appeal is limited, you'll quickly need to get the names of attorneys who are familiar with appeals. Even if you're not happy with your trial attorney, ask him for names of appellate attorneys, and push to get more than one name. You should, as when you hired your trial lawyer in the first place, interview at least three lawyers to get a feel for who would work with you best. Try contacting your state's licensing board or bar association to see if there's a referral service that includes appellate lawyers. Also ask if there is a group specifically for appellate attorneys in your state. Some state bars have committees or smaller bar associations for particular practice areas like appeals.

The tips in Chapter 4 for hiring a lawyer are just as valid in hiring a lawyer for an appeal as they were for hiring a lawyer for the trial. If you used the tips in that chapter to hire your trial lawyer, and you aren't happy with what you ended up with, review the notes you took as you interviewed various lawyers. Ask yourself the following questions:

- What was the main reason you hired this particular trial lawyer?

- Why did you like this trial lawyer better than the others?

- How much did price factor into your decision?

- How much did a time crunch factor into your decision?

- What did the trial lawyer do, specifically, that disappointed you? Why?

- What could the trial lawyer have done to avoid disappointing you?

Be sure you've got answers to these questions before you begin looking for an appellate lawyer. Be very aware of why you hired the trial lawyer. If a classy office or aggressive reputation lured you in, you'll know how much weight to give those factors this time.

What you're looking for in an appellate lawyer is usually a little different from what you want in a trial lawyer. You want someone who can meet the time deadlines set by the court for the appeal, and who is comfortable with the appellate process. Often appellate lawyers are very intellectual types, and not terribly impressive looking. You should be more interested in experience than appearance in appeals.

Will the Court of Appeals Hear My Case?

There are two ways that courts of appeals hear cases: by right and by leave.

When an appeal is by right, it means you have an automatic right to appeal. You don't have to show anything special to get a review by the appeals court. All you have to do is follow proper procedure.

An appeal by leave means that you have to get permission from the court of appeals to file the appeal.

In cases where you're appealing by leave, generally you have to file a document with the court explaining why your case should be heard. Is it a new or uncharted area of the law? Is there such clear error that justice cries out for the case to be heard? Is there a chance to reverse some other law? These are the types of reasons why leave would be granted.

You will need to check with your attorney to see whether or not your case is appealable by leave or by right. Generally, it's easier to have a case heard by right rather than by leave, because as long as you follow the right procedure, the court has no choice; your appeal has to be heard. On the other hand, appeals by leave give the court a choice, and the court can easily choose not to hear your appeal.

PITFALLS

You don't want to have a case that was originally appealable by right turn into one that can only be filed by leave. How does that happen? Usually, someone (you or your attorney) misses a filing deadline. It is not a position you want to be in. File on time, every time!

Taking It to the Supreme Court

Before your case can go to the Supreme Court of the United States, it first has to go through all other possible appeals. If your case is a state case, it likely has to go to two appeals courts before it can go to the U.S. Supreme Court—the intermediate state court of appeals, and the highest state court of appeals, often called the state Supreme Court. From the state Supreme Court, you can try to bring your case to the U.S. Supreme Court. If your case is in the federal system, it will first go to the federal court of appeals for your district. After that, it can go to the Supreme Court of the United States.

This isn't a quick process, nor is it cheap. You'll have to pay fees for the appeal at every court of appeal you go to, unless you manage to get the fees waived due to your lack of money. As mentioned in Chapter 5, getting permission to file "as a pauper," or *in forma pauperis*, usually means you have to be at or below the federal poverty level, not that you've spent all your income on the lawsuit. The expectation is that if it's important enough to you, you'll somehow find the money.

State courts of appeal only require that the attorney be licensed to practice in their state in order to appear before the court to make an appeal. The Supreme Court of the United States has an additional licensing requirement for attorneys to be allowed to appear in front of the Supreme Court. The attorney must not only be a member of a state's bar, but also a member of the bar of the Supreme Court of the United States.

Most attorneys aren't members of the bar of the Supreme Court, although it's not difficult to join as long as the attorney is in good standing with his home state's bar association. The attorney has to find a current member of the Supreme Court bar to sponsor his admission, and pay an additional fee for membership. Many law school alumni associations have annual trips to Washington, D.C., so that their alums can join the Supreme Court bar. If it's so easy to join, why don't more lawyers do it? For one thing, it's not necessary to the everyday practice of law. For another, the application process—and the trip to D.C.—take time away from the lawyer's practice.

In addition, if membership does become necessary to the lawyer's practice, it's easy enough to join then.

Procedure

There are two ways that cases get to the U.S. Supreme Court, and it's very similar to how ordinary appeals are brought: appeals as of right, and appeals that are granted based on a petition for review. Both ways require that a full appellate brief be provided to the Supreme Court for its review, meaning that the majority of the work is done without knowing whether the court will actually agree to hear the case.

IN THE KNOW

Most cases that try to get to the U.S. Supreme Court do it by petition for review, known as asking for a writ of certiorari. Most lawyers call it "asking for cert" because pronouncing certiorari (*sir-show-rare-eye*) is so difficult!

The Supreme Court isn't required to hear every case that gets proposed to it. The estimate is that of the approximately 10,000 petitions sent to the court each year, between 1 percent and 5 percent get some kind of attention from the court. Only about 75 to 100 cases are actually heard by the Supreme Court each year. There is no constitutional requirement that a specific number of cases be heard or decided.

Because of the huge number of cases that try to get a review from the Supreme Court, the court is very picky about which cases it will hear. The Supreme Court tends to pick cases that deal with issues of first impression, as discussed in Chapter 13, to give guidance to all the other courts within the United States. There's also a tendency to pick cases that deal with major issues that will affect large numbers of people. The Supreme Court tries to use its limited resources—only 9 justices and 24 hours in a day—to provide the greatest benefit to the greatest number of people. It also tries to use its power to guide the judicial system in a way that increases justice and the efficiency of the system as a whole. Because of that, there would have to be something really unusual about your small claims case concerning your mailbox being run over by your neighbor's riding mower in order for it to be heard by the Supreme Court of the United States, no matter how deeply you feel about it.

The Least You Need to Know

- Appeals have to be made quickly, within the time period allowed by the courts.
- You may want an attorney who's an appellate specialist to work on your appeal.
- Appealing your case won't change the way the facts were decided, unless there's something really unusual about your case.
- Getting your case heard by the Supreme Court of the United States has odds of 1 in 10,000 or worse.

After the Dust Clears

In This Chapter

- Dealing with the legal fallout from a lawsuit
- Repairing your business and personal relationships
- Protecting your credit
- Putting the pieces back together

What are you going to do after the lawsuit is all over? Chances are good that you've been spending a lot of time and attention on the lawsuit, and once it's over, you may feel a little disoriented—even if you get everything you want. What will you do to return to normal? Or how will you adjust to a new normal? This chapter addresses those questions.

Legal Consequences of a Lawsuit

Once the lawsuit is over, it's time to evaluate the effects of the lawsuit on your legal situation. If you won your suit, hopefully you are in the legal situation you wanted to be in at the beginning of the case. The problem is that winning a lawsuit doesn't necessarily mean you got everything you wanted. For example, you may have been awarded money, but not all the money you originally asked for. By the same token, if you lost, you might not have lost as much as you could have.

The Judgment

At the end of the lawsuit, the judge will make his decision, possibly along with the jury if there was one in your case. The final decision in the suit is called the "judgment," and it's more than just "you win, they lose" or "they win, you lose." The judgment states who won and lost, but it also announces how much and what was won or lost, and what each party is ordered to do as a result. You may have won money, in which case the judgment will state how much and the time frame in which it must be paid. It may even state how the payments should be made—cashier's check, installments, from a specific account.

The judgment may also order that someone do something specific, like return a piece of property. Again, the judgment is usually specific; it doesn't just say "give back the diamonds," it says "give back the diamonds on March 20 at 3 P.M. at the First Bank on Main Street." The advantage to this level of detail is that it's going to be clear when everyone has lived up to, or "satisfied," the judgment. The disadvantage is that if you miss one of the details—like you show up at 3:15 P.M. instead of 3 P.M.—you're in violation of the judgment. The consequences, if your violation is extreme enough, can include monetary fines you must pay to the court and to the other side, as well as criminal contempt of court charges.

Be sure that whatever else happens, you've tied up all the loose legal ends of your lawsuit. The dust hasn't really cleared until you've swept it all away.

What Has This Lawsuit Done to Your Relationships?

Any lawsuit takes up a great deal of time and energy—both physical and emotional. Chances are good that this expenditure of energy came at the expense of some very important relationships in your life. Now is the time to make amends with those people. The best way to do so is to evaluate what happened throughout the litigation, and be honest about how it affected you and the people around you.

Friends and Family Members

Your friends and family have probably heard the most about the lawsuit, and dealt with the most personal fallout from it. If your suit was against a friend or family member, or if a friend or family member had an interest in the suit, your relationship changed the moment you started the lawsuit. Now is the time to ask yourself how you behaved toward these people during the litigation process and to decide who needs apologies and who needs thank-yous.

Part of getting your feet under you again after a lawsuit is mending the relationships you rely on for support in your daily life. Lawsuits are particularly stressful, and the people who supported you during that time are especially deserving of your thanks.

The friends and family who have been distanced from you because of the lawsuit may need time to forgive, if not forget, the effects of the lawsuit. Do not be surprised by resentment or outright anger from those nearest and dearest to you. Be particularly aware of what they expected to get at the end of the lawsuit. Did they expect to get money along with you? Why or why not? Did they expect that once the suit was over, everything would go back to the way things were before the suit? Talk openly with your friends and family, and work to help them understand the way things are now that the suit is over. Give them a chance to help—or to back off completely, if that's their preference.

In particular, now that you've had this experience, ask yourself who was able to support you and how, and what you'd do differently with your friends and family if a new lawsuit were to come up. Chances are excellent that this won't be the only lawsuit in your life. You can use your experience in this suit to help you prepare for, or prevent, the next one.

Business Partners

Business relationships are greatly affected when someone is involved in a lawsuit. It's inevitable. You're spending time and money away from your core business, which affects your profits and those of your partners. The decisions you made about the lawsuit might not be the decisions your partners preferred. Your partners might not have even agreed with your decision to pursue the suit in the first place. Worse yet, your partners may have been on the other side of the lawsuit.

What do you do to fix your business partnerships? Much the same things you do to fix your personal relationships. For one thing, talk to your partners. Find out what they're happy about and what they're not so thrilled about. What do they wish you had done differently? What do they wish they had done differently? Be as up front as possible here. This discussion may be a good start for a revision of your partnership or business agreement.

It's unavoidable that during the lawsuit events came up that you never anticipated in your original business agreement. It's common for standard partnership or business agreements to say something about taking a vote if a decision is worth more than a certain amount of money, but most standard agreements don't specify how emergency decisions are to be made. And your agreement probably doesn't say anything about what happens when one partner is involved in a major event outside of the business, like a personal lawsuit. If you've been head-down in your divorce for almost a year, you may have been neglecting your business. What is your partner entitled to do? What are you entitled to from the business?

Again, as with your personal relationships, ask yourself who is entitled to thanks— and who deserves an apology. The faster you take care of those two things, the faster you can get back to your usual business life. Allow some time for healing, but know that with business, people are more ready to forgive once the productivity and profit start to roll in again. It's important to attend to the etiquette, but the best possible way to fix your business relationships post-lawsuit is to buckle down to work and get things back on track as soon as possible.

Business Associates

Employees, employers, vendors, clients, and customers have all been affected in some way by your lawsuit, if only because you weren't available during the time taken up by the lawsuit. Once again, apologies and thanks are due to some of these people, but certainly not all of them. This is an area that requires real thought and careful action, because some people have no need to know why you were less accessible than usual. In particular, you may not want clients, customers, and vendors to be aware of even the existence of the lawsuit.

If the lawsuit was in the public eye, you will have to make some statement about the lawsuit and its outcome. No matter how bad you think the outcome is, you need to approach your statement from the best possible light. If you were found negligent or lost a great deal of money, you can't lie and say you won. However, you can focus on your continued strength in other areas. You can also say that you think the decision was wrong. For example, "We have the capacity to meet the judgment's requirements, but we believe we were correct in _____." You may want to state whether or not you're going to appeal; if you're not, think about how you can make that statement without sounding like you agree that you should have lost. Perhaps you might say that you're conserving your resources for more important business goals, or, if the other side is particularly liked by the public, you might say that you'd like to spare them any further litigation.

Your Lawsuit's Effect on Your Personal Finances

The most obvious effect the lawsuit will have on your personal finances is the money you personally spent on the suit. You may have gone deeply into your savings—or even gone into debt—to pay for it. However, the suit can have other effects on your financial life as well.

Your Credit

If you lose a lawsuit, the amount of the judgment goes onto your credit report. Why? Because the judgment amount is a debt, just like the debts you may have on credit cards or for the mortgage on your house. The amount of debt you carry, compared to your ability to pay it off, affects the decisions potential creditors make about how much money they can safely lend you. This is one reason that *recording a judgment* or settlement is such a big deal. The world will know (if it cares to find out) exactly how much money you have to pay the other party.

DEFINITION

Recording a judgment (or settlement) means putting it on the public record. This is done so that the judgment can be easily enforced and also to give the public notice that someone owes a specific amount of money and why.

It's not usually possible to avoid recording a judgment, because the entire litigation proceeding was likely to be public in the first place. Confidential settlements, on the other hand, need not be recorded with the court. Many parties are eager to avoid making settlement information public, and so will agree not to record the settlement with the court. The parties who want to record the settlement usually want to make the settlement more enforceable in the event that the other side doesn't live up to the settlement agreement. Discuss the advantages and disadvantages with your attorney before making a decision about recording the settlement.

Typically, if the lawsuit was for an unpaid bill or unpaid taxes, the effect on your credit will be particularly bad. This tells potential creditors that if they expect to be paid back, they're likely to have to take you to court to get their money. That likelihood makes lending you money a riskier and more expensive proposition.

If you borrowed money to pay for your lawsuit, be careful to pay it all back in a timely manner. A lawsuit for nonpayment over a lawsuit is a consequence you don't want to have to deal with after everything you went through with the original lawsuit. Losing a lawsuit for nonpayment of your debts from your original lawsuit can also affect your credit report and credit score.

Your Financial Future

If you won a great deal of money in a lawsuit, congratulations! If you lost a great deal, well, better luck next time. Either way, your financial future is affected. In addition to consulting with your attorney, it's a good idea to talk with an accountant to see how the money you won or lost will affect your finances.

In particular, you need to find out how the judgment is going to affect your tax situation for the year it was declared, as well as the years to come. Your judgment or settlement may be set up in a particular way so that you get income over a long period of time, or so that you pay over a long period of time. This is called a "structured judgment" or "structured settlement." Structured judgments are often set up so the winner avoids having one big tax payment and the loser has time to get the money together. Structured judgments are also used to make sure the winner has a consistent income over a period of time in order to pay for needs as they arise.

If you have to pay on a judgment, it's much better to make the payments yourself rather than to allow the other side to start collection proceedings against you. For one thing, in collection, the other side can go after all your assets, regardless of what they are. You may think of a particular bank account as your child's college fund, but unless it's specifically protected, it might be available to the other side to satisfy the judgment. The same holds true for brokerage accounts, boats, cars, and just about anything else you own, including your home. Different states have different rules about using homes and essential business equipment to satisfy a judgment debt, so check with your attorney about whether your house is safe from seizure.

> **IN THE KNOW**
>
> There are companies that will buy your future right to be paid on the structured judgment or settlement for a discounted amount. For example, if you won $100,000 to be paid over 10 years, the company might pay you $65,000 immediately. The reason you're getting less than the full value of the settlement or judgment is that the company isn't getting the $100,000 up front; it has to wait the full 10 years to get it all. You're giving them money in exchange for them waiting for the full amount. This is also where they make their profit; this is a business transaction, after all, and they're not doing it because they love you! If you're someone who needs cash immediately, this may be a good trade-off. However, you may end up with even less money than you anticipated because of the tax bill you're hit with for the large lump sum you receive.

Bankruptcy

The most severe scenario for someone who owes on a judgment involves declaring bankruptcy. Bankruptcy won't eliminate all judgment debt; for example, you can't get out of making payments on a judgment of fraud. Bankruptcy is an option for some judgment debt, though, and it's an option that has to be considered very carefully. Take the following into account before you decide to declare bankruptcy:

- Whether it's truly impossible to pay the judgment debt, or just uncomfortable
- What other debt you have
- Your plans for purchasing houses, cars, and other major assets in the near future
- Your plans for starting any businesses in the near future
- What your assets are, and whether bankruptcy would protect them or result in their loss
- What your overall financial situation is, realistically assessed by an accountant
- What your litigation attorney advises
- What a bankruptcy lawyer advises

It's particularly important to consider the advice of your litigation attorney and bankruptcy attorney. The rules on which debts are cleared by bankruptcy are complex and constantly changing. What other people tell you about their experiences with bankruptcy may be completely out of date by the time you're considering doing it yourself.

Monday Morning Quarterbacking

After the lawsuit is over is the time to indulge in "if onlys," but with a purpose, and only for a brief period of time. Take advantage of the clarity of hindsight to see what went wrong and how it might have been prevented. Reviewing the case might lead you to consider malpractice charges against your attorney (see Chapter 17 for more on legal malpractice), but that's not the point of this exercise.

Who Did I Listen To?

Your advisors are an important part of how you made your decisions. Who were they, other than your attorney? Why did you select them? Were they relatives? Friends? Friends of friends? Business acquaintances? Business partners? Employers? You might not even remember talking to some of the people you asked for advice about the lawsuit, but some advice will stand out.

The advice you'll remember will have been very good or very bad. Why did you trust—or mistrust—specific people? Were you right to do so? Should you do it again? Who do you wish you had listened to, and why didn't you? The point of this review is to help you make better decisions the next time around.

What Would I Do Differently?

People discover surprising things about themselves during a lawsuit. They're more vindictive than they thought, or they're more willing to negotiate than they believed. Lawsuits can teach these types of life lessons. On a more practical level, after considering the lawsuit with the benefit of hindsight, you probably wish you had done some things differently.

Regarding the emotional aspects of the lawsuit, some people say they wish they had known how draining the lawsuit would be; they'd have settled earlier. Others find the process surprisingly invigorating, because they feel they're doing something positive to solve their problems.

Regarding the process itself, many people look back and wish they had kept better records, or had kept a closer eye on their money and bank accounts. Following the advice given in this book, particularly on taking notes and keeping track of dates, will help reduce these kinds of "if onlys" as much as possible.

> **IN THE KNOW**
>
> If you're reading this before a lawsuit starts, get a review of your insurance poli-cies. Contact attorneys who do personal injury cases and ask which insurers are easiest to work with. The easier an insurance company is to deal with, the more likely you are to be able to avoid a lawsuit to get your damages covered.

Frequently, people wish they had done the following:

- Taken their attorney's advice

- Settled

- Been more active in their case

- Not started the whole thing in the first place, especially if they lost

- Kept running notes on their discussions with their attorney

- Kept receipts in general, but particularly from the lawsuit

- Not tried to contact the other side after an attorney was involved

- Frozen their shared accounts the minute they learned of a lawsuit from the person they shared the account with

> **PITFALLS**
>
> Once a party is represented by a lawyer, other lawyers are ethically prohibited from contacting the party directly. It's not an ethical violation for a party in a lawsuit to contact another party in the lawsuit directly, but it's a very bad idea. You're likely to say something you later wish you hadn't. In fact, lawsuits have been lost because of statements made between the parties without their lawyers present.

There's no way you'll get through a lawsuit without regrets, just as there's no way you'll make it through life without regrets. The best you can do is to promise yourself that you'll make the best decisions you can based on the information you have. If you can say you've done that, you can safely say that you don't regret what you actually did; you only regret how things turned out.

Does One Lawsuit Lead to Another?

When you're finished with your lawsuit, don't get too comfortable. Your recent lawsuit might lead to another lawsuit. How can that be?

Some failed lawsuits lead to malpractice lawsuits against the attorney who represented you. (Again, see Chapter 17 for more information on legal malpractice.) Others lead to lawsuits to collect the money or items owed on the judgment. In either event, the lawsuit you thought was in your past can live on in a separate but related lawsuit in your future.

Far less common is a separate but factually unrelated lawsuit brought in revenge for having started the first lawsuit. Grudge suits are difficult for people to do, as the new lawsuit can't have any legal or factual issues in common with the first lawsuit. It's also difficult to do because lawsuits intended merely to harass the defendant are generally not permitted, both because they lack the factual or legal standing necessary to qualify as a lawsuit and because it's hard to get a lawyer to represent someone who doesn't have a reasonable case, at least on the surface. Remember, the lawyer doesn't evaluate the truth of the claims, just whether the claim is one that has a legal remedy. (See Chapter 2 for more information on what makes up a lawsuit.)

You can't count your legal problems as completely finished until every part of the judgment is completely satisfied. When the judgment is satisfied, you're likely to be safe from further litigation on that topic.

Limiting Collateral Damage After a Lawsuit

It's pretty clear that a lawsuit can cause all sorts of problems in areas of your life that don't even seem related to the suit. There's no such thing as a "surgical strike" in law; every action you take affects something else, potentially creating collateral damage. After the lawsuit is over, you should try to limit the damage.

As mentioned previously, relationships often suffer during high-stress times, and lawsuits are notoriously high-stress events. Limit the damage to your relationships by identifying who was hurt by the suit, and if appropriate, try to fix the wrong done by the suit.

Your finances can also take a serious hit by a lawsuit. Be ruthlessly realistic about your financial situation, and try to focus on how you can make up for the loss rather than mourning the money that's already gone.

Damage to reputation is trickier to deal with. For one thing, you may have a more negative view—or a more positive view!—of things than is warranted. How can you tell whether your perception of your reputation is spot on? Ask other people for their honest opinion.

If you really have taken a hit to your reputation, remember that you can't control what other people think about you. You can try to influence it, but there is no effective mind-control device out there to make people believe what you want them to believe. The best you can do is present yourself in as positive a manner as possible. Act as if you are the honorable person you know yourself to be, and hold your head high. Know that it may take a while for people to trust or believe you again, but it can happen if you're consistent in being truthful and honorable in your dealings with others.

If the lawsuit has affected your business reputation, you may want to consult a public relations expert. Businesses have bounced back from events that seemed impossible to overcome. You can, too. Think of the Tylenol poison scare: some crazed person put poison in Tylenol capsules that were sitting on the shelves of drugstores. People bought it, took the Tylenol, and died. Even though Tylenol wasn't the one responsible for poisoning people, their reputation took a huge hit. Tylenol made a tremendous effort, changed from capsules to caplets, and even changed its packaging to make it safer. Not only that, Tylenol did a great deal of public relations work to assure the world that their product was the safest on the market. Years later, the story is pretty well forgotten, and people "trust Tylenol" again.

You and your business can earn the public's trust again as well, but it won't be an easy road. One thing that rarely works in improving reputation is explaining why you're not at fault, or why everything is someone else's fault. Stick to simple statements and take responsibility for what you need to do to improve people's belief in you and your business. Give it time, too. You won't repair your reputation overnight.

The Least You Need to Know

- Give thanks and make apologies to the people in your life who were affected by the lawsuit.
- The lawsuit isn't really over until the judgment is completely paid and satisfied.
- Review what happened and decide what you'd do differently next time.
- If your reputation was damaged by the lawsuit, take careful, consistent steps to improve it.

Legal Malpractice

In This Chapter

- What malpractice is—and isn't
- Complaining to the attorney licensing boards
- How to sue a lawyer
- Benefits and costs of malpractice lawsuits

Even though you go into a lawsuit knowing there's no guaranteed outcome and knowing that one side will lose, you're probably not anticipating that you'll be the loser. If you thought you were going to lose, you probably wouldn't have taken your case this far! But if your case doesn't turn out the way you hoped, you're likely to be very unhappy. You're also likely to take out some of that unhappiness on your lawyer and decide that the loss (or less-than-perfect outcome) is your lawyer's fault.

It's entirely possible—in fact, probable—that your lawyer did make a mistake in your case. Even in successful cases, lawyers make mistakes. The question is whether the mistakes "count" as malpractice. This chapter discusses malpractice and the alternatives for getting what you are owed from an attorney who made an actionable mistake.

What Is Malpractice?

At its simplest, legal malpractice is when an attorney makes a sloppy mistake that causes you to lose your case. Common mistakes leading to malpractice claims include not filing a motion on time or missing a court hearing. It's not enough for the attorney to make the mistake, however; other conditions must apply.

Most important, to even begin considering filing a malpractice suit, you must have had an attorney-client relationship with the attorney you're planning to sue. Think about what your interaction with the attorney was like. Was it in the attorney's office? Was it over the phone? Was it at a party? The more formal the meeting, the more likely there's an attorney-client relationship. If you've got an actual contract or retainer signed by both you and the attorney, then you've definitely got an attorney-client relationship, and you can move on to the next step.

Furthermore, for the mistake to be malpractice, it has to be more than just a mistake in judgment. As long as the judgment was the kind of decision that was reasonable to make given the knowledge the attorney had at the time, a choice of strategy that doesn't work out is not grounds for malpractice. For a malpractice charge to stick, the attorney must have made a careless mistake, failed to live up to a contract, or behaved in a manner that's against the rules of professional conduct. Not only that, the mistake has to have directly caused you damage. Once you can prove those things, you can start thinking about suing for malpractice.

IN THE KNOW

Don't get malpractice confused with "ineffective assistance of counsel." That's only for criminal appeals, and only for the purpose of trying to get a new trial. It won't get you anything in a civil case.

Three kinds of mistakes or behaviors lead to successful malpractice charges:

- Proof of negligence
- Breach of contract
- Breach of fiduciary duty

Each of these mistakes and behaviors are covered in detail in the following sections. For all of them, the following conditions must be met:

- The behavior you're complaining about had to be one that a reasonable attorney would not engage in.
- The behavior caused your injury (loss of money, etc.).
- But for your attorney's behavior, you would not have suffered an injury.

If you can show that these three conditions apply, together with proof of negligence, breach of contract, or breach of fiduciary duty, you've got a legal malpractice case.

Negligence

In everyday English, the term *negligence* means carelessness. Carelessness is an element of legal negligence as well, but that's not all there is to it. Legal negligence also requires that there be a relationship between the parties that makes one party responsible for behaving with reasonable care toward the other. This is called a "duty of care" toward that other person. The attorney-client relationship fits that requirement.

In addition, to prove legal negligence you have to show that the responsible person didn't live up to her duty to act reasonably carefully, or "breached" her duty of care. This is the part where you have to show that the lawyer didn't do what a reasonable attorney would have done in this particular case. What a reasonable attorney would've done is decided by determining the "standard of care" that should be used. To do that, you're likely to need an expert witness, like another lawyer, to testify as to what that standard of care should be and how the accused lawyer violated that standard.

You also have to show that the attorney's failure to act with reasonable care was the direct cause of what happened next. Believe it or not, this is often the weakest link in the negligence case. There are lots of reasons that a case doesn't go the way you hoped. Narrowing those reasons down to one main reason can be hard for a jury when they're presented with all the problems that a case presents. Expert witnesses can be useful in establishing a link between the attorney's breach of duty and what went wrong in the case.

Finally, you have to show that you were injured as a result of the attorney's failure to act with reasonable care. This seems easy, but like everything else in negligence, it's not a cut-and-dried matter. Your injury has to be one that can be measured and that wouldn't have happened without (or "but for") the attorney's failure to act reasonably in your case. For example, you might have lost the case anyway, based on other issues.

This brings up the issue of the *case within a case*. In many states, in order to win a malpractice case based on negligence, you have to show that you would have won the original case had the attorney not made careless mistakes. This means that you'll have to conduct the trial for your original case all over again. This makes malpractice cases take longer than many other kinds of court cases.

> **DEFINITION**
>
> A **case within a case** is the process of proving that you would've won the case that the malpractice charges are based on.

Breach of Contract

To win a malpractice suit based on breach of contract, you have to prove there was an agreement between you and the attorney, and that the attorney didn't live up to her end of the agreement. You can see how this fits with the idea of negligence: with negligence, you have a relationship with requirements that the attorney didn't live up to; with breach of contract, you have an agreement that the attorney didn't live up to.

Hopefully, you signed a written retainer agreement with the attorney at the beginning of the representation. (See Chapter 5 for more on letters of representation and retainers.) This is a contract between you and the attorney under which you both have obligations. For example, you agree to pay the attorney for her work, and she agrees to do specific things for you, like file your case with the appropriate court on time.

> **PITFALLS**
>
> Unfortunately, many attorneys who get sued for malpractice have poor office organization, which is often one of the reasons they make mistakes and end up being sued for malpractice.

The retainer agreement should list what the attorney agreed to do and what you agreed to do in exchange. Check through the list and look for what the attorney didn't do that he was supposed to do according to the contract. For instance, the attorney may have promised to return calls within a certain time period or may have listed a series of actions he was going to take.

Even without a written contract, you may be able to argue that you had a verbal or oral contract that required the attorney to do specific things. The difficulty here is not that oral contracts aren't enforceable; it's that they're hard to prove. They're not impossible to prove, though, so don't give this up as a possible way to recoup your losses unless your malpractice attorney tells you it's not worth it.

Breach of Fiduciary Duty

"Fiduciary duty" isn't just about money. It's actually about loyalty, which can include dealings with money but certainly isn't limited to it. When someone has a fiduciary duty toward you, he has a duty to act in your best interest, not his own. Lawyers have a fiduciary duty to their clients that requires them to give up opportunities for themselves if those opportunities conflict with the client's needs.

This is where temptation can lead to malpractice. Lawyers keep client money in trust for the client; the lawyer's fiduciary duty means that he can't use the client's money for anything other than the client's case, even if the lawyer plans to (and does) later replace it. Because lawyers are officers of the court, and because of their fiduciary duty, they are trusted to keep a client's money safe. When it's discovered that the lawyer broke that trust, it's definitely the basis for malpractice. (It's also the basis for losing his license to practice, but that's a separate issue.)

Again, it's not just money that leads to fiduciary issues. If an attorney is involved in negotiating a business deal for you and takes a portion of the deal for himself, that's a breach of fiduciary duty. If he were truly loyal to you, he would've tried to get that portion of the deal for you, not himself.

Other Sources of Malpractice

Attorneys promise to follow rules of professional ethics in exchange for permission to practice law. These are not optional rules, and while they may differ slightly from state to state, they are, for the most part, consistent in their underlying goals. Essentially, the rules state that an attorney has several duties, including …

- A duty of loyalty to a client (fiduciary duty).
- A duty to keep client communications confidential.
- A duty to provide competent service.
- A duty of honesty in all dealings.
- A duty to act in a timely fashion.

The rules break these concepts down into more specific, complex issues, like the rules about conflict of interest between one client and another, but for the most part, the preceding list summarizes the major ethical rules.

Why should you care? Because if the attorney violates one or more of the ethical rules, not only is she subject to discipline by the state licensing board (up to and including losing her license to practice law), but she's also open to malpractice charges. Remember, in order for a malpractice charge to work, you have to show injury. Ethical violations will be punished regardless of whether they result in an injury or not.

What Kinds of Mistakes Can Lead to Malpractice?

The number of mistakes that can lead to malpractice is almost infinite, but some mistakes tend to lead to malpractice claims more than others. These include …

- **Incompetence.** This doesn't mean bad judgment; it means missing deadlines or not doing legal research on a case.

- **Revelation of client confidences.** This can support a malpractice claim if the disclosure damages the client's case.

- **Misleading advertising or unethical "solicitation."** If an attorney's ads are misleading, or the attorney improperly pursued the client to get her business, it can lead to a valid charge of malpractice.

- **Mishandling client money.** After incompetence, this is one of the most common charges in malpractice cases.

"Grieving" Your Lawyer

Along with, or even instead of, malpractice claims, you may want to complain to the state attorney licensing board, sometimes called the "state bar," about your attorney's behavior. This is called "grieving" your attorney, and the complaint you file is called a "grievance." (See Appendix B for websites for your state's attorney complaint process.) The grievance process is handled by a state organization called an attorney disciplinary board or an attorney grievance commission. Whatever it's called, it has the power to force attorneys to respond to client complaints and to punish attorneys who have violated the rules of ethics.

It's important to know that grievances are entirely separate from malpractice, and that you can successfully grieve an attorney you might not be able to successfully sue for malpractice.

The Grievance Process

Typically, once you file your grievance against your attorney, the attorney disciplinary board notifies the attorney that a grievance has been made against her. She is then required to formally respond to your claims in writing, and the attorney disciplinary board begins an investigation. The investigation process can involve depositions and requests for documentation, much like any lawsuit. (See Chapter 10 for more on depositions and requests for production of documents.) Both your testimony and the attorney's will be taken under oath, sometimes by creating a sworn document, or affidavit. Usually, the testimony is reviewed by the staff at the disciplinary board and then presented to a judge or a panel of judges. The judge or judges weigh the evidence and come to a decision about whether or not the attorney violated the rules of ethics.

There's a possible twist to all this: if the attorney does not respond, the investigation doesn't go forward. This is actually good news for you, because it means you win by default. This is the same kind of thing that happens when a defendant doesn't respond to a lawsuit.

If the attorney does respond, the investigation proceeds as described previously. If it shows that the attorney's behavior was within the limits of the rules of ethics, the grievance is dismissed, and the attorney is not punished. If, however, the investigation shows that the attorney's behavior violates the rules of ethics, the attorney will be disciplined.

What Do You Win?

At the end of a successful grievance, you win the satisfaction of knowing that the attorney has been publicly punished for her mistakes. Typically, you won't win any money. In some cases, the attorney is ordered to pay back money she took from a client, but it's rare that the attorney will have to pay the client money for other reasons.

IN THE KNOW

Most state bar associations have a fund for clients who have been injured by their attorney's unethical behavior. Check with your state bar to find out if your case qualifies for reimbursement through this fund.

No matter how big your state is, its legal community is actually pretty tight-knit. Even in states like New York and California, which have thousands of lawyers, the legal community is more like a really big high school than anything else. Why do you care? Well, in most high schools, it's hard to live down an embarrassment, because there's always someone happy to remind you of when and how you made a fool of yourself. That's what the legal community is like when it comes to attorneys who've lost grievances. Even the lightest punishment is a big deal within the legal community, no matter how minor it seems to the outside world.

The least serious punishment is a "reprimand," which is a public statement that the attorney made a very bad mistake. It may be called "censure" in some states. It's not a mere slap on the wrist; it's part of the public record, and anyone doing research on the attorney will be able to find it. The vast majority of attorneys make it through their careers without any form of public punishment at all, so the existence of a reprimand or censure on an attorney's record is a big deal.

The next most serious punishment is suspension of the attorney's right to practice law for a specified period of time. While the suspension is not permanent, it's hugely embarrassing for the attorney because not only does the entire legal community know about it, but the attorney has to notify all of his clients that he has been suspended and cannot handle his cases for the period of the suspension. Most clients don't come back after that kind of notice. If the attorney wants to go back into practice, the conditions of the suspension determine what he must do. While reinstatement may be automatic, the lawyer usually has to reapply for permission to practice law once the suspension is over. He may also have to get recommendations from other attorneys swearing that he has changed for the better. Many attorneys are reluctant to have their name associated with someone who was suspended, so it's not easy to get back into the practice of law after a suspension.

The most serious punishment is disbarment, which permanently takes away the attorney's right to practice law in the state. If an attorney has been disbarred in one state, no other state will permit him to practice law either. Although some states will allow a disbarred attorney to reapply for permission to practice law, often after five or more years, it's even more difficult to do than beginning to practice again after a suspension. There will be an in-depth investigation as to the disbarred attorney's character, the original incident or incidents that got him disbarred, and the attorney's behavior during the period of disbarment. For the most part, once an attorney is disbarred, it's the end of his career.

Why Suing an Attorney Is Complicated

There's a joke about a doctor, a lawyer, and a bartender stuck on a deserted island, just a few hundred yards from shore. It's close enough to swim, but the waters are infested with sharks. The three can see them plainly, ominously circling the island. "No problem," says the lawyer, and walks across the backs of the sharks to the shore. The doctor and bartender see this and are amazed. "I can do that!" the doctor says, and sets foot into the water. The sharks immediately attack and eat him up. The bartender shouts to the lawyer, "How come the sharks helped you across and not the doctor?" The lawyer shouts back, "Professional courtesy!"

The concept of professional courtesy is only one reason that suing an attorney is difficult. Historically, lawyers were reluctant to sue other lawyers for malpractice because they didn't want to be sued for malpractice themselves. However, that's changing, with the emergence of attorneys who specialize in legal malpractice as the focus of their careers.

Many of these legal malpractice specialists will not take cases involving divorce, child custody, or criminal law, because more often than not, a bad result in those kinds of cases has very little to do with the kinds of attorney behavior we discussed previously. It's also difficult to find a legal malpractice specialist who will take your case if you believe your lawyer settled for too little money or didn't perform well at trial.

The Attorney Judgment Rule

Part of the reason you may have difficulty finding a legal malpractice attorney to take your case is the attorney judgment rule. This rule protects attorneys from malpractice as long as their decisions in technique and strategy were made with sincere good faith and were based on the law as it was at the time. Unless the attorney's decision was clearly against the client's best interest, or had no legal basis, the lawyer is protected against malpractice charges. If this rule didn't exist, attorneys would never make any decisions at all, fearing that every step they took would result in malpractice charges. The rule doesn't protect attorneys from ignorance or sloppy work, only reasonable decisions that just didn't work out. That's why, as mentioned earlier, dissatisfaction with the amount you settled for or overall performance at trial aren't the strongest bases for malpractice claims.

Am I Even Allowed to Sue?

If you were not the actual client of the attorney, your claim against the attorney for malpractice isn't likely to succeed. There are a couple exceptions, like people who should have received something under a will but didn't because of an attorney's malpractice. The other major exception is for people who have guardians; the guardian can sue on the client's behalf. Overall, though, you need to be the attorney's client to be able to sue successfully. This means that your son may have suffered from an attorney's malpractice, but it's up to him to sue.

Fees

Keep in mind that you will have to pay the malpractice attorney her fees directly. After you've paid for your original case, there may not be as much money available to pay for still more lawyer fees. In some states, malpractice attorneys are allowed to take these cases on a contingent fee basis, meaning that their fees will be taken out of any money you win or settle for; if you don't win or settle, they don't get paid. (See Chapter 5 for details on contingent fees.)

PITFALLS

Not all states require attorneys to maintain malpractice insurance. If your state doesn't require it, the attorney you want to sue may not have it. That means you'll have a much more difficult time finding an attorney to take your case on a contingent fee basis, since there may not be a ready fund of insurance money to collect from.

Benefits and Costs

The benefits of suing your attorney for malpractice can be significant. Among other things, you may get the money you should have won in the original case, plus get paid back for the money you spent on attorney fees. You might even get the attorney fees for your malpractice attorney paid for, too. This is, of course, the best-case scenario.

The downsides of suing your attorney for malpractice include the amount of time you'll spend continuing to fight and the amount of money this new fight will cost you. There's also the very real risk that you may lose your malpractice case. In that event, you've lost not only the time and money from the first case, but from the malpractice case, too. Talk about throwing good money after bad!

Some people are afraid that if they sue an attorney for malpractice, they'll never be able to get another attorney to represent them. While it's true that the attorney you sued is unlikely to want to represent you again (and would you want that attorney anyway?), there are plenty of attorneys who will be willing to represent you even if you've lost a malpractice case. There is no database of "bad" clients that you'll land on if you file a malpractice suit. However, you probably don't want to discuss your past malpractice case with a prospective attorney. Hearing about your past bad experiences will not make an attorney want to work harder to make up for the lousy experiences you've had before. It's more likely that the attorney will think you're going to be a difficult client, and think twice about taking your case.

Instead, use your malpractice case as a learning experience. Make sure the mistakes that happened in that case aren't going to happen in your new case by telling the attorney what your concerns are—without going into detail about how awful your previous attorney was.

Withholding Fees

Your duty to pay your attorney is not connected to the attorney's duty to provide competent services; they're two separate things. Your attorney cannot use your non-payment of fees as a defense for his malpractice. Withholding fees from the attorney you're suing for malpractice is very common. So is a counterclaim from the attorney you're suing asking for payment of those withheld fees. (See Chapter 6 for a discussion of counter-plaintiffs and counter-defendants.)

If your attorney counterclaims for the money you owe for services, it's a good idea to ask the court to put your money into a court escrow account. Escrow accounts hold money so that neither side can take it until the court makes a decision. In some cases, if you win, the amount that you "owe" can be used to decrease the amount you get as damages from the malpractice in the judgment. This is called a *set off*.

Effect of Malpractice Suit on Appeal

Your malpractice suit has no real effect on any appeal you make to a higher court for review. You won't get more time to appeal, and you won't get any special consideration. In civil cases, if an attorney commits malpractice at trial, you're stuck with what he did for the purposes of the appeal. Unfortunately, you cannot get a new trial because of the malpractice. Worst of all, the appeals court will not accept an argument that you would have won the trial if it hadn't been for the malpractice, so you should win on appeal. The only things a civil appeals court reviews are the mistakes made by the court in interpreting and applying the law, not the mistakes made by attorneys.

The Least You Need to Know

- Malpractice requires that the attorney both performed badly and caused you injury.
- Violations of attorney ethical standards may justify malpractice claims if they also cause you injury.
- If there's no injury but attorney ethical standards were violated, you can file a grievance against the attorney.
- Your right to competent representation is separate from your duty to pay your attorney fees.

Alternatives to Filing Suit

While the main focus of this book is on lawsuits, three alternatives to lawsuits cannot be ignored. Negotiation happens throughout the entire process of litigation, and this part discusses the best ways to negotiate to preserve your position. Many courts now require mediation before you can even proceed with your lawsuit; you'll learn what mediation is and how it can help and hurt your case. Finally, more and more contracts you sign require that you use the true alternative to a lawsuit, arbitration, to resolve any problems you have because of the contract. You'll discover this hidden solution to conflicts and how to work with it in this part.

Negotiation

In This Chapter

- Negotiation defined
- Successful negotiating techniques
- Dealing with difficult people
- When to settle

At the heart of every lawsuit is a problem that one of the parties wants to solve. Usually, they've tried to solve it themselves before going to a lawyer and taking the case to court. Without being aware of it, most people try to solve these problems through the process of negotiation, whether it's formal or informal.

What Is Negotiation?

Negotiation is a back-and-forth process of two or more parties offering possible solutions to a problem. It is often very informal, and done without much thought. If you're owed money, you contact the person who owes you the money and try to work out when you'll get paid. Maybe you'll offer to wait until the end of the week for your payment. Negotiation can be as simple and unglamorous as that.

Negotiation also can get much more formalized and rigid. As other people get involved in solving the problem through some form of negotiation, the name of the process changes, as do the rules governing the process. For example, mediation, discussed in Chapter 19, is a form of assisted negotiation. Arbitration, discussed in Chapter 20, and even lawsuits can be seen as a form of very formalized assisted negotiation, because they're both basically a back-and-forth process of two or more parties trying to solve a problem.

Ultimately, negotiation is an opportunity to try to resolve a problem. It may be easier to think of negotiation as the opposite of a trial. In a trial, a decision is made for you; in a negotiation, you get to make the decision.

What's the Secret to Successful Negotiation?

The secret is that there is no secret. There is an old saying, "Pigs get fat; hogs get slaughtered." That means that you have to advocate for yourself, but you also have to keep in mind that the other side needs to eat as well, so to speak. If you act like a hog by trying to get too much out of the negotiation, you're likely to end up with nothing.

Negotiation is often seen as very intimidating, and something for which there must be a secret method of success. This is because some people always seem to get what they want by negotiation with very little trouble. There are tons of books, courses, and Ph.D. dissertations written about how to be one of those people who consistently succeed in negotiation.

Before we go any further, we have to recognize something here: success is relative. Someone can claim to be a successful negotiator, but what does that actually mean? If someone owes you $1,000, and the other side acknowledges that they owe $1,000, is that a successful negotiation? Or is that simply acknowledging an undisputed truth?

What if there's a dispute over whether or not the money is actually owed? What if there's a condition that has to be met, and there's a dispute over whether the condition has been met?

Boiled down to three main principles, here are the big secrets to success in negotiation:

- Help the other side understand how it is to their advantage to resolve a dispute under certain terms.

- Remember, getting too greedy will leave you with nothing.

- Know your alternatives.

Many books and studies talk about power in negotiation, and how to change the perception of who has the power. Power in negotiation is essentially having what the other side wants or needs. If the other side has something that you desperately want or need, the key is to put aside your feelings of desperation and think about what the other side could get in exchange that they might want—or want to avoid—as much as or more than what you want. That's how you can shift the power from one side to another.

Don't Limit Yourself to Solving the Current Problem

The biggest mistake in negotiation is limiting yourself to the current problem in front of you. By expanding the definition of the problem, you can bring in other elements that might give you power or leverage for negotiation.

IN THE KNOW

Professional negotiators bring up secondary issues to help change the focus of the dispute, and you can, too. Point out how one solution can solve more than one problem, and you're more likely to sell the other side on that particular solution.

How Can I Get Help Negotiating?

Because of the importance of the topic you're negotiating about, you're likely to feel somewhat stressed, to say the least. Stress often has a very negative effect on your ability to perform the way you'd like to, so it makes sense to get some help. At the least, the help will make you feel more confident. Some people feel more comfortable having someone else, like a lawyer, do the negotiating for them. The downside is that this is one of the more expensive options.

Another way to get help is to check your local adult-education course offerings. There are often classes in negotiation that might give you good ideas for how to go about solving your problem through negotiation. The big plus is that you'll be able to discuss your current situation with an expert in negotiation as you go along, and get suggestions. The big minus is that the course might not be offered in time to give you the help you need. You might consider contacting the instructor through the group offering the course, to see if you could have a few hours of private instruction.

Community groups with names like the community ombudsman or mediation centers also offer assistance in negotiation. Try contacting local community centers to see what programs they offer. Also try contacting your county and state governments;

many of them have received grants for negotiation and mediation programs. You might be surprised to find the resources available to you.

Finally, and probably most simply, you can practice your negotiation skills and techniques with a friend. Have your friend pretend to be the other side, and try your offers and counteroffers on them before you try them out in real life. It's definitely worthwhile because not only will it give you more ideas for how to approach your negotiation, it will also increase your confidence. Practice tends to do that.

Negotiating Techniques

There are as many negotiating techniques as there are people and personalities. The most successful techniques tend to work regardless of who uses them. This means that because yelling works well for some but doesn't work for all, it's not a consistently successful technique and isn't one that can be recommended.

The major techniques have to do with looking at the problem and thinking about as many different solutions as possible. This gives you the most flexibility in discussions, and keeps you from being stuck in one spot with nowhere to go. The difficulty is that there is no technique that guarantees you'll get the thing that's most important to you.

Is There Always More Pie?

The first technique is based on the theory that most people see things as they are on the surface, with definite limits. They think of the options in front of them as slices of pie; if there are eight slices of pie, and they take five, then there are only three slices left for the other side. This is officially referred to as a "zero-sum game," because once you've given out all the pieces of pie, there are zero left.

Rather than seeing the pie as all there is, the first negotiating technique suggests that you make the pie bigger. If you can't make the pie bigger, add ice cream. Heat the pie up. Do something to increase the available goodies. The technique is often referred to as "increasing the pie," "avoiding a zero-sum game," or a "win-win scenario." If you only see an either-or, limited solution, there can only be one winner. But by changing the focus of your negotiation from the original, limited scope to a broader vista, you broaden the available rewards, and create the possibility that more than one winner exists. Ultimately, you are showing the other side why it would be to their advantage (and yours) to resolve a case.

The problem, of course, is that sometimes there is nothing more you can think of that would make the pie bigger. Some things really are either/or, where there's only so much to go around. For example, if you're fighting over who gets Grandma's pearl necklace, either you have the pearls or you don't.

The best you can hope for in such situations is compromise. People try to "make the pie bigger" in these circumstances by figuring out why the people want the pearls, and trying to address those desires by compromising. Maybe the pearls can be split up and made into new jewelry so that everyone has some of them. Maybe the pearls can be shared on an agreed-upon schedule. Creativity is key, and so is being reasonable and recognizing the other side's interests. By coming up with a compromise that recognizes the other side's interests, you are showing the other side why it would be to their advantage (and yours) to resolve a case.

Unfortunately, there may be situations in which you're absolutely convinced that there is no "fair" negotiated alternative in your mind. It might involve physical danger, or it might involve an inability to work with the other side. In cases like this, there is no negotiation possible as far as you're concerned. You'll simply need to accumulate enough evidence to prove to the court that the law and the facts are on your side and you must win. This is why you need to know the alternative—which in every case includes going to trial.

Have Alternatives Available

Alternatives don't just make the pie bigger; they are a major tactic in your overall negotiation plan. For one thing, the bigger the number of alternative solutions you can come up with, the more likely you are to have an outcome you can live with. For another, the more alternatives you can present, the more likely it is that you can hide your true goal from the other side. You'll give them things to refuse and shoot down without putting your basic needs in jeopardy.

Here's how to use this technique. Make a list of all the things you want to get out of the situation, from the reasonable to the unreasonable. Think about why you believe that the reasonable items really are reasonable, and why the other side might disagree. This helps you get in their head and predict what they're going to do during the process. Come up with answers to their reasons to deny you your reasonable requests.

Now think about why some of your alternatives are unreasonable. Are they something the other side will never agree to? Why? Do they seem too greedy—do they turn you into a hog? Is there a way to phrase your outrageous request to make it seem perfectly normal? This gives you a wider range of things to ask for in negotiation, and also gives you things that the other side can refuse. This is where you give the other side something to say no to without hurting your position. These wild requests, phrased reasonably, give the other side something to focus on and feel that they've won when you give in.

Any situation in which a party has a deeply held belief that there is only one proper solution means that they're not likely to see alternatives. Actually, they will see alternatives; they just won't believe they're valid or just. The key to these kinds of negotiations is to find the underlying issues to create a compromise. The accused in a sexual harassment case won't see any compromise as possible, because he believes it would show he was guilty of really bad conduct. The accuser won't see any compromise as possible, because she believes it would show she was lying about the harassment. The underlying issues here are public honor and future credibility. How can those issues be satisfied for both parties? Creativity is definitely called for here, and a tailor-made solution is required.

Having alternatives available really is the professional's winning strategy for negotiation. Even in the few situations where there is no appealing alternative, recognizing that there are still plenty of alternatives out there will help you maneuver to the best available alternative if you don't get what you really want. The key is to not get your heart stuck on just one solution, if at all possible.

Know Your Worst-Case Scenario

What's the worst thing that can happen at the end of this negotiation? This is an important question to answer honestly, because this is what you want most to avoid. You may not want the other side to know what you believe is the worst possible outcome. They're likely to hold it over your head as a negotiating tactic, saying, "If you don't agree with me on this point, your worst case will happen."

Again, think of alternatives. What will you do if the worst case actually happens? The old saying, "Plan for the worst, but hope for the best," is an excellent tactic in negotiation. In fact, try to think of several possible reactions and strategies to deal with the worst case. If you've got a way—or more than one way—out of the worst, you'll have greater confidence throughout the negotiations.

JUST THE FACTS

Creating alternatives to the worst-case scenario is important enough that professional negotiators even have a jargon-y phrase for it. They call it the "best alternative to a negotiated agreement," or BATNA.

It's important to recognize that part of the worst-case scenario involves feeling emotional. The feeling of loss is very powerful, and is often accompanied by a sense of humiliation. People go to great lengths to avoid those twin emotional crushers, and often react very badly when they feel them. Plan for a period of upset after negotiations are over, even if you've "won." For one thing, no one ever really wins everything they want in a negotiation. For another, many people resent that they had to argue or negotiate to get what they believe they should've gotten in the first place without having to make a fuss. That leads to a sense of anger and loss even when you come out on top. If you know it's coming, you're better able to deal with it when the emotional upheaval hits.

Along those lines, remember that no matter how obnoxious the other side is, they fear loss and humiliation, too. If at all possible, give people a way out of the conflict that doesn't emphasize that they've lost or that they've humiliated themselves, even if you desperately want to hurt them. You're more likely to get what you want and need from someone who isn't looking for revenge for the hurt you inflicted on them. Even after the negotiation is concluded, you still have to deal with the other side to get whatever was promised. Try to set things up so that those dealings will be as smooth as possible.

Start High—or Low

The biggest mistake people make in negotiations is failing to recognize when they are in a negotiation. If you start out with a bottom line, there is no negotiation. It's a "yes" or "no" situation. If you don't get what you want, your only other option is litigation. This is not where you want to be.

Some people have trouble with this concept, because they feel it is dishonest not to tell the other person everything about their position. But not revealing everything up front is not being "dishonest." Instead, it's the best way to get you to where you honestly want to be.

If you can at all avoid doing so, never start with what you're willing to settle for. Ask for more, so you can reduce your request and still get what you need. Offer less, so you can increase your offer without giving up everything. Often, the person who makes the first offer gets the most benefit out of the negotiation. It's probably because the first, high offer defines the upper boundary of where the negotiation is going to go.

There is no hard-and-fast rule about how much more or less you should begin with. You'll read suggestions that you should start 20 percent higher, or 40 percent higher. If only it were that easy! It's impossible to give a guaranteed successful starting point that always works. The starting point is different for each situation. That's why books are written with titles like *The Art of the Deal*. Negotiation is an art, not a science, and the more negotiations you enter into, the better you'll get at sensing where to start. Of course, that's not terribly helpful when you've got an important negotiation coming up and you don't know where to begin.

Here's what will help: you have already come up with alternatives. Start with your best alternative, the one that gives you the most. Who knows? You might get it! The big problem is that if you start much too high, the other side may well think you are nuts, and walk away. You might then have to lower your price, so to speak, but now you have lost credibility. If you know what you are dealing with, you will have the ability to justify your request and withstand the criticism.

Another potential pitfall with starting the negotiation too high is that you'll anger the other side into stopping negotiations, or get the other side so mad that they increase their own starting point beyond anything reasonable. The fact is that the other side will get angry no matter what you offer, unless your offer is to roll over and give them everything they want. Let them get angry. It's part of the process. Not to be all pop-psych, but you're not responsible for how they feel. Besides, when they're angry, you've got the upper hand.

How should you respond to their reaction to your offer? Whatever you do, don't start apologizing for your "unrealistic" offer! If you absolutely feel that you have to respond to their emotions, you could say something like, "I didn't realize you'd feel that way." Immediately follow up with "What do you think would be more reasonable?" Often, their response will be "I don't know, but not that!" You can start offering some of your less desirable alternatives. Chances are, they haven't prepared alternatives themselves, so you'll be in the enviable position of directing the negotiation along your chosen lines.

You can also use this phase of the negotiation to get them to start giving you possible alternatives, and to ask them to define their priorities. This will give you an idea of where their limits are, so you can tailor your alternatives into something they'll accept. This is another professional negotiator's technique that has a double benefit:

it's likely to result in both sides getting a better outcome than if you don't ask for their input. If you can maneuver things so it sounds like you're accepting their alternative and their priorities, you've done a top-level job of negotiation.

PITFALLS

Don't get locked into a particular solution. Falling in love with one answer and sticking to it is a recipe for disappointment in negotiation. The more alternatives you can come up with where you feel like you win, the happier you'll be at the end of the negotiation.

Dealing With Unreasonable People

Almost all negotiation advice assumes you're dealing with someone who can be bargained with. Truthfully, when people say they have to deal with an unreasonable person, what they're really saying is that the person is being stubborn about giving them what they want. They might also mean that the person they're dealing with is rude. Face the fact that many people are just plain obnoxious in negotiation situations. They won't go as fast as you want, or in the direction you want, but they can be bargained with.

How to Deal With Obnoxiousness

Dealing with obnoxious behavior is part of the process of negotiation. The best advice available is to stick to your plan of negotiation and recognize that the other side's rudeness and obnoxiousness is probably a strategy to get you to give in. There are some people whose negotiation style is to bully the other side into submission. They stick with it because it often works. People compare how important the object of the negotiation is to them with the unpleasantness of the negotiation itself, and just give up.

Being aware that obnoxiousness is a strategy helps. As mentioned previously, sticking to your own strategies of having realistic alternatives to offer and work with is a big help, too. Sometimes pointing out the rudeness of the behavior can stop the other side for a moment, as can refusing to deal with them until they lower their voice. Staying calm while the other side is screaming is difficult, but it can really unsettle someone who's used to getting under people's skin with their bullying. Responding in a composed, calm way to their hysteria really upsets them, and makes them look even worse to any bystanders. On the other hand, some obnoxious people actually respond best to people who yell back, strangely enough. Try that if the calm, collected approach isn't working, and if you're comfortable with it.

Whatever you do, don't start swearing or name-calling, even if the other side does, and even if you think it's the best way to get them to react the way you want them to. When you have to report the negotiations to someone like a judge, it helps to be the one who acted like a responsible, rational adult. If the other side is really difficult to deal with in person, you might want to suggest that all offers and counteroffers be made in writing. Last, if the person is really horrible for you to deal with, hire a lawyer to deal with them.

Dealing With Impossibility

The reality is that there are plenty of people out there who are genuinely unreasonable, in the sense that they aren't able to bargain reasonably. They might have an untreated mental illness, or be too intellectually challenged to think logically. Sometimes, no matter what your best effort is, it's not going to be good enough. Here's how to handle those situations.

The most important thing in dealing with completely unreasonable people is to make sure you yourself are physically safe. If you believe that the person you're in a dispute with is violent, contact the police and ask for help. You may need to obtain a personal protection order, sometimes also known as a restraining order, to keep that person away from you throughout the conflict and afterward. These orders are successful in protecting people in the vast majority of cases.

Keep track of everything that happens throughout the negotiation. You should do that anyway in every negotiation, but it's particularly important when you're dealing with an unreasonable person. Your record of the reasonable offers you've made and the crazy responses you've gotten may be very helpful in getting a court to help resolve the problem quickly.

Recognize that some of the strategies that work with ordinarily obnoxious people might not work with people who are unreasonable. For example, moving the negotiations from spoken to written form often works well with the obnoxious, but your unreasonable opponent might not be able to focus enough to read or write. Remaining calm while the other side blusters works well with people who can control themselves; people who are out of control can't change their behavior no matter what you do. Accept that there is no special technique guaranteed to work, and do your best to stay focused on finding a solution.

A lot of the art of dealing with the unreasonable is accepting that you're not going to have an easy time of it, and staying focused on what you can do, rather than on what you can't. Getting outside help is particularly important when you're dealing with someone who's completely impossible. Expect that the outside help will cost you more, in both time and money, because the outside help won't have any magic wand that will suddenly turn the crazy person sane, or make the process go any faster. The best the outside help will do is shield you from dealing with the person as much or as closely as you were before—and to be honest, that's a lot.

Negotiation as Part of the Lawsuit

All of the negotiation you've gone through before you decided to file suit is going to be repeated as part of the suit. As discussed in Chapter 19 on mediation, and also in Chapter 8 on the process of lawsuits, you're likely to be required to participate in some form of assisted negotiation at an early point in the process.

Don't be surprised if suggestions you made during your informal negotiations are made again, and even accepted. Sometimes, having the reality of the time and money of a lawsuit in front of a person makes him rethink things he previously didn't want to consider. This can work both for and against you, as you may be the one who ends up deciding to go with a solution you previously discarded.

No matter what the requirements of the court are for some form of assisted negotiation, you and your attorney will be negotiating with the other side throughout the litigation process. As both sides find the facts through the process of discovery, offers will be made to settle, or to end the lawsuit by compromise. The new facts you find through discovery will affect your negotiation and may change the alternatives you are willing to consider.

How Do I Know When to Settle?

There is no special test to use to decide when it's time to settle the lawsuit. There are plenty of questions to ask yourself, and things to consider, and they're the same considerations you'd have in deciding to agree to any negotiated conclusion to a dispute.

The first step is always to consider your alternatives. When you're thinking about settling a lawsuit, your major alternative is going through to trial. The thing you always have to take into account is that you can't guarantee any particular outcome for a lawsuit. That's what makes decisions about settlement so difficult; they're basically a gamble.

Here are some questions to think about in deciding whether or not to settle:

- How likely do you and your attorney think a win at trial really is?

- Is the offered settlement within the range of your acceptable alternatives?

- Is it financially smarter to take the offer on the table than to continue to spend money on the trial?

- How will you feel if you don't continue on to trial?

- How will settling affect your business or career?

- How will settling affect your relationships?

Some people avoid settlement because they want a full-on, court-ordered win. Others don't want to settle because they're afraid it makes them look as if they didn't believe they could win their case. The reality is that settlement is just another part of the process of solving your dispute. Settling doesn't mean your side would've lost, nor is a settlement less of a victory if you get something that's within your range of acceptable alternatives.

The most difficult thing about settlement is the same thing that's difficult about all phases of negotiation: the pull of emotion over logic. You've spent a lot of time, energy, and resources on this dispute, and that creates a major emotional investment. For most people, their response to a settlement offer is mostly emotional, and the emotion is often anger. This is normal, but not helpful in the long run.

Before you respond to the settlement offer, give yourself time to cool down, even if it's only five minutes. Frequently, settlement offers are made "on the courthouse steps," outside the courtroom just before the trial begins. That doesn't give you much time to think or calm down, but you'll certainly have a few minutes to step away from the other side and talk to your attorney about the offer. Hopefully, you've done your homework and come up with a wide range of alternatives so that this offer falls somewhere within the range of what you've already considered. If it is, you'll have a good idea of what the advantages and disadvantages of accepting the settlement offer will be.

Instead of focusing on your emotions *during* the settlement, consider how you'll feel *as a result of* the decision. Your emotions after the decision will be affected by how the decision affects your day-to-day life. If you have less money than you need to live on as a result of the settlement, you'll be angry, stressed, and generally unhappy. But notice that your anger and unhappiness are likely to be a direct result of the financial and other consequences of the settlement, not necessarily because of the fact that you settled. Focus on the end result and how it will make you feel, not on how it makes you feel while you're settling.

The Least You Need to Know

- You'll be negotiating throughout the litigation process, so don't shy away from it.
- Know all your alternatives before you start negotiating.
- Expect obnoxious behavior from the other side.
- Don't be afraid to settle when it makes sense.

Mediation

In This Chapter

- Mediation explained
- Types of mediation
- The good and the bad side of mediation
- How to find mediation services

A trend over the last 25 years has been to move away from solving problems through litigation and the courts and toward alternatives. A whole field has developed, called Alternative Dispute Resolution, or ADR, which tries to solve problems or disputes through alternatives like mediation and arbitration. Mediation, the most common and least expensive form of ADR, is discussed in this chapter.

What Is Mediation?

Mediation puts a third party in the middle of someone else's dispute or conflict to help the original parties solve their problem. If you think about it, that's sort of like what a court does: puts a third party—a judge or a jury—in the middle of the plaintiff and defendant's conflict, so that the judge or jury can solve the problem. The big difference between what a court does and what mediation does is that the court solves the problem for the parties; mediation helps the parties solve the problem for themselves.

The big focus in mediation is in helping the parties come to a compromise. Both sides have to be willing to move from their original positions in order for mediation to work. Even if the parties aren't willing to shift at first, sometimes the process of mediation can help people see the advantages to changing their position.

Often, mediation is a good next step to offer as part of a negotiation. It can help people feel that the dispute is being taken seriously. It can also help to bring some perspective to the problem by allowing a fair third party to make suggestions and help each party see the way the land lies.

The way mediation works varies depending on the style of the mediator, or the person providing the mediation service. One of the most common ways for a mediation session to work is for both parties to get together with the mediator at a neutral place. This might be the mediator's office, a public facility like a library meeting room, or a courthouse meeting room. The mediator will ask each side to tell his story, often starting with the person who's sort of in the plaintiff's position, having brought the problem up. That person tells his side of the story, without interruption. The mediator might repeat back the main points of the story to make sure he's got them right. Then the other person tells her side of the story. Again, the mediator might repeat the main points of the story to be sure he's clear on them.

At this point, techniques vary. Some mediators will keep both parties in the room and start suggesting solutions to see how the parties react. Others will ask one side to leave the room so the mediator can speak privately to one side to suggest a solution. The mediator will then ask the first person to leave and ask the second person to come back in, and suggest the same solution to that person. Some mediators put the parties in two separate rooms, and go back and forth between the rooms themselves.

The reason mediation sometimes works better than plain negotiation is that the mediator is neutral. The mediator doesn't get angry, doesn't get offended, and doesn't have any real interest in the case, other than helping to try to resolve it. Because the mediator has no emotional involvement in the process, it's easier for him to focus on solving the problem. When one party expresses anger over a suggested solution, the mediator doesn't get angry back or make the new solution even tougher. He just waits until the anger blows itself out, gets the actual response from the person, and moves on.

Mediation can also work better than ordinary negotiation because sometimes the parties both want to resolve an issue, but their own personal issues make it too difficult to try to settle the case. All they really need is some help. For example, the parties may be so angry at each other that they can't even be in the same room together. However, if the mediator uses the technique of keeping the parties apart during the process, the anger each party naturally feels and expresses doesn't end up creating a sort of loop, each feeding the other party's anger.

When the mediator makes a suggestion that one party agrees to, he checks with the other party to see if he can get them to agree to the same thing. If he can't, he asks what needs to change for an agreement to happen. This goes on, back and forth, until an agreement is reached. There's no telling how long this will take, as it depends on the individual parties.

PITFALLS

Don't let the mediation drag on so long that you miss the ability to file your case within the statute of limitations! You can even use the deadline as a help in mediation, to increase the pressure on the other side.

Sometimes the parties cannot come to an agreement. No matter how good the mediator is, if one side absolutely refuses to give an inch, there can't be a fair resolution. Even if you think the other side isn't going to give a quarter of an inch, much less an inch, mediation is worthwhile if only to get a feeling for how the other side is thinking. The other side may accept bits and pieces that never seemed possible, or they may even agree to end the entire dispute. You'll never know unless you try!

What you get at the end of a successful mediation process is an agreement. This agreement is basically a contract, which you should write out clearly, including consequences for either side's violation of the contract. You might want to use an attorney to write up the contract to conclude the mediation, or you might let the mediator write up the agreement. Double-check the agreement to make sure it reflects your understanding of what you agreed to throughout the mediation. Don't sign it unless it's exactly what you wanted. It's okay if that throws you into another round of mediation! Better to be clear that you're getting what you agreed to than to be stuck with something that doesn't solve the problem to your satisfaction.

Voluntary Mediation

Mediation is often very successful in resolving disputes between parties. It's significantly cheaper than filing a lawsuit, and much faster, too. There are no penalties for failing to come to an agreement, and you can continue on to the courts and a trial if you like. Having gone through voluntary mediation won't excuse you from court-ordered mediation if your local courts require it as part of the process of litigation. On the plus side, voluntary mediation will give you a better idea of where the other side is coming from for the purposes of negotiation throughout the lawsuit, if it does come to that.

Court-Ordered Mediation

Because mediation is such a good alternative to resolving problems through the courts, many courts have decided to reduce their overwhelming caseloads by ordering parties to go into mediation before bringing their dispute before the court. It's often a part of the court rules (as discussed in Chapter 8) that you have to take your case to mediation after you file the lawsuit but before the court schedules a trial. It's very common for mediation to be required for small claims court cases, as they are frequently easily resolved through mediation.

The court may require that you use the court's official mediation services in order to fulfill the mediation requirement. Some courts have full-time mediators on staff; many others use attorney volunteers to act as mediators. If you believe that the mediator is not neutral, first let the mediator know, and tell her why you believe she is not neutral. For example, if the mediator knows the other side, she might not be neutral toward either side. She might favor the other side—or might favor you because she knows too much about the other side. The mediator should be able to excuse herself if there is such a conflict. If you believe there is such a conflict, and the mediator won't excuse herself, contact the court clerk's office or the judge's clerk immediately. Ask to be assigned a new mediator, and explain why. You may have to file a motion to request a new mediator, or submit a written request for a new mediator. Usually, a "feeling" that the mediator doesn't like you, or favors the other side, isn't enough to show bias. You need to show actual circumstances, behavior, or words that can be legitimately seen as bias.

IN THE KNOW

Some people actually prefer a mediator to have ties with one side, thinking that the inside knowledge they have will make them better able to persuade that side to be reasonable!

With formal court-ordered mediation, as with ordinary mediation, there is always the option to go to trial if the mediation process doesn't work. Generally, there's no penalty for not settling the case through mediation, and you can continue on through litigation with no problems. However, this means there is no incentive, other than trying to avoid the time and expense of a trial, to solve the dispute through mediation. Because of that, some courts have moved to a different form of quasi-mediation, often called "case evaluation."

Court-Ordered Case Evaluation

Case evaluation is more like arbitration, discussed in Chapter 20, than mediation, because a decision is made by a third party rather than come to by agreement between the original parties. However, because some courts use case evaluation and call it mediation, it will be discussed here as well as in Chapter 20.

Whatever it's called, case evaluation usually has a panel of attorneys, experienced in the area of law that your lawsuit falls under, who review both sides of the case. They then give the case a dollar value. This isn't a prediction as to what the case is worth or what will happen if the case goes to trial. It is a dollar amount that they hope both parties can accept to settle the case. It might be less than the one side wants, or more than the other side is willing to pay, but it's supposed to be a compromise.

The evaluators come up with their decision based on two things. The first is a document called a "case-evaluation summary" or "mediation summary" prepared by each side. It summarizes the facts that each side intends to prove and the cases and statutes that support each side. The second thing the evaluator's prediction is based on is a short presentation by each side, which sort of hits the high points of the summary. The evaluators can also ask questions of each side at the presentation.

Using the summary and the presentation, the panel then discusses the case's strengths and weaknesses. Based on their experience, they arrive at a case-evaluation figure. The announcement of the panel's decision might happen the same day as the presentation, or it might be mailed to the parties some time later.

What gives this process more bite than ordinary mediation is that there are often penalties if it turns out the party who rejected the case-evaluation figure ends up with a judgment that is worse for them than if they had accepted the case evaluation. The penalties usually come in the form of having to pay the other side's attorney fees, which can run into the tens of thousands of dollars, or some other monetary measure of punishment. That's a real incentive to carefully examine your evaluation of your case's strengths and weaknesses and compare them to what the evaluators thought of them.

Mediation-Arbitration

The last variant on mediation services is mediation followed by arbitration, called mediation-arbitration, or "med-arb." If the parties can't come to an agreement through the mediation process instead of going to court, they go to *binding arbitration*. Although arbitration will be discussed in greater detail in Chapter 20, basically arbitration is a non-court-based trial. A third party, called an arbitrator, acts like a judge and makes a decision in favor of one side or the other. With binding arbitration, the case will not go to court at all.

> **DEFINITION**
>
> **Binding arbitration** results in a final decision that cannot be brought to a trial court for review or retrial. The choice between binding arbitration and nonbinding arbitration is made at the time you sign the contract agreeing to arbitration in the first place.

Some people think med-arb gives the parties a greater incentive to work things out through mediation, so they can avoid having a decision made for them. Other people see the mediation portion of med-arb as a sort of formality that they just have to get through in order to get to the arbitration. Whichever position you take, the mediation portion of med-arb works exactly like any other mediation. A third-party mediator tries to get the parties to come to agreement, going back and forth between them, trying to get them to see each other's point of view. The difference, of course, comes if the mediation isn't successful, when the parties move on to binding arbitration instead of a trial.

Do I Need a Lawyer for This?

Typically, a lawyer isn't required or even allowed in traditional voluntary mediation. For court-ordered mediation or case evaluation, a lawyer isn't necessary but can be very helpful, especially for case evaluation. One of the things that makes traditional voluntary mediation so attractive is that you really don't need a lawyer. You can easily and effectively represent yourself in the traditional mediation process. The only outside party you'll have to pay is the mediator, and you might not even have to do that. You might be eligible to use free community mediation services, which brings your out-of-pocket cost to zero.

What Are the Pros and Cons of Mediation?

Mediation is almost all upside and next to no downside. When mediation works, it's very cheap and very fast. Your problem is solved and you can move on with your life. You avoid the costs of litigation and save a great deal of time and stress. What could be better than that?

Mediation also enables you to work with the other side to create your own solution, rather than having a solution imposed on you from the outside. This gives you more control over the final decision than what you would have in arbitration or the courts. If it's done right, and both sides feel they came to a fair agreement, people often stick to the decision made through mediation better than they do to an outside decision, like one made through arbitration or the courts.

The downside comes when mediation doesn't solve your problem. The time you thought you'd save through mediation was instead wasted, because you still have a problem that will take still more time to solve. Whatever money you spent on mediation, such as any fees charged by the mediation service or the mediator, now gets added to the money this problem is costing you. Worse than that, though, is that through mediation, you might have revealed more about your position and strategies than you wanted to in an effort to reach an agreement. That might make later negotiation more difficult.

Mediation Services

There are many professional mediation services available, as well as plenty of volunteer associations that provide mediation services. It might take a bit of research to find the service that's right for you, but it's well worth the effort in order to resolve your problem quickly and effectively.

Community Mediation

The first place to try for finding mediation services is within your community. Many charitable organizations have set up neighborhood mediation services that are available for free or for very little cost. These are particularly good for disputes you might have with neighbors, as it's a much lower-key process than going to court, even small claims court. When you have to work with or live near the people you share a problem with, it's often better for the relationship in the long run to try a relatively nonconfrontational way of solving the problem. Community mediation tries very hard to help you maintain a relationship with the people on the other side of the conflict.

Check with community centers; your town, city, or county government; and charitable groups like the United Way or the various YMCA-type organizations. They're likely to have contacts with the groups you're looking for.

Professional Mediators

Retired judges, attorneys, and social workers often start mediation businesses in an effort to help people solve problems while the problems are still relatively small. They might have had special training through classes or seminars, or they might just rely on their years of experience helping people solve problems on the job. The advantage to having a retired judge or an attorney as a mediator is that they're likely to be able to put a fairly accurate value on the case as far as what you'd get in court. Based on their experience and authority, they can often persuade both sides that their judgment is correct.

JUST THE FACTS

Many retired judges go on to become mediators or arbitrators. They're easier to check out than other mediators or arbitrators because you can research their history in public documents. Plus, you can easily find out about their reputation based on the kind of behavior they've shown over their years on the bench.

The disadvantage to using a retired judge is that if you really want to do a classic-style mediation, you want a mediator who can help you explore different solutions to your problem. Mediation isn't supposed to be about someone coming in and imposing a solution on you, which is what judges are used to doing.

For that reason, before you hire a professional mediator, ask what her background is and how she runs her mediations. If you'd prefer someone who will run the mediation more like a trial, definitely go for a retired judge. If you'd rather go for a more holistic, win-win problem-solving approach, be sure that's the mediator's style.

PITFALLS

Although there are associations for professional mediators, mediators aren't licensed, so belonging to an association is no guarantee of quality service.

When interviewing potential mediators, ask lots of questions and ask for references. If it's at all possible, talk to the references to see how they feel about how the mediation went. Be sure to ask not only the people you contact as references but also the mediator herself a lot of questions about the mediator's style and what she does to get her results. And don't forget to ask about the money. Does the mediator charge a flat fee or an hourly fee? Is there a separate fee for the meeting place? What happens if the agreement falls through? Will the mediator meet with you again at no charge, or will there be a separate charge for that service?

Online Mediation

There are two kinds of online mediation. The first is used when you know who is responsible, but you're still arguing about the amount. This is called a "blind-bidding" form of mediation. As of this writing, it's limited to disputes individuals have with large corporations or to parties represented by attorneys. It works like this: the parties sign up with the online mediation service, and send in "bids" that are the amount of money for which each side is willing to settle. Most services allow you a limited number of bidding or submission rounds.

The service keeps the bidding secret from each side, which is why it's called "blind" bidding. The parties can agree ahead of time to settle if the bids are within a specific range of each other, whether the range is a percentage or measured in actual dollars. When that range is reached, the difference is split and a settlement is declared. If the bids never get close enough to reach a settlement, either or both parties can walk away from the process. The other side will never know how little you would have settled for because every offer, or bid, remains secret.

Ordinarily, the corporation or insurance company pays the majority of the fees for this kind of service. Most of the time, individuals only pay a fee if a settlement is reached. The amount that an individual would pay is generally based on the amount of the settlement. The range of payment fees is from $100 to $1,000, with the lower end for settlements under $5,000.

The second kind of online mediation is a more traditional back-and-forth with a third party in the middle. This kind of mediation can take place in a chat room or via e-mail. Online mediation is particularly helpful when the parties are physically far apart. Most of these online programs focus on resolving disputes with online merchants. Those tend to be situations where one side is thousands of miles away from the other, and the two parties may never have even met. Fees tend to be relatively low, around $50 to start, and can go up depending on the amount of time spent on the mediation or the amount of the settlement. There are many more traditional back-and-forth online mediation services available than there are blind-bidding mediation services. This may be because blind-bidding mediation involves specialized software, for which one company holds a patent.

Online mediation is an excellent solution to the problem of settling disputes that arise online. You don't have to travel to get to the courts of another state or try to learn the rules of that court. Not to mention that you can experience the entire mediation process in your pajamas if you choose, and no one will be the wiser. The downside to online mediation is that if you don't come to some kind of settlement, you've still got a long-distance problem that requires much more time and money to settle than the same problem would locally. That's actually more of a downside to getting involved with anything online than it is a direct result of online mediation; if the transaction goes bad, it's a long-distance transaction, not a local one, and the consequences are long-distance ones, too.

Can I Still Sue If This Doesn't Work Out?

The best thing about mediation, regardless of whether it's traditional voluntary mediation or court-ordered mediation or case evaluation, is that you absolutely can continue on with a lawsuit if the mediation doesn't work out. Remember that this isn't true for med-arb with binding arbitration, but otherwise, the courts are open to you after an unsuccessful attempt at mediation.

The Least You Need to Know

- Mediation brings a third party in to help the disputants solve their own problem without going to court.
- Mediation can be the fastest, cheapest way to solve a problem between parties.
- Be sure to follow the rules in court-ordered mediation.
- Mediation is often the first formal step to solving a problem; you can still sue if mediation doesn't work for you.

Arbitration

In This Chapter

- Arbitration explained
- How arbitration works
- The advantages and disadvantages of arbitration
- How to get your award enforced

Even though arbitration is considered a form of alternative dispute resolution, it's run very much like an actual court proceeding, only without a government judge and courthouse. It has been around for a long time, but it's only recently that it's become more widely used, especially in consumer-business transactions. Arbitration is often used in the sports world for the same reasons it's spreading into ordinary people's lives: it's fairly quick, it's relatively cheap, and most importantly, it can be kept confidential.

What Is Arbitration?

Arbitration is a way of solving disputes by bringing in a neutral third party, called an arbitrator, who listens to both sides of the problem and applies the appropriate law to come to a decision for one side or the other. If that sounds like a trial, that's because arbitration works a lot like a trial. It's done by agreement of the parties either at the time you sign a contract or after a dispute arises.

There are two main kinds of arbitration: nonbinding arbitration and binding arbitration.

Nonbinding Arbitration

With nonbinding arbitration, you're not required to abide by the arbitrator's final award. You're free to decide not to follow the award and to instead go to a regular government court to have your dispute resolved by a trial. Nonbinding arbitration is similar to case evaluation discussed in Chapter 19. An expert gives her opinion as to what the case is worth, and if the parties agree, the dispute is over. If they disagree, the parties can continue on to regular litigation. The freedom to try again with regular litigation is the major advantage to nonbinding arbitration. It's also the major disadvantage. If you go to trial after nonbinding arbitration, your costs increase significantly because you're essentially going through two trial-like procedures instead of one.

Binding Arbitration

Most contracts you sign that include arbitration for resolving disputes are for binding arbitration, where you agree to abide by the arbitrator's final award whether you like it or not. If the arbitration award is binding, there are no further costs in trying the case again in front of a court. Arbitration is often specified in contracts specifically to avoid the high cost of litigation. By making the arbitration binding, the aim of lowering overall costs is more likely to be achieved.

There are subcategories of arbitration, which can be binding or nonbinding. For example, there is "bracketed" or "high-low" arbitration. This is used when the parties agree about what happened and who is responsible, but disagree about how much should be paid. A high dollar amount and a low dollar amount are set by the parties as "brackets" for the potential award. The party to be paid will get no less than the lower amount and no more than the higher amount, but might get something in between. Sometimes the arbitrator knows how much the bracketed or high-low amounts are, and sometimes he doesn't.

Another subcategory of arbitration is "pendulum" or "baseball" arbitration, in which the arbitrator can't come up with her own solution for the problem. Instead, she has to pick one side or the other to agree with. A further variant is called "night baseball arbitration," because the arbitrator is working in the dark as far as the actual amounts involved are concerned.

Regardless of the differences among types of arbitration, there are significant differences between a trial and arbitration. For one, the rules of procedure aren't set by the government. Instead, they're created by the groups that offer arbitration services, and may be different depending on which group you use. In many cases, the parties to the arbitration can even make up their own rules. Another difference is that in a trial, you're assigned a judge; in arbitration, you and the other side pick your arbitrator, who acts as a judge.

Another big difference between arbitration and a trial is that you don't get a judgment that can be enforced by the courts at the end of an arbitration. Instead, you end up with an *award*, which is the end result of the contract you signed that got you into arbitration in the first place. Whether you agreed to arbitration as part of a contract that you're arguing about now or agreed to arbitration later, agreeing to arbitration creates a contract that says you agree to be bound by the arbitrator's decision before you know what the decision is.

DEFINITION

An **award** is a new contract created at the end of the arbitration process. Awards are the arbitration version of a court's judgment.

This leads to another big difference between trials and arbitration: with a trial, if the other side doesn't follow the judge's order, the court can immediately order compliance. In arbitration, if the other side doesn't follow the arbitrator's award, you have to start a new lawsuit in a regular trial court to enforce the arbitration contract and its award.

The most significant legal difference between arbitration and trials is that you can't appeal the binding arbitration award the way you can appeal a court's judgment. For the most part, the only way to challenge the binding arbitration award is to claim there was fraud in the process of arbitration. A mistake in the way the arbitrator applied the law can't be challenged the way you can challenge a judge's mistake in applying the law.

What Types of Disputes Can Go Through Arbitration?

Almost any kind of dispute can be brought to arbitration, although some things are reserved solely for the courts. For example, only a court can clear up the title to a piece of property, and only a court can grant a divorce. That doesn't mean other parts of those cases can't be arbitrated. For example, while only a court can grant a divorce, the parties can agree to arbitrate any property division disputes. Arbitration is particularly popular in business-to-business problems, and is especially good for international business transactions. It's proven useful in cases ranging from Internet domain name (.com) disputes to construction controversies to personal injury or torts.

You've probably agreed to arbitration yourself without being aware of it. For example, if you have an account with a stock broker, your agreement most likely requires you to settle any disputes through arbitration rather than the courts. Don't recall agreeing to that when you opened your account? That's where the controversy surrounding arbitration and consumers comes in. Your contract with the brokerage house, cell phone provider, or other large corporation was probably filled with fine print. You were probably presented with the contract as a "take it or leave it" proposition. Some consumer advocates see this as denying you the right to free access to the courts by forcing arbitration on you through a contract you couldn't negotiate. They also see arbitration as favoring big business, which has more experience and more financial investment in the arbitration process than individuals do.

The arbitration community disagrees, saying that arbitration is so much cheaper and faster than the courts that consumers come out ahead. They point to studies that show that business doesn't win at arbitration more than individuals do, and that most individuals who participate in arbitration would recommend the process to other people in the middle of a dispute.

Advantages of Arbitration

Arbitration is perceived by many, especially in the corporate community, as having significant advantages over ordinary trial court procedures. First, arbitration can be faster than a trial, and is often more flexible in terms of setting up times for the hearings.

IN THE KNOW

Unlike court hearings, which have to be held during business hours, you can request that arbitration proceedings be held after work or on weekends to fit your own schedule. This can save you money and work hassles.

Next, arbitration may be cheaper than a trial, in part because it may take less time and so cost less in terms of attorney fees.

Arbitration is often less stressful for the parties because while there is formality involved, there isn't the same stress as appearing in a courthouse, before a judge on the bench in his robes, with court officers with guns, in front of a jury and an open courtroom.

Because arbitration also allows the parties to create their own rules, it is in many ways easier to present your case. For example, typically, in an arbitration, the rules of evidence are relaxed so that the arbitrators can consider any evidence presented and put any weight or level of believability on that evidence. For example, suppose a doctor wrote a statement about his treatment of a person who was in an accident. Ordinarily, that doctor would have to be called to testify in court at a trial because the statement is hearsay. However, at an arbitration, the arbitrator could consider that statement without requiring the doctor to appear.

Another advantage is that arbitrators who have expertise in highly technical fields can be selected, which can make a hearing over a technical dispute go more smoothly.

Finally, and often most important to the participants, it's easier to make the arbitration proceedings private and confidential than it is a trial in open court. Mediation shares many of these advantages, and has the additional advantage of bringing the parties together to create a solution that can be a win for everyone. However, if the problem's too far gone for the parties to cooperate, you're right back at the kind of adversarial fight that trials—and arbitration—are designed to deal with. Like a regular court trial, arbitration is also more effective than mediation if solving the problem requires that facts be decided or the law be interpreted.

Disadvantages of Arbitration

Arbitration's disadvantages are similar to the disadvantages of going to trial, with a few arbitration-only issues thrown in the mix.

Like a trial in court, arbitration is adversarial, so it's not designed to help find a mutual solution to the parties' problem the way mediation is. It's intended to find one solution, which will favor only one side. This can be a disadvantage to both sides because the arbitrator's solution may not be one both sides are happy with, just as both sides may not be happy with a court's decision.

The major disadvantages to arbitration stem from the fact that arbitration is not a true court procedure. In the majority of arbitration cases, the arbitrator's decision is binding. Remember that means the parties cannot later get access to the courts for a judge or jury to decide the case. Not only that, there is no procedure available for appealing the award, unless you can show fraud. While this saves time and money, it doesn't contribute to a sense of fair play or allow much flexibility.

The cost of arbitration may not be as low as its advocates claim because of the requirement to pay for the arbitrators. For example, if arbitration is to be held through an already existing arbitration company, then money has to be spent to use those services, which in many cases are prohibitively expensive.

In some circumstances in the court system, it's possible to get your attorney fees paid; that isn't an option usually available in arbitration.

Discovery, discussed in Chapter 7, is usually much more limited in arbitration, so it's possible that important information may be overlooked.

There is also something called the "outrage" factor, which is sometimes lost in arbitrations. Sometimes a case is so outrageous that if it was in front of a jury, the jury likely would be so outraged at the other side that you could pretty much expect a huge award. In arbitrations, however, you are not dealing with a jury. Rather, you've got an arbitrator who has seen it all before. Because of that, he or she is not going to be so easily swayed or outraged, and so will be far less likely to be guided by passion.

Finally, there may be a perception of bias if the arbitration group or arbitrator gets a lot of business from a particular party. Although it's true that some judges are also perceived as biased, there are established methods for dealing with such problems that aren't permitted in arbitration.

Costs

Just as with court cases, there are costs associated with arbitration. Unfortunately, as with court cases, it's very difficult to predict exactly what the costs will be, but for very different reasons. With arbitration, this is because the costs vary widely from provider to provider and are often based on the value of the case as well as how long the case lasts. There is a perception that the cost of arbitration is lower than the cost of going to court. This may be true for cases worth little money that can be resolved quickly, but as more and more complex cases go to arbitration, the costs can quickly approach—or even exceed—the costs of going to trial.

Who Pays the Fees?

Typically, both sides have to pay half the fees in arbitration. However, some states, like California, have laws that require the retailer or business on the other side to bear the full cost of the arbitration if the consumer in an arbitration case is at 300 percent of the federal poverty level. The American Arbitration Association has voluntarily provided free arbitration services when possible for people at 200 percent of the federal poverty level. They also have provisions limiting the amount that the consumer has to pay in terms of administrative fees, which makes using them more attractive to consumers.

Arbitrator's Fees

Unlike a court case, where the cost of the judge is underwritten by taxes and requires no separate payment, the arbitrator, who acts as judge, gets paid an additional fee on top of whatever administrative fees are required. The amount charged depends on the organization the arbitrator is affiliated with. As of late 2009, the American Arbitration Association had an in-person daily rate of $750 per day for disputes worth up to $75,000. For any dispute worth more than $75,000, American Arbitration Association arbitrators can determine their own fee.

Other organizations, like the World Intellectual Property Organization, have their arbitrators charge a flat fee for the entire arbitration, again based on the value of the dispute. At $20,000 per arbitrator for a dispute up to $2.5 million, arbitration does not seem to be the cheap alternative to trial that its advocates claim it to be. However, other advantages of arbitration—like secrecy—might outweigh the cost in some types of cases, such as intellectual property cases dealing with secret formulas and patents.

You can see why determining which arbitration organization to use is so important. Your costs and ability to force the other side to pay them vary with the organization and its rules, as well as your state's rules on arbitration.

Other Fees

You'll probably have to pay an initial fee, which may be called a case service fee, a registration fee, or an administrative fee. Depending on the organization, in a consumer-business dispute, the business may have to pay this fee or the majority of the fee. The amount will probably depend on the value of the case, the same way that the arbitrator's fees depend on the value of the case. The amounts seem to range from about $125 to several thousand dollars, again depending on the value of the case and the organization used.

Do I Need a Lawyer for This?

As with court cases, there is no requirement that you have to have an attorney in order to go through arbitration. In fact, some arbitration services promote the cost efficiency of arbitration by pointing out that you do not need a lawyer. Realistically, you need a lawyer for arbitration as much as you'd need one for a court case. What that boils down to is that you might need a lawyer; then again, you might do fine on your own.

Advantages and Disadvantages

The advantages of going with an attorney for arbitration are the same as they are in a court case. You'll have someone who's more familiar with the system than you are and who's set up for dealing with a conflict and tracking all the papers and issues. You'll also have someone able to negotiate for you and appear before the arbitration tribunal when you're not able to leave work.

The major disadvantage to using an attorney in arbitration is purely monetary. You will not only have to pay for the arbitration fees and for the arbitrator, you'll have to pay your attorney for his time and expenses. As with court cases, you'll need to evaluate how comfortable you are with arguing your own case and how much time you have available to deal with the dispute. The more time you have to work on the case yourself, the less you'll need a lawyer's time. The more comfortable you are with arguing on your own behalf, the less you'll need a lawyer's assistance for that particular aspect of arbitration.

Costs

The costs of having an attorney for an arbitration are the same as the costs of having an attorney for a court case. Once again, how much it will cost depends on the attorney and your agreement with the attorney. See Chapters 4 and 5 for a thorough discussion of finding an attorney and discussing costs with her.

When Would I Go to Arbitration?

People go to arbitration the same way they go to court, and at the same stage in the conflict. You're likely to go to arbitration rather than court when a contract requires it of you. Many of the contracts you sign have an arbitration clause in them. For example, your cable television provider and cell phone providers probably have somewhere in the contract you signed that in the event of a conflict about the service, you have to use arbitration rather than the courts.

You might also choose arbitration if you'd rather not have the details of your conflict made public. Although you'll have to go to a regular court for a divorce, for example, you could use arbitration to decide the division of your assets so that no one knows those details.

Why Would I Go to Arbitration If I Had a Choice?

The major advantage arbitration has over the courts is that it is a private proceeding. The courts are a public forum, and anyone with any interest in knowing about your case can find out all about it unless the court "closes" the case to the public. In the pre-Internet days, it wasn't easy to find out anything about what was going on in a courthouse without physically going to the court and asking to see a particular case file. With the Internet, it's not difficult at all to discover other people's legal business, or at least the fact that there is some sort of legal proceeding going on.

Because arbitration is private in the first place, it's easier to enter into an agreement that the entire arbitration proceeding be kept secret. When you're concerned about information leaking out, arbitration reduces the number of people who have access to the case. If there are issues of business secrets, or property that is essentially information-based, arbitration is the best way to keep important information private.

Another reason to go to arbitration is if you believe that your case is very specialized. If your case involves technical information you don't believe a general court will easily understand and be able to make an intelligent decision on, arbitration is the way to go. You can select arbitrators who have expertise in your area so you spend less time educating the decision-maker about the basics underlying your case.

If you believe arbitration will be faster and less expensive than going to court, consider several factors before making your decision. First, the more complex your case, the longer it will take regardless of whether you go to court or to arbitration. There isn't anyone out there who can wave a magic wand to make an intricate case fast and easy. Second, the longer your case will take, the more expensive coming to a decision will be, regardless of whether you go to court or to arbitration. You'll still be paying for the attorney fees, if you're using one, and your time and expenses should be taken into account as well.

How Should I Pick an Arbitrator?

Unlike the random assignment of a judge to your case in the court system, with arbitration you can actually pick the person who will decide your case. If you're going to arbitration because you signed a contract that specifies arbitration as the way of solving a dispute, chances are pretty good that you won't be able to pick the organization with which the arbitrator is affiliated. The arbitration organization that will be used is usually named in the contract. The reason that's important is because, as discussed previously, the costs vary with the organization used, and so will the rules that are used to decide the case.

The selection of an arbitrator is the first thing both parties have to agree upon. Most of the organizations that sponsor arbitration have biographies and resumés of their arbitrators, which you can read either online or in a brochure or pamphlet published by the organization. What you're looking for is experience in your kind of dispute in terms of the topic, and perhaps experience as a judge or mediator as well.

Don't assume that because the other side has selected a particular arbitrator there's a secret reason they've done so. The other side is using the same criteria you are to pick an arbitrator, and it's likely they've picked one who has experience with this topic. In fact, this person may be the same one you would have picked, too.

What Do I Get at the End of Arbitration?

At the end of arbitration, you get an award, which is sort of like the verdict or judgment you get at the end of a trial. The important difference is that an award isn't immediately enforceable by itself the way a court judgment is. An award is basically a new contract that says who gets what. To enforce the award or contract, you have to go to court and file an "action to confirm the award." This is very similar to suing someone for not living up to a contract and adds more expense to the process if the other party doesn't live up to the award voluntarily.

PITFALL

If you win at arbitration, make sure your award states when you should be paid and what happens if you don't get paid on time. Go to court as soon as possible to enforce your award if it's not being honored by the other side. This is another time when waiting too long can cost you everything.

Can I Still Sue If This Doesn't Work Out?

As mentioned previously, unless you've participated in a nonbinding arbitration, your ability to go to court to challenge the arbitrator's decision is very limited. The main ways you can challenge the decision is by showing fraud or bias. The only thing you ordinarily go to the courts for after an arbitration award is made is to have the award enforced, the same way you would sue to enforce any contract. Like everything in law, you have to move quickly if you want to challenge the arbitrator's decision. Statutes of limitation still apply, and there may be court rules that require you to make your challenge to an arbitrator's award within a certain period of time. Whatever you do in any dispute, don't sit on your rights and wait until you feel you've got the time or energy to deal with the problem. Deal with it right away to make sure that you're not timed out of your recovery.

JUST THE FACTS

It's not just individuals who are unable to challenge an arbitrator's decision. The MassMutual Financial Group lost in arbitration against their former chief executive, Robert J. O'Connell, to the tune of $50 million. They sued to overturn the award and lost because the court found no evidence of fraud or poor procedures in the hearings.

The Least You Need to Know

- Arbitration is like a trial, but without the court's power behind it.
- Arbitration can be cheaper and more flexible than a trial.
- You've probably agreed to arbitration in several of your consumer contracts without even knowing it.
- Binding arbitration means you cannot sue if you are unhappy with the outcome of the arbitration.

Glossary

ADR   *See* alternative dispute resolution.

alternate service   The process of posting court documents in prominent places as an alternative to physically presenting or serving the party with the documents.

alternative dispute resolution (ADR)   Any method of solving a problem that doesn't involve going to court. ADR is very popular as a low-cost, low-conflict alternative to traditional adversarial court proceedings. It includes negotiation, mediation, and arbitration.

American rule for damages   The winning party cannot receive attorney fees from the other side unless there's a specific statute or rule allowing it.

appeal by leave   An appeal that requires the court's permission to file.

appeal by right   An appeal that the court must hear.

appeals court   A court that reviews decisions of law made by trial courts.

appellate brief   A summary of the facts and law that apply to a particular case on appeal, written by each side to present their case in the best possible light.

appellate process   The course a trial case takes after judgment when it goes through the appeals courts. This is when the case is reviewed for errors in the application of the law.

arbitration   A private, trial-like proceeding not held in a regular courtroom to decide a dispute between two parties.

arbitration award   The end result of an arbitration; the arbitration version of a judgment.

associate attorney   An attorney who works for one or more attorneys but is not a partner in the firm.

attorney discipline   Proceedings to punish attorneys who do not live up to ethical and legal requirements in practicing law.

attorney fee   The money paid to an attorney for his or her work.

award   A new contract that is created at the end of the arbitration process. Awards are the arbitration version of a court's judgment.

bailiff   Court officer responsible for maintaining order in a courtroom.

bar   A way of referring to attorneys as a profession or group, or a group made up of attorneys.

baseball arbitration   Type of arbitration in which the arbitrator (decision-maker) must choose between two possible solutions and cannot come up with any alternative solutions.

BATNA   *See* best alternative to a negotiated agreement.

bench   Raised desk where the judge sits throughout any court proceedings.

bench trial   A trial held without a jury, where a judge decides both what facts are true and how the law applies to those facts.

best alternative to a negotiated agreement (BATNA)   A negotiating technique involving knowing what your alternatives are so that you're not forced into one solution.

best-evidence rule   Evidence rule that requires that original documents or objects be used in court whenever possible.

beyond a reasonable doubt   The standard of proof for criminal cases only.

bill out   To charge for legal services.

billable hour   The portion of an hour in which an attorney or paralegal actually worked on a particular case.

binding arbitration   Arbitration that results in a final decision that cannot be brought to a trial court for review or retrial. The choice between binding arbitration and nonbinding arbitration is made at the time you sign the contract agreeing to arbitration in the first place.

bracketed arbitration   Arbitration in which the parties agree about what happened and who is responsible, but disagree about how much should be paid. The arbitration is set to determine payment within a range—high dollar amount and low dollar amount. Also known as "high-low" arbitration.

breach   Broken, violated, or contrary to what was supposed to happen.

brief   A document written for the court explaining the facts and legal theories of a case, written by each side to support their view of the case.

burden of proof   A party's responsibility for finding and showing that a fact is true.

calendar days   A method of figuring out due dates that includes every day on the calendar.

calling a witness   The process of announcing the name of someone who is to stand as a witness in court; usually performed by the attorney or the bailiff.

case evaluation   A formal appraisal of the value of a case before trial by a panel of experts. The parties in the case can accept the recommendation of the evaluation panel, in which case no trial need be held.

case law   Law created by appellate cases, usually describing how statutes should be interpreted.

case of first impression   A case with facts and legal questions that have never before been decided by a court.

case within a case   Within a legal malpractice case, the process of proving that you would've won the case that the malpractice charges are based on.

censure   The least severe punishment a lawyer can receive from an attorney disciplinary board; also called a reprimand.

cert   *See* certiorari.

certification of a class   A requirement for a class action suit, in which a group of people are certified by the court as having a problem in common that can best be solved by a class action.

certiorari   Certification that a case will be heard by an appellate court like the Supreme Court of the United States; also called "cert."

chambers   The judge's office.

civil lawsuit   A lawsuit brought by an individual to enforce his or her rights.

civil procedure   The rules of court that govern how a lawsuit will proceed.

class action suit   A lawsuit brought by a group of individuals with a common problem or complaint against a defendant.

clean hands doctrine   Rule stating that if you come to court guilty of bad behavior, you cannot get equitable or nonstatutory relief.

clear and convincing evidence   Standard of proof for civil cases; highest civil standard, and hardest to prove.

client trust account   Bank account required for lawyers who receive client monies; keeps client money separate from the attorney's money.

closing statement   Speech made at the end of a trial to summarize what happened and to influence the decision of the finder of fact (judge or jury).

collection   Process of getting money owed to you from the person or entity that owes it.

common law   Law created by appellate courts, usually describing how statutes should be interpreted; also called case law.

compensatory damages   Money or other things given to make up for harm that was done to a party; usually puts the party in the position they were in before the damage was done.

competence   The legally recognized ability to take care of yourself and make your own decisions; also, a lawyer acting with reasonable preparation and forethought.

consent judgment   An order ending a lawsuit according to the agreement (or consent) of both parties.

consequential damages   Money or other things given to make up for the harm that happened after the initial injury.

consideration   In contracts, the exchange or the thing exchanged.

constitution   The source of all laws in a state or country.

contempt of court   A criminal judgment finding that a person has behaved disrespectfully to the court.

contingency fee   An agreement that a lawyer's fee will not be paid unless the case is won; other fees, like court costs, must still be paid by the plaintiff.

contract   An agreement between two or more people to do (or not do) a specific thing that is enforceable under the law.

counsel   To advise; also used to refer to an attorney.

counselor   An attorney.

counter-defendant   A plaintiff who is being sued by a defendant in the same case.

counter-plaintiff   A defendant who sues the plaintiff in the same case.

court clerk   Officer of the court whose job involves making sure that all papers are properly accepted, paid for, and filed.

court costs   Fees charged by the courts to cover part of the cost of filing a lawsuit (taxes pay for the majority of the costs of filing a lawsuit).

court of record   A trial in which everything that happens is recorded so that the application of law can be reviewed at the appeals level.

court reporter   Court officer who records, word for word, the proceedings in court or at a deposition.

credible   Something that one can believe or trust; credible evidence is trustworthy and believable by the finder of fact in a trial.

criminal lawsuit   A lawsuit brought by the government against an individual who is accused of breaking a criminal law.

cross-defendant   A defendant who is being sued by another defendant in the same case.

cross-examination   Part of the trial in which a witness is asked questions by the other side.

cross-plaintiff   A defendant who sues another defendant in the same case.

damages   Loss to property or the amount of money awarded by a court because of a loss.

declaratory relief   Court judgment that states who has what rights in a particular situation.

default   Failing to do what is required by law.

default judgment   Judgment by the court that a party has lost because they failed to respond as required by law.

demonstrative evidence   Physical evidence that shows how something works or how an event might have happened.

deponent   A person who gives testimony at a deposition.

depose   Verb used to describe the deposition proceedings.

deposition   Out-of-court hearing, held to obtain testimony from witnesses before a trial begins; it is always recorded by a court reporter so that the testimony can be quoted accurately later.

derivative action   A lawsuit brought by a corporate shareholder to enforce the corporation's rights; usually done because the corporation refuses to sue to enforce its rights on its own.

direct examination   Initial questioning of a witness at trial by the party who called that witness.

disbarment   Most severe punishment meted out by an attorney disciplinary board for an attorney who violates ethical codes; it prevents the attorney from ever practicing law again.

discovery   Process at the beginning of a trial to find out, or "discover," important facts about the case.

dispute   Argument or problem between two or more parties.

diversity jurisdiction   A form of federal jurisdiction requiring that the plaintiff and defendant be from two different states and that the amount argued about (the "amount in controversy") be more than $75,000.

docket   The court's schedule or calendar; many attorneys refer to their own schedule or calendar as their docket, too.

documentary evidence   Evidence that is written down, whether on paper or electronically.

due process   Basic right under the U.S. Constitution requiring that everyone be given notice that he is being sued and that everyone be subject to the same procedures under the law.

duty   An obligation or requirement that the law will enforce.

e-filing   Sending and registering documents with the court via computer and Internet, rather than on paper and in person.

elements   The basic parts of a law.

emancipation   Freedom, particularly the freedom given to a minor who is judged by law to be able to care for him- or herself.

equitable relief   A court-ordered remedy under which someone is told to do or not do something specific.

evidence   Information used to determine the truth in a case.

expenses   Part of a legal bill that is separate from legal fees; these include things like copies and delivery fees.

expert witness   A witness who has particular skills, education, or experience that will help the court understand technical evidence.

Federal District Court   Federal trial court.

fiduciary   Having to do with loyalty, not finances.

fiduciary duty   A duty of loyalty.

filing fee   Money paid to the court to begin a lawsuit.

finder of fact   Responsible for deciding which pieces of evidence presented to the court are true; may either be a judge or a jury.

flat fee   A set amount of money to be paid to an attorney for a particular piece of work.

foreperson/foreman/forewoman of the jury   Head juror responsible for keeping the jury on track in its discussions and for announcing the decision of the jury.

foundation   Basis for evidence, which shows why it should be believed and why it's relevant.

frivolous   Describes something not based in law; making a claim not recognized in law.

garnishing/garnishment   Taking something from a third party who owes it to a defendant before the third party gives it to the defendant.

grievance   Complaint made against an attorney to the state agency that controls attorney licensure.

grieving   Process of complaining about an attorney to the state agency that controls attorney licensure.

guilt   Criminal responsibility for an act that is against the law.

hearsay   A statement made outside of court, not under oath, that a party tries to get the court to accept as truth.

high-low arbitration   An arbitration proceeding in which the arbitrator (person who will make the decision) can only pick a monetary amount between a high and low number that the parties have already agreed to.

hourly fee   The most common way attorneys get paid, by the hour and only for the part of the hour spent working on that particular client's case.

in forma pauperis   In the way of a poor person; the court waives the fees that are usually paid because the person is too poor to be able to afford them.

in pro per   *See* in propria persona.

in propria persona   In the proper person, or suing without an attorney; also called *in pro per.*

incompetence   Not being able to do something because you're considered legally incapable; also, when a lawyer doesn't do basic things properly, like meeting deadlines.

ineffective assistance of counsel   A concept applying only to criminal law that claims that the outcome of the criminal trial would've been different had the attorney been competent.

injunction   A court order requiring a party to do (or not do) something specific.

Interest on Lawyer's Trust Account (IOLTA)   A bank trust account that holds client money separately from the law firm's money; known as IOLA in some states.

interlocutory appeal   An appeal made to a higher court before the end of a trial.

intermediate appellate court   An appeals court set up to hear cases before the highest court hears them.

interrogatory   Written questions submitted only to the parties in a lawsuit; part of the discovery process.

irrelevance   Having nothing to do with the question at hand in a lawsuit.

judge's clerk   The judge's legal secretary; may be a lawyer, law student, paralegal, or legal secretary. Controls access to the judge.

judgment   Court order that declares one party the winner of a lawsuit and usually awards the winner money that the loser must pay.

judgment creditor   Someone who is owed money on a judgment.

judgment debtor   Someone who has to pay a judgment who owes money on a judgment.

judgment interest rate   The state-set interest rate that is added to unpaid judgments.

judgment-proof   When someone has no assets and cannot pay a judgment against him or her.

jurisdiction   The power to hear and decide a case.

jurisdictional amount   The limit to the amount of money in question in a case that a particular court can hear.

juror   A person who sits on a jury.

jury   Group of people who make decisions about the facts in a case, and may make decisions about whether those facts fulfill the requirements of the law.

jury fee   Money paid to the court to have a jury in a lawsuit.

jury instructions   Directions to the jury about the law in a particular case.

justice   Another name for a judge on an appellate court.

law clerk   Law student who works, usually part-time, at a law firm.

law firm   Company that provides legal services.

lay witness   Ordinary person with firsthand knowledge of an event in a case.

legal assistant   Sometimes called a paralegal; a person with training in law who assists a lawyer.

legal entity   Any person or business that the law recognizes as having rights.

legal malpractice   Failure to provide legal representation at the level required by community standards.

legal secretary   Person who helps an attorney with paperwork and office organization.

liable   Responsible.

lien   Claim against an asset that allows the asset to be taken if the underlying claim is unpaid or unsatisfied.

liquidated damages   Damages that have been translated into cash.

litigation   Process of taking a claim against another party through the legal system.

local court rules   Rules that only apply in one particular court, that solve a problem local to that court.

magistrate   A judge.

making a record   Putting information in a form that the public can refer back to later.

med-arb   *See* mediation-arbitration.

mediation   Negotiation between two or more parties with a neutral third party helping them come to a decision.

mediation-arbitration   Mediation followed by arbitration if the mediation is unsuccessful; also known as med-arb.

mediator   A neutral third party who directs a mediation and helps the parties come to a decision.

medical malpractice   A form of personal injury or tort that occurs when a medical professional doesn't use proper procedures in caring for a person.

mistrial   A trial that is ended early because of mistakes; mistrials are treated as if the trial never happened.

mitigate   To make better or to reduce.

monetary damages   Damages that are expressed in a dollar amount.

motion   Plaintiff's or defendant's formal demand that the court take a specific action and order that something be done.

motion day   Day of the week when most courts hear formal requests for action, or motions.

motion fee   Money paid so that a court will hear a formal request for action.

motion for a new trial   Formal request for a new trial.

motion for additur   Formal request to increase the dollar amount of a judgment.

motion for judgment notwithstanding the verdict (motion j.n.o.v.)   Formal request that the judge ignore the jury's decision and rule against the jury.

motion for remittitur   Formal request to reduce the dollar amount of a judgment.

motion in limine   Formal request to the court to limit the evidence that can be used to decide the case at trial.

motion to compel discovery   Formal request to the court to require the other side to answer questions or produce documents.

motion to dismiss   Formal request to the court to end the case.

motion to dismiss with prejudice   Formal request to the court that the case be permanently dismissed and never allowed to be brought before any other court ever again.

motion to dismiss without prejudice   Formal request to the court that the case be dismissed now, but allowed to be brought back before this or another court.

negligence   Failing to live up to the duty to be careful in action and causing injury to another.

negotiation   Process of coming to an agreement between two parties.

nondisclosure agreement   Contract agreeing that aspects of your dispute that led to the case being filed will remain confidential; usually provides financial and legal penalties for breaking the agreement.

nonmonetary damages   Harm that cannot be measured in monetary terms.

objection   Request to the court made to prevent information from being put on the record.

of counsel   An attorney who acts as an advisor to a firm or another attorney.

opening statement   Speech made by the parties at the beginning of a lawsuit, to map out what the suit will be about.

overruling an objection   The court's denial of a request to prevent information from being put on the record.

paralegal   Person with training in law who assists a lawyer; sometimes called a legal assistant.

party or **parties**   Another way of referring to the people directly involved in a lawsuit; plaintiffs or defendants.

personal jurisdiction   Power of a court to bring an individual before the court to answer a lawsuit.

personal protection order   Order issued by a court to protect an individual from harm by another.

physical evidence   Evidence that can be touched, as opposed to testimonial evidence, which can only be heard.

plaintiff's lawyer   A lawyer who starts personal injury cases, like medical malpractice and auto injuries.

precedent   Appellate court decisions that give guidance to other courts about how to make decisions in specific circumstances.

preponderance of the evidence   A standard of proof in civil cases; usually expressed as "more likely than not" to be true.

pretrial   Everything that happens before a trial; also, the procedures put in place that take the parties from filing the lawsuit to the trial itself.

prime rate   The interest rate at which the U.S. government lends money to banks.

privileged   Information that's legally protected because of the kind of relationship it came from.

probate   The court that makes decisions on wills, trusts, and sometimes family law issues like guardianships.

probative   Something that can prove or disprove a fact.

process fee   Money paid to a process server to deliver papers to another party.

product liability   A tort caused when a manufacturer creates a product that will hurt people even if it's used properly.

proffering   Producing and offering something to the court, like a piece of evidence or a motion.

punitive   Punishing.

recess   Formal break in court proceedings when the judge and parties can leave the court room.

recording a judgment (or settlement)   Process of putting the judgment or settlement on the public record so it can be easily enforced, and to give the public notice of the debt.

relevance   Something that has a direct relationship to the question being discussed.

remedy   The "fix" or solution provided by the law for a specific problem.

reprimand   The least severe punishment a lawyer can receive; also called censure.

restraining order   Order issued by a court preventing a party from doing something specific.

retainer   Money paid to hire an attorney; may be considered a prepayment of fees and may or may not be refundable.

rules of civil procedure   Rules that govern how cases go through the process of litigation.

rules of court   Another way of referring to the rules of civil procedure; the rules that govern how cases go through the process of litigation.

satisfied   A duty that is completed or discharged.

SCOTUS   Supreme Court of the United States.

seizure of assets   Legal process in which a court orders that something owned by the defendant be taken (and possibly sold) to pay off a legal debt.

sequester   To keep witnesses out of the courtroom so that they don't hear other witnesses' testimony and consciously or unconsciously change their own testimony because of it; also used to keep juries away from outside influences during their deliberation.

service fee   Money paid to a process server to deliver papers to another party.

settle   To reach an agreement in a lawsuit before the end of the trial.

settlement   The agreement ending a lawsuit before judgment, or the things agreed to in order to end the lawsuit.

shareholder suit   A lawsuit against a corporation claiming that shareholder rights were not protected by the corporation.

sidebar   Any discussion held next to the judge's bench or desk, usually out of the hearing of the jury and not recorded by the court reporter.

small claims court   A court specializing in deciding civil cases that are worth a relatively small amount of money.

standard of proof   The level of proof required to prove or disprove a fact.

standing   The right to sue or the right to be heard in a lawsuit.

statute   Law passed by a legislature, such as the United States Congress.

statute of limitations   Law that requires a suit be started within a specific period of time after the event complained of; if the lawsuit isn't started before the end of the time period specified in the statute of limitations, it cannot be started at all.

strike   To take out or remove something from a lawsuit or part of a lawsuit; when an attorney says "strike that," after a statement, it means ignore that statement.

structured judgment   A judgment set up so that payment is made over a period of time.

structured settlement   A settlement set up so that payment is made over a period of time.

subject matter jurisdiction   Power of a court to hear a particular type of case; bankruptcy courts have subject matter jurisdiction over bankruptcy cases.

summary disposition   Ending or disposing of a case because there is no argument between the parties about the law or the facts; also known as summary judgment.

summary judgment   *See* summary disposition.

suspension   An intermediate punishment for attorneys who violate ethical rules; the attorney is not permitted to practice law for a specified period of time.

sustain an objection   The court upholds or agrees with the objection made by a party.

test case   A case that "tests" whether the appeals court is willing to change the law on a particular topic; test cases often create major changes in the law.

testimony   Evidence given by a witness in court by speaking under oath.

toll   To stop or pause; usually used with statutes of limitation when the time period for suing is "tolled" or paused to extend the amount of time available to start a lawsuit.

tort law   Law dealing with injuries to people and property.

transcript   Written record of a hearing, deposition, or trial created by a court reporter.

trial   Formal procedure in a government court for deciding which party is right in a lawsuit.

trial court   A court in which a lawsuit is filed, and which hears and decides evidence and makes a final decision in the case.

venue   The location in which a trial takes place.

verdict   Final decision of a jury.

verdict form   Form on which the final decision of the jury is written; it guides the jury in stating its decision.

working days   A method of figuring out due dates that includes only days on which a court is open and working.

writ   Order of a court.

zero-sum game   Situation in which there is a limited range of solutions; if one person wins, another must lose.

Resources

This appendix gives you the resources you need to find an attorney and check out that attorney using publicly available information. You'll also find basic information links for small claims courts in each state if that information is available online. Because all of this information is published by individual associations and state governments, this author cannot take responsibility for the content of the websites listed here.

Many states have a lawyer referral service that can help you find an attorney. Check for those resources on their websites. Most state bars won't guarantee that you'll be happy with the attorney you're referred to, but most will give you more than one name so that you can interview them and pick the one that you're most comfortable with.

If you already know of an attorney that you're interested in hiring, you can check to see whether they're actually licensed to practice law. Look for a directory or member listing on the website. Some states have separate sites for licensing look-up, and that's noted for those states.

Finally, you should check to see whether the attorney you're interested in hiring has been censured. Look for something called "discipline," "complaints," or "grievances" on the websites. Not all states publish the names and reasons for discipline for attorneys on the Internet. Some states only publish information on how to file a complaint against an attorney. Some states require you to make a phone call to get disciplinary information, but it's well worth your time to make that call.

Attorney Information Resources

Alabama

To find an attorney to help you, find out if an attorney is licensed, and/or find out if an attorney has been disciplined:

> Alabama State Bar Association
> www.alabar.org
> 415 Dexter Avenue
> Montgomery, AL 36104
> 334-269-1515
> 1-800-354-6154
> Fax: 334-261-6310

Alaska

To find an attorney to help you, find out if an attorney is licensed, and/or find out if an attorney has been disciplined:

> Alaska Bar Association
> www.alaskabar.org
> 550 West 7th Avenue, Suite 1900
> Anchorage, AK 99501
> 907-272-7469

Arizona

To find an attorney to help you, find out if an attorney is licensed, and/or find out if an attorney has been disciplined:

> Arizona State Bar
> www.azbar.org
> 4201 North 24th Street, Suite 200
> Phoenix, AZ 85016-6288
> 866-482-9227

Arkansas

To find an attorney to help you:

> Arkansas Bar Association
> www.arkbar.com
> 2224 Cottondale Lane
> Little Rock, AR 72202
> 1-800-609-5668

To find out if an attorney is licensed:

> http://courts.arkansas.gov/attorneys/attorney_search.cfm

To find out if an attorney has been disciplined:

> http://courts.arkansas.gov/professional_conduct/index.cfm

California

To find an attorney to help you, find out if an attorney is licensed, and/or find out if an attorney has been disciplined:

> State Bar of California
> www.calbar.ca.gov
> 180 Howard Street
> San Francisco, CA 94105
> 415-538-2000

Colorado

To find an attorney to help you:

> Colorado Bar Association
> www.cobar.org
> 1900 Grant Street
> 9th Floor
> Denver, CO 80203
> 303-860-1115

To find out if an attorney is licensed or has been disciplined:

www.coloradosupremecourt.com/Registration/Registration.asp

Connecticut

To find an attorney to help you:

Connecticut Bar Association
www.ctbar.org
30 Bank Street
PO Box 350
New Britain, CT 06050-0350
860-223-4400

To find out if an attorney is licensed:

http://civilinquiry.jud.ct.gov/AttorneyFirmInquiry.aspx

To find out if an attorney has been disciplined:

www.jud.ct.gov/SGC/decisions/default.htm

Delaware

To find an attorney to help you or to find out if an attorney is licensed:

Delaware State Bar Association
www.dsba.org
301 North Market Street
Wilmington, DE 19801
302-658-5279

To find out if an attorney has been disciplined:

http://courts.delaware.gov/odc/

District of Columbia

To find an attorney to help you, find out if an attorney is licensed, and/or find out if an attorney has been disciplined:

> District of Columbia Bar
> www.dcbar.org
> 1101 K Street NW, Suite 200
> Washington, DC 20005
> 202-737-4700

Florida

To find an attorney to help you, find out if an attorney is licensed, and/or find out if an attorney has been disciplined:

> The Florida Bar
> www.floridabar.org
> 651 East Jefferson Street
> Tallahassee, FL 32399-2300
> 850-561-5600

Georgia

To find an attorney to help you, find out if an attorney is licensed, and/or find out if an attorney has been disciplined:

> State Bar of Georgia
> www.gabar.org
> 104 Marietta Street NW, Suite 100
> Atlanta, GA 30303
> 1-800-334-6865

Hawaii

To find an attorney to help you, find out if an attorney is licensed, and/or find out if an attorney has been disciplined:

> Hawaii State Bar Association
> www.hsba.org
> Alakea Corporate Tower
> 1100 Alakea Street, Suite 1000
> Honolulu, HI 96813
> 808-537-1868

Idaho

To find an attorney to help you, find out if an attorney is licensed, and/or find out if an attorney has been disciplined:

> Idaho State Bar Association
> http://isb.idaho.gov
> PO Box 895
> Boise, ID 83701
> 208-334-4500

Illinois

To find an attorney to help you:

> Illinois State Bar Association
> www.isba.org
> Illinois Bar Center
> 424 South Second Street
> Springfield, IL 62701-1779
> 1-800-252-8908

To find out if an attorney is licensed or has been disciplined:

> www.iardc.org

Indiana

To find an attorney to help you:

> Indiana State Bar Association
> www.inbar.org
> One Indiana Square, Suite 530
> Indianapolis, IN 46204
> 317-639-5465

To find out if an attorney is licensed:

> http://hats2.courts.state.in.us/rollatty/roa1_inp.jsp

To find out if an attorney has been disciplined:

> www.in.gov/judiciary/discipline/

Iowa

To find an attorney to help you:

> Iowa State Bar Association
> http://iabar.net
> 625 East Court Avenue
> Des Moines, IA 50309
> 515-243-3179

To find out if an attorney is licensed:

> www.iacourtcommissions.org/icc/SearchLawyer.do

To find out if an attorney has been disciplined:

> www.iacourtcommissions.org/icc/SearchDiscipline.do?action=recentSearch

Kansas

To find an attorney to help you:

> Kansas State Bar Association
> www.ksbar.org
> 1200 SW Harrison
> Topeka, KS 66612-1806
> 785-234-5695

To find out if an attorney is licensed:

> www.kscourts.org/appellate-clerk/attorney-registration/default.asp

To find out if an attorney has been disciplined:

> www.kscourts.org/Rules-procedures-forms/Attorney-discipline/default.asp

Kentucky

To find an attorney to help you, find out if an attorney is licensed, and/or find out if an attorney has been disciplined:

> Kentucky State Bar Association
> www.kybar.org
> 514 West Main Street
> Frankfort, KY 40601-1812
> 502-564-3795

Louisiana

To find an attorney to help you, find out if an attorney is licensed, and/or find out if an attorney has been disciplined:

> Louisiana State Bar Association
> www.lsba.org
> 601 St. Charles Avenue
> New Orleans, LA 70130
> 1-800-421-5722

Maine

To find an attorney to help you:

> Maine State Bar Association
> www.mainebar.org
> 124 State Street
> Augusta, ME 04330
> 207-622-7523

To find out if an attorney is licensed or has been disciplined:

> www.mebaroverseers.org

Maryland

To find an attorney to help you:

> Maryland State Bar Association
> www.msba.org
> 520 West Fayette Street
> Baltimore, MD 21201
> 1-800-492-1964

To find out if an attorney is licensed:

> www.courts.state.md.us/cpf/attylist.html

To find out if an attorney has been disciplined:

> www.courts.state.md.us/attygrievance/sanctions.html

Massachusetts

To find an attorney to help you:

> Massachusetts Bar Association
> www.massbar.org
> 20 West Street
> Boston, MA 02111-1204
> 877-676-6500

To find out if an attorney is licensed or has been disciplined:

> http://massbbo.org/bbolookup.php

Michigan

To find an attorney to help you, find out if an attorney is licensed, and/or find out if an attorney has been disciplined:

> State Bar of Michigan
> www.michbar.org
> Michael Franck Building
> 306 Townsend Street
> Lansing, MI 48933-2012
> 1-800-968-1442

Minnesota

To find an attorney to help you:

> Minnesota State Bar
> www.mnbar.org
> 600 Nicollet Mall #380
> Minneapolis, MN 55402
> 1-800-882-6722

To find out if an attorney is licensed or has been disciplined:

> www.mncourts.gov/mars/default.aspx

Mississippi

To find an attorney to help you or to find out how to file a complaint against an attorney:

> The Mississippi Bar
> www.msbar.org
> PO Box 2168
> Jackson, MS 39225-2168
> 601-948-4471

To find out if an attorney is licensed:

> www.mssc.state.ms.us/barroll/barroll.html

Missouri

To find an attorney to help you, find out if an attorney is licensed, and/or find out how to file a complaint against an attorney:

> The Missouri Bar
> www.mobar.org
> 326 Monroe Street
> Jefferson City, MO 65101
> 573-635-4128

Montana

To find an attorney to help you, find out if an attorney is licensed, and/or find out if an attorney has been disciplined:

> State Bar of Montana
> www.montanabar.org
> 7 West Sixth Avenue, Suite 2B
> PO Box 577
> Helena, MT 59624
> 406-442-7660

Nebraska

To find an attorney to help you, find out if an attorney is licensed, and/or find out how to file a complaint against an attorney:

> Nebraska State Bar Association
> www.nebar.com
> 635 South 14th Street, 2nd Floor
> Lincoln, NE 68508
> 402-475-7091

New Hampshire

To find an attorney to help you, find out if an attorney is licensed, and/or find out if an attorney has been disciplined:

> New Hampshire Bar Association
> www.nhbar.org
> 2 Pillsbury Street, Suite 300
> Concord, NH 03301-3502
> 603-224-6942

New Jersey

To find an attorney to help you:

> New Jersey State Bar Association
> New Jersey Law Center
> www.njsba.com
> One Constitution Center
> New Brunswick, NJ 08901-1500
> 732-249-5000

To find out if an attorney is licensed:

> New Jersey Board of Bar Examiners
> 609-984-2111

To find out if an attorney has been disciplined:

> www.judiciary.state.nj.us/oae/discipline.htm

New Mexico

To find an attorney to help you, find out if an attorney is licensed, and/or find out how to file a complaint against an attorney:

> State Bar of New Mexico
> www.nmbar.org
> 5121 Masthead NE
> Albuquerque, NM 87109
> 505-797-6000

New York

To find an attorney to help you:

New York State Bar Association
www.nysba.org
One Elk Street
Albany, NY 12207
518-463-3200

To find out if an attorney is licensed:

http://iapps.courts.state.ny.us/attorney/AttorneySearch

To find out how to file a complaint against an attorney:

www.courts.state.ny.us/ip/attorneygrievance/complaints.shtml

North Carolina

To find an attorney to help you, find out if an attorney is licensed, and/or find out if an attorney has been disciplined:

North Carolina State Bar
www.ncbar.com
PO Box 25908
208 Fayetteville Street Mall
Raleigh, NC 27611
919-828-4620

North Dakota

To find an attorney to help you or to find out if an attorney has been disciplined:

State Bar Association of North Dakota
PO Box 2136
Bismarck, ND 58502-2136
701-255-1404

To find out if an attorney is licensed:

www.court.state.nd.us/lawyers/

Ohio

To find an attorney to help you:

> Ohio State Bar Association
> www.ohiobar.org
> 1700 Lake Shore Drive
> Columbus, OH 43204
> 614-487-2050

To find out if an attorney is licensed:

> www.sconet.state.oh.us/AttySvcs/AttyReg/default.asp

To find out how to file a complaint against an attorney:

> www.sconet.state.oh.us/DisciplinarySys/

Oklahoma

To find an attorney to help you, find out if an attorney is licensed, and/or find out how to file a complaint against an attorney:

> Oklahoma Bar Association
> www.okbar.org/public/
> 1901 North Lincoln
> Oklahoma City, OK 73105
> 405-416-7000

Oregon

To find an attorney to help you, find out if an attorney is licensed, and/or find out if an attorney has been disciplined:

> Oregon State Bar
> www.osbar.org
> 16037 SW Upper Boones Ferry Road
> Tigard, OR 97281
> 503-620-0222

Pennsylvania

To find an attorney to help you:

> Pennsylvania Bar Association
> www.pabar.org
> 100 South Street
> PO Box 186
> Harrisburg, PA 17108-0186
> 1-800-932-0311

To find out if an attorney is licensed or has been disciplined:

> www.padisciplinaryboard.org

Rhode Island

To find an attorney to help you or to find out if an attorney is licensed:

> Rhode Island Bar Association
> www.ribar.com
> 115 Cedar Street
> Providence, RI 02903
> 401-421-5740

To find out how to file a complaint against an attorney:

> www.courts.ri.gov/supreme/disciplinary/defaultdisciplinary.htm

South Carolina

To find an attorney to help you or to find out if an attorney is licensed:

> South Carolina Bar
> www.scbar.org
> 950 Taylor Street
> PO Box 608
> Columbia, SC 29202-0608
> 803-799-6653

To find out how to file a complaint against an attorney:

www.judicial.state.sc.us/discCounsel

South Dakota

To find an attorney to help you, find out if an attorney is licensed, and/or find out how to file a complaint against an attorney:

State Bar of South Dakota
www.sdbar.org/
222 East Capitol Avenue
Pierre, SD 57501-2596
605-224-7554

Tennessee

To find an attorney to help you:

Tennessee Bar Association
www.tba.org
221 4th Avenue North, Suite 400
Nashville, TN 37219-2198
615-383-7421

To find out if an attorney is licensed or has been disciplined:

www.tbpr.org/Consumers/AttorneySearch/

Texas

To find an attorney to help you, find out if an attorney is licensed, and/or find out how to file a complaint against an attorney:

State Bar of Texas
www.texasbar.com
1414 Colorado, Suite 300
Austin, TX 78701
512-204-2222

Utah

To find an attorney to help you, find out if an attorney is licensed, and/or find out how to file a complaint against an attorney:

Utah State Bar
www.utahbar.org
645 South 200 East, Suite 310
Salt Lake City, UT 84111-3834
801-531-9077

Vermont

To find an attorney to help you:

Vermont Bar Association
www.vtbar.org
35-37 Court Street
PO Box 100
Montpelier, VT 05601-0100
802-223-2020

To find out if an attorney is licensed:

www.vermontjudiciary.org/LC/attylicensing.aspx

To find out how to file a complaint against an attorney:

www.vermontjudiciary.org/LC/attydiscipline.aspx

Virginia

To find an attorney to help you, find out if an attorney is licensed, and/or find out if an attorney has been disciplined:

Virginia State Bar
www.vsb.org
707 East Main Street, Suite 1500
Richmond, VA 23219-2803
804-775-0500

Washington

To find an attorney to help you, find out if an attorney is licensed, and/or find out how to file a complaint against an attorney:

Washington State Bar Association
www.wsba.org
Puget Sound Plaza
1325 4th Avenue, Suite 600
Seattle, WA 98101-2539
206-727-8240

West Virginia

To find an attorney to help you or to find out if an attorney is licensed:

West Virginia State Bar
www.wvbar.org
2006 Kanawha Boulevard East
Charleston, WV 25311
304-558-2456

To find out if an attorney has been disciplined:

www.wvodc.org

Wisconsin

To find an attorney to help you or to find out if an attorney is licensed:

State Bar of Wisconsin
www.wisbar.org
5302 Eastpark Boulevard
Madison, WI 53718
608-257-3838

To find out how to file a complaint against an attorney:

www.wicourts.gov/about/organization/offices/olr.htm

Wyoming

To find an attorney to help you, find out if an attorney is licensed, and/or find out how to file a complaint against an attorney:

Wyoming State Bar Association
www.wyomingbar.org
PO Box 109
Cheyenne, WY 82003-0109
307-632-9061

Small Claims Court Resources

All 50 states have small claims courts of one sort or another. The federal courts do not have a small claims court at all.

For general information on all 50 states, visit the National Center for State Courts website, and do a search for "small claims." Their website is at www.ncsconline.org. Their small claims court information page is: www.ncsconline.org/wc/CourTopics/statelinks.asp?id=79&topic=SmaCla.

Alabama

No specific information is available from a reliable source.

Alaska

www.dced.state.ak.us/dca/LOGON/admin/admin-smallclaims.htm

Arizona

www.supreme.state.az.us/info/brochures/smclaims.htm

Arkansas

http://courts.state.ar.us/documents/small_claims_info.pdf

California

www.courtinfo.ca.gov/selfhelp/smallclaims/

Colorado

www.courts.state.co.us/Self_Help/Local_Small_Claims.cfm

Connecticut

www.jud.ct.gov/faq/smallclaims.html

Delaware

No specific information is available from a reliable source.

Florida

http://circuit8.org/sc/

Georgia

Georgia small claims courts are called magistrate courts. Search for "magistrate court" at this site:

www.georgia.gov

Hawaii

www.courts.state.hi.us/self-help/small_claims/small_claims.html

Idaho

www.courtselfhelp.idaho.gov/smclaims.asp

Illinois

Search for "small claims court" at this site:

www.illinoislegalaid.org

Indiana

www.in.gov/judiciary/pubs/small-claims.html

Iowa

www.iowacourts.gov/Court_Rules_and_Forms/Small_Claims_Forms

Kansas

www.ksbar.org/public/public_resources/pamphlets/small_claims_court.shtml

Louisiana

Small claims courts are called city courts. There is no single website for all city courts. Here's a sample website:

http://brgov.com/dept/citycourt/

Maine

www.courts.state.me.us/maine_courts/specialized/small_claims/smallclaimsguide/

Maryland

www.courts.state.md.us/district/forms/civil/dccv001br.html

Massachusetts

www.mass.gov/courts/courtsandjudges/courts/districtcourt/smallclaims.html

Michigan

http://courts.michigan.gov/scao/selfhelp/smallclaims/sc_help.htm

Minnesota

Small claims courts are called conciliation courts.

www.mncourts.gov/selfhelp/?page=313

Mississippi

Small claims courts are called justice courts.

www.justicecourt.com

Missouri

www.courts.mo.gov/page.jsp?id=704

Montana

www.doj.mt.gov/consumer/consumer/smallclaimscourt.asp

Nebraska

www.supremecourt.ne.gov/small-claims/

Nevada

There is no single overall state website on small claims courts, which are also called justice courts. A good resource is:

www.clarkcountycourts.us/lvjc/small-claims.html

New Hampshire

www.courts.state.nh.us/district/claims.htm

New Jersey

www.judiciary.state.nj.us/prose/index.htm

New Mexico

No specific information is available from a reliable source.

New York

www.courts.state.ny.us/courts/townandvillage/

North Carolina

www.nccourts.org/courts/trial/sclaims/default.asp

North Dakota

Only forms are available from the courts, at this site:

www.ndcourts.com/court/forms/small/forms.htm

Ohio

www.clelaw.lib.oh.us/public/misc/FAQs/Claims.HTML

Oklahoma

www.okbar.org/public/brochures/sccbroc.htm

Oregon

www.osbar.org/public/pamphlets/smallclaims.html

Pennsylvania

No specific information is available from a reliable source.

Rhode Island

www.courts.ri.gov/district/smallclaims.htm

South Carolina

Called magistrates court or magistrate small claims court.

www.scbar.org/public_services/lawline/magistrates_small_claims_court/

South Dakota

Search this site for "small claims":

http://ujs.sd.gov/

Tennessee

No specific information is available from a reliable source.

Texas

Search for small claims courts on this website:

www.texasbar.com

Utah

www.utcourts.gov/howto/smallclaims/

Vermont

www.vermontjudiciary.org/gtc/Superior/smallclaims.aspx

Virginia

www.courts.state.va.us/courts/gd/home.html

Washington

Search this site for "An Introduction to Small Claims Court":

www.courts.wa.gov

West Virginia

Small claims courts are called magistrate courts.

www.state.wv.us/wvsca/magistrate.htm

Wisconsin

www.wicourts.gov/about/pubs/circuit/smallclaimsguide.htm

Wyoming

www.courts.state.wy.us/CourtRules_Entities.
aspx?RulesPage=SmallClaimsCases.xml#top

Index

B